T0392273

All About Agni

The Many Fires of Agni

The Secret History of the Vedas, Volume III

James Kalomiris

BALBOA.
PRESS
A DIVISION OF HAY HOUSE

Balboa Press books may be ordered through booksellers or by contacting:

Balboa Press
A Division of Hay House
1663 Liberty Drive
Bloomington, IN 47403
www.balboapress.com
844-682-1282

Because of the dynamic nature of the Internet, any web addresses or links contained in this book may have changed since publication and may no longer be valid. The views expressed in this work are solely those of the author and do not necessarily reflect the views of the publisher, and the publisher hereby disclaims any responsibility for them.

The author of this book does not dispense medical advice or prescribe the use of any technique as a form of treatment for physical, emotional, or medical problems without the advice of a physician, either directly or indirectly. The intent of the author is only to offer information of a general nature to help you in your quest for emotional and spiritual well-being. In the event you use any of the information in this book for yourself, which is your constitutional right, the author and the publisher assume no responsibility for your actions.

Any people depicted in stock imagery provided by Getty Images are models, and such images are being used for illustrative purposes only.
Certain stock imagery © Getty Images.

Print information available on the last page.

ISBN: 978-1-9822-2557-5 (sc)
ISBN: 978-1-9822-2558-2 (e)

Balboa Press rev. date: 10/13/2020

DEDICATION

To my children, Kelley and Alex, my
inspiration and my reason for being,

and

To Niki, my Flaming Star, my Love, my partner in crime.

CONTENTS

FOREWORD

Agni may be an overwhelming Vedic force and energy to comprehend simply due to his own vast powers, capabilities, manifestations, aspects and epithets —all of which are an accurate reflection of his true nature but must be taken in small portions to be fully appreciated. A great deal can be learned about Agni by the most simple method. If you read the opening rcs (mantras) of the First Mandala of the Rg Veda, you would be well on your way to learning about Agni's nature and characteristics. But first let's consider the place the divine Vedic power of Agni occupies in the Vedic dharma. It's true that the Vedas speak of the world of Light, but it also is a world of Fire. Fire plays a more important role, because what is Light but a by-product of Fire? Without fire could there possibly be light?

Perhaps the best introduction to the Vedic force of Agni can be found in the Five Fires doctrine articulated in the early Upanishads. In this doctrine, Prajanya recycles the worshiper's soul as well as and in the manner of rain. This process is described in the Five Fires of the Vedas. According to the Upanishads there are five fires:

- There is the Heavenly Fire. In this Fire, humans are sacrificed at death by cremation, becoming food for the divine Vedic energies and principles and transformed by the heavenly fire into Soma, the purified mind. This fire transforms the human body at death and upon the funeral pyre. The smoke, ciders, and ashes carrying the soul upwards to the heaven. (BU, 6.2.14, Ch.Up., 5.4.1.) This Fire of Agni will be found in various contexts, including, but not limited to the following:

- As a manifestation of Agni, the Heavenly Fire is found in Agni Bharati and Agni Vaisvanara.
- The Vedic force of Agni, repeatedly, is spoken as representing the existential level — and sublevels — of Heaven.
- Agni Suci is the manifestation of Agni as the Celestial Fire.

As the Fire of Parjanya, the Heavenly Fire transforms Soma and the souls in its command into rain. Parjanya is the Vedic divine force for rain. The soul carried upwards to the heavens to be met by Parjanya. (BU, 6.2.10, Ch.Up., 5.5.1, 5.6.1.) This type of Fire encompasses but is not limited to several aspects and manifestations of Agni:

- The Vedic force of Agni, even though commonly associated with Fire, is intimately linked with all Vedic things watery. Namely, Agni is known as the "Child of the Waters," is "Born in the Waters," and so on as discussed hereafter. This is not physical water, as much as Agni is not simply physical fire. Water, the Water element, the concept of essential fluidity, is the very subtle basis of the Vedic dharma.
- Agni is the "Bull." Again, Agni is not a simply associated with bovines. Agni is the Bull, *Vrsti*, signifying Rain. The Bull is *Vrsan(aa)*, the Showerer of Benefits. Just as in this type of Fire, the "Showerer" is not precipitation, but the acquisition of spiritual benefits.

In the Vegetative Fire, Soma, the divine food, releases the rain, its essence, to earth. There, it is transformed into vegetation. Rain is the essence of Soma (Purification), as divine food, falls to the earth with the souls in transmigration. (BU, 6.2.11, Ch.Up., 5.4.2.) Agni is repeatedly associated with all things watery and with the product of that water, vegetation. Vanaspati is the power of Vegetation. Vegetation, as we will see, is a much deeper, complex, concept which, while associated with the Vedic force of Soma, is also associated with the Vedic force of Agni:

- Agni Vanaspati is the manifestation of the Fire of Agni in the Mid-World or Firmament.

- Vanaspati is a Terrestrial manifestation of the Vedic force of Agni.
- The Vedic force of Agni, in his Aspect as the Mystic Fire, is also associated with Vanaspati, "Lord of the Plants."

As the Digestive Fire, when these food plants containing the human remains are eaten, they are transformed into seamen by the man-fire, the digestive fire. The rain containing the seeds of the souls in transmigration are transformed to semen and are absorbed by the plant life and fauna and eaten by man or animal. (BU, 6.2.12.) As revealed in what follows, the digestive fire is found in varying contexts:

- The Vedic force of Agni as the Eater.
- As the "Eater," the Vedic force of Agni encompasses everything from the dissolving agency of the Vedic dharma, to the Vedic force which superimposes the material universe, to obtaining knowledge, enlightenment, or consciousness and everything in between.

As the Female Fire, the semen is transformed into a Purusha, a person, by the woman-fire. The semen is transformed into a Purusha. (BU, 6.6.2.13.) The Vedic force of Agi is *Vrsabha*, signifying the Bull, as related to *Purusa*.

Fire however is a vast concept and assumes many forms. Another resource on Agni may be read from the opening rcs (mantras) of the First Mandala of the Rg Veda. Let's look at these opening rcs of the Rg Veda and what they have to say about Agni.

- Agni is *Agi/m,* the Sacrificial Fire, found in RV 1.1.1.
- Agni is *Agni/h,* the Mystic Fire, found in RV 1.1.2.
- Agni is *Agnina,* the Celestial Fire, the Fire of the Inner Vedic dharma, found in RV 1.1.3.
- Agne is *Agne,* the Terrestrial Fire, Physical Fire, the Digestive Fire, found in RV 1.1.4.
- Agni is *Agnir,* the Fire of Divine Will, found in RV 1.1.5.
- Agni is *Agna,* the Spiritual Fire, found in RV 1.14.2.
- Agni is *Agnau,* the Fire of Self-Surrender, found in RV 1.169.19.

RV 1.164.46 establishes the One, a monistic, divine, spiritual presence. RV 1.164.46 represents a fundamental truth. This well-known rc (mantra) says, in effect, that the Wise know the One ("Ekam") by many names, and they call the One Agni, Indra, etc. The many deities mentioned in the same breath as the One are simply the many manifestations of the One. The fundamental truth is that there is but One God, and the deities associated from the One are its manifestations. Similarly, there are many forms of fire. Fundamentally, however, all are called Agni in the Veda and all the permutations of fire share a common core. In each of these forms of Fire, the divine Vedic force of Agni serves as a catalyst for the variations of spiritual experience encountered by the worshiper during the spiritual journey. During that journey Agni in the capacity of the Sacrificial Fire protects the worshiper (RV 3.27.6) and provides the flame to guide the worshiper along the spiritual path. (RV 3.27.12.) Yet these are only names, categories of the fire of spiritual experience. These categories tell us nothing of the contours of each fire and how the fire changes the worshiper to achieve the goal of spiritual liberation and salvation. These fires contribute to the incredible omnipresence of Agni. This omnipresence in Agni runs across every level:

- On a material, microcosmic level Change represents the digestive fire which supports the individual and operates the material world.
- In a mental level Change represents the light of knowledge.
- On a spiritual level, Change represents the fire which burns away impurities, sins, of the worshiper, providing the forgiveness of sins.
- On cosmic level Change represents the Cosmic Fire.

The Veda speaks of many Agnis. The Veda speaks of the names referring to the inherent, essential powers (*svadha*) of Agni:

- Agni represents the Sacrificial Fire, *Agnim.*
- Agni represents the Mystic Fire in all its permutations which is inherent in the universe, signified in the Rg Veda as *agnih.*
- Agni represents the Fire of Divine Will, called *Agnir.*
- Agni represents the Celestial Fire, or Fire from Heaven, called *Agina.*

- Agni represents the Fire of the Mid-World, *Agner*.
- Agni is the Terrestrial Fire, *Agne*.
- Agni is the Agnaye, the Fire of Transcendence.
- Agni is the Fire of Self-Surrender, *Agnau*.
- Agni represents the source of the light of consciousness, or awareness, signified in the Rg Veda as *agnii/na, agnii/,* and *agna*.

Agni of course represents the physical element of Fire, *Agne*. There are four components to this element of Fire:

- Agni as the Digestive Fire.
- Agni as the Vegetative Fire.
- Agni as the Fire Altar.
- Agni representing physical fire.

As you can see, there are many sides to the theogony of the Vedic force of Agni. How can a subject like Agni be neatly summarized in a few pages? These subjects are only the highlights to what is contained herein. The pervasion and omnipresence of the Vedic force of Agni is incredible even for Vedic standards. There will be a tremendous amount of information in this treatment. The amount of that information matches the importance of this Vedic force. The Vedic force of Agni has many fires. Those fires follow.

INTRODUCTION

Surely, one of the greatest developments in the course of human civilization is the discovery of fire. Fire, of course, had always existed, human beings had only discovered how to create a burning flame and use it for their own purposes. When that moment happened, the individuals at the time of discovery were probably surprised and shocked to the bone. What they had discovered did not appear to have a stationary presence. It constantly changed shape. They could not grasp it, could not hold it, in fact, if they could it would be positively harmful. This substance had the ability to cause burns and injure anyone who got too close to the flame. Yet, it proved very beneficial. It cooked the food, it provided illumination in the darkness, it would ward off all wild animals or marauding humans who attempted to attack them; indeed, it would ward off any enemy, animal or human. And it was mesmerizing to gaze upon. The flame would dance around in front of their eyes and make a soft, crackling noise as it consumed the wood, twigs or scrub-brush. And yet, it had to be watched very carefully, because if it got out of control, it would destroy everything, including the humans who purportedly discovered the flame. Fire is one of the most powerful, terrifying, yet beneficial, forces in the Vedic dharma.

Agni is the first among equal Vedic dynamic forces and energies. It is the first Vedic force for good reason. There are three deities, divine Vedic forces, which dominate the Vedas: Agni, Indra and Soma. While identifying divine force which predominates the most is like asking someone who is their favorite Beatle, and even if Indra has been called the "first among equals," there is good reason why personage of Agni holds special standing. While Indra is arguably more powerful and Soma more

1

spiritually uplifting, Agni is everywhere, in every reference and rc, yajur or saman. Agni is omnipresent. (RV 4.1.1.) This quality has to do with the pervasive nature of this divine force. Agni's preeminence is reflected in the way in which the Vedas are organized. Except for the Ninth Mandala which is concerned solely with Soma, every Mandala in the Rg Veda begins with Suktas praising and extolling Agni. The Presiding Deity of the beginning Suktas of every Mandala is Agni. Indra can only claim this distinction in the Eighth Mandala.

Yet, for all its importance, the divine force of Agni remains a mystery. Ask anyone about Agni, and if he or she knows anything, it's that Agni is the God of Fire, and that will be it. The cognate of the Sanskrit word, "Agni" means literally, "to be maintained," that is, a fire kindled must be maintained or it will extinguish. (*https://en.wikipedia.org/wiki/List_of_Rigvedic_tribes*.) What does all this really tell us? What does it mean to be the "God of Fire"? To say that Agni is fire and leaving it like that doesn't really tell us anything substantive about this Vedic force or about the nature of fire. Is Agni simply physical fire, the fire burning the logs in the fireplace? At least the internal meaning of Agni as something to be maintained tells us something, that Agni is eternal, born of humanity, or eternally born of humanity. The main theme of this book is that Agni represents the dynamic force of Change and Transformation. As Yogi Baba Prem writes, "Agni manifests on many levels of being. Within our physical body, Agni is the digestive fire called Jatharagni. On the level of the mind, Agni is our will power. It is the ability to digest experience and activities in or life. Agni is the deity of the fire element providing transformation, as Agni does purify the mind and body. Agni is the kundalini energy when active." (Yogi Baba Prem (2011) *Yogic Secrets of the Vedas*, pp. 88 – 89.) But this does not tell us a great deal about this Vedic force. The concepts of Change and Transformation themselves are too generalized as concepts to give us a true or complete picture of the full array of powers, manifestations, or capabilities of Agni.

In the Vedas the presence or references to Agni are seemingly ubiquitous. It is therefore difficult to make sense of the powers, capabilities and nature of Agni. This book strives to describe the many aspects and manifestations of Change and Transformation, always with an eye with what the Vedas say about Agni. More importantly, this book attempts to discover the true nature of fire and how Fire is expressed in inner essence of the Vedic force of Agni. Moreover, this book attempts to sift through the many, many references to Agni and put those powers in an understandable context.

Other than Agni, Indra and Soma are two of the other most important divine forces. The divine force in Indra, while varied and multi-faceted, encompasses a narrow band width in the scope of divine powers. Soma is an incredibly important divine force, yet its divine range is narrower than Indra's. What sets Agni apart from Indra and Soma or the other divine Vedic forces for that matter, is his *scope*. The divine powers of Agni are incredible and vast, and in the grandest tradition of the inter-mutuality of Vedic divine powers, shares, but does not subsume, the divine Vedic forces of Indra or Soma, and, for that matter, the other divine Vedic forces. Agni is another primal divine force, perhaps the most important, and therefore this book must — and will — dig deep, much deeper than ordinary treatments, to reveal all about Agni.

The fires of Agni consists in his aspects and his manifestations. The Aspects of the Vedic force of Agni pertain to his essential, inherent nature. Those Aspects are:

- The Fire Altar.
- The Fire of Self-Surrender.
- The Sacrificial Fire.
- The Mystic Fire.
- The Fire of Divine Will.
- The Transcendental Fire.
- The Fire of Light.

The Veda then speaks of the many manifestations of Agni. These forms of Agni are called "manifestations" because these refer to the manner in which Agni appears in the Vedic dharma and are those qualities of the Vedic force of Agni which appear in the material world. Those qualities manifest themselves in various fires. They include fires located in the three worlds of existence. The Vedic Force of Agni has many manifestations. The general manifestations (B.D., 1.66.) include

- Agni Suci, the manifestation of the Celestial Fire.

- Agni Vanaspati, the manifestation of the Fire in the Mid-World and
- Agni Pavamana, the manifestation of the Terrestrial Fire.

The Celestial Fires of Agni are Agni Bharati and Agni Vaisvanara. The fires of the firmament are found in the

- Maruts,
- Agni Jatavedas,
- Rudra, and
- Saraswati,

Agne, the terrestrial aspect Agni, Agni Pavamana, presides over these divinities possessing the following manifestations. Those manifestations are:

- Agnayi.
- Ajith, Agni Pavamana symbolized as the "Guest" of human dwellings, constant presence.
- Apva, Agni Pavamana "filled," having the quality of Pervasiveness.
- Aranyani.
- Barhi, representing the inner seat (of grass) wherein the vision of Agni Pavamana is made.
- The Bull.
- Dhumaketu, "Special Vibratory" (dhuma) + "knowledge" (ketu), the vibration of Knowledge envisaging Agni Pavamana as the "smoke bearer."
- Dravinodas, the Giver of Strength.
- The Frog.
- Grhapati, Agni Pavamana as the Sacrificial Fire.
- Idhma, Agni Pavamana representing Fuel of Fire.
- Ila, an epithet of Agni Pavamana representing the Power of Consciousness to envision the truth.
- Kavi, another name for the Rishis.
- The litter and the Divine Doors.
- Narasamsa, the terrestrial aspect of Agni Pavamana as the Sacrifice.
- Pestle and Mortar.

- Prthvi (Earth).
- The Pressing Stones.
- Ratri.
- The Rivers.
- Sraddha.
- The Steed, the Horses.
- Svadha. Svadha is defined as an inherent power which upholds its own nature, following its own law or nature. Svadha also refers to the essential nature of Change and the other dynamic forces in the Vedic pantheon. On a personal level, svadha implicates the means by which the qualities present in the Vedic divine forces may be implementation into the life of the worshiper.
- Svahakritis, The maker of offerings, from "Offering" (*svaha*) + "maker" (*kriti*).
- Tanunapi. Tanunapi is that aspect of Agni Pavamana meaning "The summer sun" or "Son of the Body of the aspirant."
- Tvasta.
- Tvastr, the Architect, "Fashioner of Forms," of the Universe, Demiurge.
- Usasanakta, "Dawn and Night."
- Vaisvanara, a principal aspect of Agni Pavamana.
- Vanaspati, defined as the "Lord of Beauty."

This present volume will be concerned with the aspects and manifestations of Agni. The aspects of Agni pertain to the *svadha*, or essential, inherent, essence of Agni, basically those qualities which make Agni the Vedic force that he is. The remaining manifestations of Agni pertain to how Agni appears — or is manifested — in this material world.

To paraphrase that famous rc, there are many forms of Agni, but the wise call Agni only as One. This book, however, analyzes, dissects, and explains the many fires, or forms, of Agni. The many forms of this Vedic divine force are described in what follows.

This book will reveal that for all of Agni's rage and fury, once the curtains are drawn and the true nature of Agni is revealed, then, much like what occurred in the climax of The Wizard of Oz movie when the curtains were drawn to reveal the terrible Wizard to be a diminutive, gentleman, the fiery presence of Agni is not so terrible after all. Awesome, yes; all-encompassing in his power, certainly; terrible, no. Neither will the personage behind that curtain be the diminutive, likeable old man as in the movie. Agni commands a presence and notice will be taken. That presence is magisterial and pervasive. However, as primal and atavistic as is the Vedic force of Agni, so are the rewards that may be gained. Getting to that point will require some patience. This is not an ordinary examination of a Vedic deity. The path to the truth will be circuitous. The Vedas are full of symbols and this book will attempt to decipher those symbols as much as possible. But once there, the effort is well worth it. So buckle your safety belts, we are all in store for a bumpy ride. But first, there are a few issues about Agni to clarify. The true breadth of Agni cannot be properly appreciated without a description and understanding of the structure of the Vedic dharma.

The Vedic Dharma

You will see three recurring, inter-linking, terms in this book. They are "natural order," or derivations therefrom, the word used many, many times in the Veda to signify the natural order, *Rta*, and the Vedic dharma. These words refer to objects, all of which are in essence the functional equivalent to the Vedic dharma. "Dharma" is, of course, the series of moral and ethical laws regulating the daily life of the worshiper. The word itself, "dharma," however, is infrequently found in the Rg Veda. In its place, the Rg Veda spoke of *Rta*, the dynamic cosmic natural order. References to *Rta* in the Vedas are legion. *Rta*, or derivatives of *Rta*, occur well over two hundred times in the Veda. Dharma also has a wider meaning. In the Vedas, dharma is the totality of the natural order. (VS, 1.1.1.) In other words, it is everything, both great and small, gross and subtle, and macrocosmic and microcosmic. Those objects include the Sun, Moon and the Stars, the three existential levels of Earth, Mid-World, and Heaven. It includes the material we all live in. All those objects we see, feel, touch, and smell. It ranges from the outermost edges of the cosmos, to the most minutest sub-atomic particle. It is not only the material world, but it includes the subtle, intangible world which serves as its foundation. It is, quite simply, Everything. Not only everything, but the theory of everything.

6

In the Vedic Dharma the anchor of the natural order is *Rta* itself as reflected in the Vedic deities, themselves the dynamic forces of that natural order which are incorporated into the lives of worshipers. The aim is that we all learn from the dharma (*rta*). It was assumed that the human population is not only composed of the same ingredients of the universe but is also ruled by the same universal principles. The purpose of individuals and not simply the worshiper is to discover the relation of the cosmos to the natural order of things (*rta*) and relate that natural order to the material world and to the people who inhabit it who incorporate those precepts into their lives. This quest is essentially the purpose of the worshiper's spiritual journey. Dharma is that enlightenment and understanding obtained from the natural order (*rta*). (VS, 1.1.2.)

The universe is a complex organism. Numbers play a significant role in the composition of the universe by making that universe more intelligible. The Vedic multi-universe is premised on the physical complexity of matter itself. To everyday eyes, physical matter is solid and while malleable, seemingly impenetrable. As modern physics demonstrates, however, the deeper one delves into the essence of physical matter, the less and less solid is it found to be. The seeming solidity is found to be far more rarified and subtle, the surface solidity pocked with abscesses and canyons, the surface placidly charged with electrical sparks. Modern physics has found that the deepest recesses of solid matter are not solid at all, but rarified, ethereal spaces. This is the basis of the Vedic universe, and it informs the Vedic dharma. It guides the worshiper to liberation from this transmigration world.

As in all things Vedic, numbers play a very significant role in the Vedic dharma. The universe is interpreted through number. The worshiper's spiritual development and very existence is measured by number. Indeed, in the Vedic dharma, everything is measured by and through number. While number is potentially infinite, there exists cardinal numbers, with which that potential infinity is reduced.

The cardinal numbers in the Vedic universe are two, three, five and seven. The cardinal numbers pertain to ever-greater levels of abstraction: As the numbers progress to higher levels, so does physical matter become ever subtle and so intensify the worshiper's journey to liberation. These numbers are coordinates which are incorporated into the structure of the universe.

The microcosm and macrocosm can be interpreted with reference to these cardinal numbers. The Vedic path to liberation and salvation, traverses these stages of creation, these manifestations of the possible universes. The spiritual progression is very much an upward climb through these universes, from the duality present in the Two-Dimensional world to the transcendent world of the Seven-Dimensional Universe. The many possible worlds are born from the single, unitary, One (Ekam). As quoted in the Tao Tse Ching, "One produced two, two produced three, three produced ten thousand."

These are the Vedic multiple universes reflect the material world:

- The Two-Dimensional Universe which is the material world itself.
- The Three-Dimensional world is the gateway, inching towards the Five-Dimensional Universe.
- The Five-Dimensional Universe is the subtle aspect of the material world. It is at this point that the spiritual journey the Agni, the Fire of Change accomplishes the world yajna in five movements, three and seven threads. (RV 10.52.4.)
- The Seven-Dimensional Universe is that which transcends the material world.

These different dimensions define different levels of reality. At a rudimentary level, the analysis begins with the visible, material, gross world we all live and breathe in, the Two-Dimensional Universe. The progression to higher stages brings the worshiper to levels of existence which are ever more and more subtle and abstract. Viewed from the bottom up, the progression can be summarized as follows:

- The Two-Dimensional Universe consists of the material world itself, roughly corresponding to *Prakrti*, the inert matter of the everyday world, and the larger macrocosm, corresponding to Purusa, Consciousness. In this world, the worshiper lives in a confused, chaotic world. It is the world we all wake up to and confront every day.
- The Three-Dimensional Universe introduces the first intervention of the Mind, consciousness. Sankhya, one of the branches of the

Vedas, describes this moment as that instant when Purusa makes contact with inert matter, *Prakrti*, energizing the evolution of the world. In this Vedic dharma, because *Prakrti* is inert and essentially cannot act on its own accord at this point, that contact is made through the Mind. Mind, Consciousness, therefore, acts as the bridge between *Prakrti* and Purusa. What this means to the worshiper is that these are the beginning "baby steps" made in the spiritual search.

- The Five-Dimensional Universe continues the process begun in the Three-Dimensional Universe. Here, the Mind, Consciousness, is more fully developed, becomes meditative, exhibits the first indicators of enlightenment. At this stage the worshiper begins and proceeds in earnest to restrain and control the mind in yoga or engage in any of the other paths to liberation or salvation.
- The highest level, at the Seven-Dimensional Universe, is the most subtle, and goes by different names, such as Heaven, *svar, rocane*, and others. It represents the liberation of the worshiper and the culmination of the spiritual journey.

The divine Vedic energy in Agni has a special role to play in every stage of the spiritual journey. For example, Agni represents the Two-Dimensional Universe. In this world there exists are entire array of Terrestrial Fires. These Terrestrial Fires are discussed in detail much later in this book.

Agni represents the broad overview of the Three-Dimensional Universe. Agni is the Light of Consciousness. He is the mediating Mind bridging the actions of Purusa to make its contact with *Prakrti*. There are three elements to this existential level; Agni has three forms. (TS, 2.2.4.2.) Representing the Purusa enlivening the inert matter of *Prakrti*, he is the perfect spokesman for the Three-Dimensional Universe:

- The Fire of Change (Agni) has a three-fold nature. (RV 1.95.3; 4.1.7.)
- This three-fold nature has sometimes been a representation of the Garhapatya, daksinagni, and Ahavaniya, the three fire altars, sometimes called the "three brothers." (RV 1.164.1; 10.51.6.) These

three altars would later be the inspiration for the three humors, the dosas, in Ayurveda, Pitta, Kalpha, and Vatta.

- The divine fashioned The Principle of Change (Agni) to have this three-fold nature. (RV 10.88.10.)
- The Fire of Change (Agni) has three heads. (RV 1.146.1.)
- Agni resides in three stations, tongue or bodies. (RV 3.20.2.)
- The Fire of Change (Agni) resides in three abodes (RV 8.39.8), meaning heaven, earth and water. (RV 8.44.16; 10.2.7; 4.6.9.)
- The Fire of Change (Agni) is lit with three kindlings. (RV 3.2.9; 3.26.7.)
- The Fire of Change (Agni) has three births (RV 1.95.3; 4.1.7), the first from heaven, the second from men, and the third from the waters. (RV 10.45.1.)
- There are three aspects to Vaisvanara, a manifestation of Agni: (1) the Fire of Knowledge, (2) the force of Vital energy, and (3) the sacrificial fire. (RV 3.2.9.)
- Agni has a triple nature. He has three Steeds (read, energies or senses), three worlds, the Heavenly, Mid-World and Earth Fires, three tongues, or bodies, three bodies desired by the other Vedic forces and energies. (RV 3.20.2.)

Sayana interprets this rc (mantra) as referring to the flame of fire originating from the three altars, the Grhapatya, Ahavaniya, and Daksinagni. On a cosmological level, Agni acts on the Three-Dimensional Universe in the Fires of the Earth, Mid-Earth, and Firmament, discussed later in this book. These will have their role to play when Agni acts on the Five-Dimensional Universe."

The Five-Dimensional Universe is an important step in the spiritual journey because it is here that it all starts go come together. This is accomplished through the agency of Agni. Agni represents the Five-Dimensional Universe.

- Agni has five forms. (TB 1.2.1.70.)
- There are five steps to purification, discussed a little later in this Introduction.

- Indeed, the Upanishads clarify that there are five fires presiding the vast swath of existence, liberation, procreation and transmigration.

Which brings the worshiper to a higher level of Heaven in the Seven-Dimensional Universe. We just saw that Agni serves many capacities when acting on the Three-Dimensional Universe. At bottom, the Seven-Dimensional Universe is a combination of the three upper and three lower levels of existence, conjoined together by the Svar. At the same time, there are three levels of sensible appearance, the earth, mid-world, and heaven. (RV 1.34.7, 1.154.4.) The Fire of Agni is the unifying force to this existential structure. The Vedic dharma then is a vast umbrella which covers two separate, wide, existential planes.

- One, it is the three-part structure of Earth, Mid-Earth, and Heaven. This is represented in the Three-Dimensional Universe.
- Two, it is a seven-layer structure consisting of the existential levels of *Sat, chit ananda, svar, dyu, Antariksha, bhuvah, and bhumi.* (R.L. Kashyap, *Basics of the Rig Veda*, p. 30.) This structure is represented in the Seven-Dimensional Universe.

In a broad, subtle sense the Vedic Field extends over these two distinct planes of Existence: One, the three-part structure of Earth, Mid-World, and Heaven, and Two, the seven-layer existential levels of *Sat, chit, ananda, svar, dyu, Antariksha, bhuvah*, and *bhumi*. Agni is the unifying agent for both of these two existential planes, the Third-Dimensional and Seven-Dimensional Universes. These two vast swaths of existence are bound together by the Vedic force of Agni. This is established in the Veda through abundant authority:

- It will be repeated several times here — if only because it is such an important point — that the Vedic force of Indra fights the serpent Vrtra as an incarnation of Agni. Once Vrtra has been overcome and as a result of conquering Vrtra, the lunar house of Indra took control of the secrets of Heaven and Earth and unlocked the power which united Heaven and Earth to create the three existential levels of Earth, Mid-World and Heaven. (RV 3.38.3.) This Vedic force of Agni is the same power which creates the Svar, that region

11

which binds Heaven and Earth This rc (mantra) reveals not only that Agni created the existential structure to support not only the Svar but the power which unites the three layers of Earth, Mid-World and Heaven with the seven existential levels of *Sat, chit, ananda, svar, dyu, Antariksha, bhuvah*, and *bhumi*.

- As the essence of the Vedic dharma is Water, Agni the Sacrificial Fire, represents the ultimate Vedic paradox. In the Vedic dharma water and fire are not mutually exclusive. They are of the same substance and they complement each other in their opposition. The Vedic force of Agni, sacrificially and as a philosophical construct, plays its own part in defining and maintaining these different universes.

Agni as the Sacrificial Fire is the overlay of these two plains of existence. The Vedic force of Agni binds together the three layers of Earth, Mid-World and Heaven and the seven existential levels of *Sat, chit, ananda, svar, dyu, Antariksha, bhuvah*, and *bhumi*. That Agni is the force binding these existential planes is evident from the epithets and descriptors given to Agni in the Vedas:

- The Fire of Agni is both the sevenfold human and the triple abode. (RV 8.39.8.)
- Agni is described as having three heads and seven rays. (RV 1.146.1.)
- Agni is given the epithet, "Thrice Seven," *trih sapta*, throughout the Vedas, in the Rg Veda in several rcs (mantras). (RV 1.72.6; 1.191.12, 14; 4.1.16; 7.87.4; 8.46.26; 8.96.2; 9.86.21; 10.64.8; 10.90.15.)

These epithets and concepts will appear in this book in varying degrees. The Fire of Agni represents the unifying agent to the Seven Rivers, symbolically meaning the seven layers of existence. (RV 3.1.4.) In addition, the Fire of Agni represents the unifying force of the three existential levels of Heaven, Mid-Earth, and Earth. (RV 10.88.3.) What this means to the worshiper is that the Vedic force of Agni, by its very nature as Change and Transformation, navigates the worshiper through these different levels of the Vedic dharma to proceed upwards

The Principle of Change and Transformation

The spiritual journey, or any journey for that matter, involves change. Change in daily habits, change in the way of thinking, change in the manner of behavior — or any other change. The dancing flames of Agni is the perfect metaphor for Change and Transformation, because, before our own eyes, the flames change and morph in ever differing shapes, sizes and forms. The first hurdle to overcome in understanding the fires of Agni is finding a workable definition. As had been stated above, Agni is associated with fire. But simply saying Agni is fire, without more, really doesn't tell us anything about the powers and capabilities of Agni. There is a deeper meaning behind fire. We just have to find it, and this is what this book is about. When we say Agni is fire, what we are saying is that he is the active Fire of Change and Transformation. Why do we say that?

Agni is associated with this material world. In his dominion over this world, Agni rules as the Fire of Change, encompassing the constant change and flux of the sensible world and informs the mental and spiritual transformation of the mind and soul of the worshiper. Lightning is an incidental characteristic for Agni.

This Fire of Change is best exhibited in Agni Vaisvanara. (SPB 10.6.4.1.) Vaisvanara is defined as the Terrestrial Fire produced from the Aerial Fire and Celestial Fire. (BD, 2.18, Nir. 7.6, T.S., 2.2.5.) Vaisvanara is elsewhere defined as the digestive fire (B.G). The Aerial, Celestial and digestive fire are the processes by which the Fire of Change is powered and regulate the other aspects of Agni's divine cosmic force. In yet other places, Agni Vaisvanara is a principal manifestation of the Celestial Fire of Agni, which will be explained in detail later.

In Sanskrit "Agne" means "fire." Agni is traditionally mentioned as the god of fire. Agni is more than simple, physical fire. Classical grammarians, however, derive Agni's name from the root, *"ang."* (Sastry, *Collected Works*, Vol. IV, (1983).) From the root ang the word angara for "charcoal" is derived. The charcoal is the remnants of the Sacrificial Fire or any form of fire. The sacrificial ritual is representative of the universe, the acquisition of Knowledge of the universe and of the worshiper's self, and Self-Sacrifice. Considered alone, the Sacrificial Fire represents knowledge in this equation. A spark becomes a flame, a flame becomes many flames, the flames die out and become embers and ash. Embers are the heated coals once the fire has subsided, and after the Sacrificial Fire has been ignited the embers have subsided, what remains is are the charcoal remains. If the Sacrificial Fire represents knowledge, charcoal represents the final irreducible essence of that knowledge.

Agni is many things with many applications in the Vedas. Agni represents Change and Transformation, this is Agni's inherent nature, and this inherent nature is reflected in its many manifestations:

- The Heavenly Fire, the fire created when humans are sacrificed at death by cremation, becoming food for the divine Vedic energies and principles and transformed by the heavenly fire into Soma, the purified mind.
- The Fire of Parjanya, the Vedic divine force for rain, the fire which transforms Soma and the souls in its command into rain.
- The Vegetative Fire, the Fire of Soma, the divine food, who releases the rain, its essence, to earth, where it is transformed into vegetation.
- The Digestive Fire, the fire transformed into seamen by the man-fire, the digestive fire.
- The Female Fire, the Fire created when semen is transformed into a Purusha, a person, by the woman-fire.

Agni is in constant motion and flux. It constantly changes form and substance to accommodate the particular purpose involved. In this constant change and transformation, Agni assumes many Aspects and Manifestations described earlier.

The relation between change and consciousness is reflected in a Sanskrit root associated with Agni, Ang. The clan of Seers, the Angirasas, were born from Agni. (RV 10.662.6.) This derivation does much to tell us about the nature of Agni and Knowledge.

- *Anga*, signifying brilliance or effulgence, specifically to describe the aspect of Change in the light of consciousness. (RV 1.1.6, 1.84.7, 8, 19, 1.118.3,1.164.7, 2.41.10, 3.33.11, 3.48.5, 5.3.11, 6.44.10, 6.50.10, 6.52.3, 6.72.5, 7.20.9, 7.56.2, 7.91.1, 8.6.26,8.7.2, 8.80.5,

8.96.13, 10.4.4, 10.42.3, 10.54.4, 10.64.13, 10.79.4, 10.129.7, 10.131.2, 10.149.3.)

- *Angdh*, the attribute of resplendence, again, expressed in association of consciousness. (RV 9.5.10.)
- *Angdhve*, signifying the flash of revelation. (RV 10.100.10.)
- The Angiras, the family of Vedic Rishis. (RV 1.1.6, 1.74.5, 2.23.8, 4.9.7, 5.11.1, 6.2.10, 8.60.2, 8.74.11, 8.75.5, 8.102.17.)
- *Angirastama*, the mystic essence of the Agniras Rishis. (RV 1.75.2, 8.43.18,8.43.27.)
- *Angiraso*, that aspect of Angiras in possession of super-human intellectual powers, a siddhi. (RV 1.62.2, 1.71.2, 3.53.7, 4.2.15,4.3.11, 5.11.6, 6.65.5,7.42.1, 10.14.6, 10.67.2, 10.78.6, 10.108.9.)
- *Angiro*, the divine reflection of Angiras imbued with the glory of Change. (RV 1.31.11, 1.112.18, 4.3.15, 5.2.8, 5.21.1, 6.16.11.)

Keep this derivation in mind for later. This root derivation signifying charcoal will be important to establish the spiritual leap from Agni to Indra. Agni has the quality of lightning. Agni, commonly related to fire, is associated with lightning. (SPB 10.6.2.11.) In a passage from a Brahmana, pregnant with individual meaning, gives one of the best descriptions of the scope of Agni. In that passage the Fire of Agni is kindled in six ways (SPB 10.6.2.11):

- By the fire, by the breath.
- By the Sun, by the winds
- By the winds, by fire,
- By the moon by the sun,
- By the stars by the moon, and
- Through the lightning of the Stars.

The important word in that passage is "Kindled." Physical fire is "ignited," but the Sacrificial Fire is "kindled." Kindling imparts all those qualities and energies from the universe and channeled those qualities and energies into the Fire. The Sacrificial Fire plays a central role in the Sacrificial ritual, it is the center of attraction. Once kindled it is beheld by the worshiper, or, as in the Soma Sacrifice, the principal means of producing the Soma juice to be consumed by the worshiper. In all sacrificial settings, the central fire is the means by which the worshiper is transformed spiritually. The Sun is the source of all life. It is the agent which destroys the old life of the worshiper, and like the phoenix rising from the ashes, a new worshiper emerges. Breath in this above passage is prana, the subtle essence of the life force permeating the universe and sustaining the life of the worshiper. In other words, in part, the Fire of Agni is powered by and empowers the elements of the Vedic dharma, the natural order (*rta*).

What this passage from the Brahmana serves to show is that fire is not simply a burning flame. It is a dynamic active force which ignites the spiritual transformation of the worshiper. This because fire is the principal medium for change. As a physical phenomenon fire constantly changes shape and form, and it is one of the few agents which is able to change another substance and reduce it to its most elemental physical substances. Agni is Fire, the image of a flame of fire constantly flickers and palpitates, which is why Agni is the Fire of Change and transformation and why he is so central to the Rg Veda. So when we speak of the manifestation of Agni as the embers from the Sacrificial Fire, Anga, we learn this about the brilliance or effulgence in the light of consciousness.

- The dynamic energy supplies the light of consciousness in the worshiper. (RV 1.1.6.)
- From that point, the divine dynamic force of Indra (RV 1.84.7, 8, 16, 8.6.26, 8.80.5, 8.96.13) or his confederates such as the Asvins (RV 1.118.3) assume the role thereafter in regulating and managing that light of consciousness.

The Light of Consciousness, then, is one aspect of Agni's divine force and energy. There are other characteristics to the active Fire of Change. It is one thing to say that Agni is the Light of Consciousness. That light must first be turned on. This is also a power of Agni.

Increase

Related to the Vedic concept of Change and Transformation is Increase. Increase is one of the most esoteric, yet important, elements in the Vedic dharma. Increase is what it is all about. There can be no development — internal development, upward movement, downward movement, spiritual or otherwise — without Increase. Increase is the practical means of the worshiper to gain the spiritual endowments provided in the Vedas. More generally the only means by which the fire of Change and Transformation may occur. Agni is the guiding force for the power of Increase.

The idea of increase is expressed in the fact that the spiritual development of the worshiper admits to the addition of qualities not present before of characteristics not previously exhibited. In many cases, previous views are modified, some are outright discarded. It is the very essence of sacrifice. Sacrifice is basically a giving and taking.

The fire of giving and taking is grounded in the Two-Dimensional Universe which serves as the basis for the material world. The rising of the Sun gives rise to the appearance of the Moon, Day rises to bring in the night, Hot is the flip side of Cold. This dynamic was not unknown in Vedic literature. The Chandogya Upanishad recognizes the dichotomy of pleasant and unpleasant smells, Truth and Falsity, pleasant and unpleasant sounds, and even pleasant and unpleasant thoughts. This dichotomy is grounded on the existence of Good and Evil. But even with these polar opposites there comes a point where there is unification. This is the purpose of Increase and implies the importance of Agni in the resolution of this push and pull.

The chaotic Two-Dimensional Universe is resolved with the worshiper's spiritual awakening. In the process of spiritual awakening, the world and its perception are different because the worshiper is different. The old worshiper is discharged in exchange of the new. The sacrifice of the higher element produces an increase of the lower is called an out-and-out increase: it indicates the spirit that alone has power to help the world. Sacrifice thus becomes a prominent feature of increase, because it is a product of a give and take process. As Richard Wilhelm, commenting on the I-Ching, once observed, "Sacrifice on the part of those above for the increase of those below fills the people with a sense of joy and gratitude that is extremely valuable for the flowering of the commonwealth. When people are thus devoted to their leaders, undertakings are possible, and even difficult and dangerous enterprises will succeed. Therefore in such times of progress and successful development it is necessary to work and make the best use of time. This time resembles that of the marriage of heaven and earth, when the earth partakes of the creative power of heaven, forming and bringing forth living beings. The time of increase does not endure; therefore it must be utilized while it lasts."

Here however is where the I-Ching and Vedas depart. The I-Ching credits the worshiper for this increase, while in the Vedic dharma, in the Vedas, Agni is the agent for increase. (RV 5.16.7, 5.17.5.) Thus, it is said that

- Agni obtains his powers of Increase from the Waters, from the foundation of the Vedic dharma itself. (RV 1.95.5.)
- The Vedic force and energy of Agni is the means of increase in every aspect of the worshiper's life. (RV 5.10.3.)
- We will soon meet Parjanya, the Fire of Regeneration. This fire Increases the spiritual Fire of Agni. (RV 7.101.3.)
- The Vedic force and energy of Agni in its manifestation as the Bull increases the life of the worshiper. As the Bull, the change and transformation effected by Agni is accomplished through regeneration, which the Bull symbolizes. (RV 1.31.5.)
- Agni's means for Increase in the worshiper is also sourced from his light. (RV 1.71.8.) It seems rather self-evident that there should be some correspondence between fire, flames and light. But this is another exercise in symbolic speech. Light is associated with Illumination and Consciousness, and as we will see in the next discussion in this Introduction, Agni is the Light of Consciousness.
- The divine force and energy of Agni, in its manifestation as Jatavedas, is the source of Increase to the Vedic dharma as a whole. (RV 1.87.5.)

The Veda states that the Increase of Agni will "prosper" the worshiper. (RV 1.92.11.) We need to be clear on what is meant by "wealth." The Veda speaks of "benefits," and "riches." These references are not to taken literally to mean material wealth. It is to obtain those spiritual benefits that guides the worshiper's spiritual journey. Ostensibly, the Vedic force of Agni, in his aspect as the Sacrificial Fire, provides these spiritual endowments and entitlements to the worshiper. (RV 7.10.3.) The worshiper receives these riches once the worshiper serves the Sacrificial Fire. (RV 8. 44.15.) These riches are interpreted to mean the specific characteristics of the spiritual increase personally experienced by the worshiper. The Spiritual Fire of Agni creates and instills in the worshiper the desire seek the same during the spiritual journey. (RV 6.1.3.) The Spiritual Fire of Agni casts the light on the path the worshiper should tread, (RV 6.1.3), although not completely. In a manner of speech relatively common in the Rg Veda, these spiritual endowments are the "treasures" obtained by Agni in his manifestation of the Sacrificial Fire. The spiritual endowments and benefits — the worshiper's prosperity — is made possible through Increase.

Agni's capacity of Increase is a demonstration of the give-and-take displayed at the sacrifice. Agni as the Sacrificial Fire is itself increased when the fire is kindled by the worshiper. (RV 2.35.11.) The "kindled" fire carries with it an entire bundle of mystic properties. The Veda states that the kindled, transcendent Agni does not simply have the characteristics of the Maruts, but those characteristics multiplied twice or three times. (RV 6.66.2.) The Maruts, even though they are more commonly associated as the "cleaners" of the Vedic force of Indra, were first empowered with their divine Vedic energies from Agni, in his manifestation as Vanaspati, the Terrestrial Agni. (BD, 1.103.) We will later see those seven characteristics of the Maruts. Briefly, those qualities are:

- The Maruts encapsulate the knowledge of how to cause the waters to descend. (RV 1.19.3.)
- The Maruts are ferocious (*ugra*). (RV 1.19.4.)
- The Maruts are radiant and powerful. (RV 1.19.5.)
- They live in the heaven above the Sun. (RV 1.19.6.)
- The Maruts have the psychic and physical strength to move mountains. (RV 1.19.7.)
- The Maruts spread and expand with the rays of an ocean (i.e., Consciousness.) (RV 1.19.8.)
- The Maruts drink Soma. (RV 1.19.9.)

This is a powerful set of qualities, you can imagine the awesome strength of these characteristics when Agni is fully empowered. After the worshiper kindles the Sacrificial Fire, these augmented powers are concentrated into the light produced therefrom and becomes food. This food is thereupon consumed by the worshiper and is incorporated into spiritual lessons the worshiper gains and incorporates for travel in the spiritual journey. In turn, Agni as the Fire Altar thereafter gives Increase in the form of strength to the worshiper. (RV 8.75.13.) It is an intricate symbiosis which ultimately accounts for the spiritual inspiration of the worshiper during the spiritual search. As a result of this give-and-take process Agni bestows much more to the worshiper:

- The worshiper's increase results from being "bathed in the flames" of Agni. (RV 1.71.6.) This is symbolic speech referring to the fire of purification. In addition to being the agent for Increase, Agni is the purifying agent. This aspect of the Vedic force of Agni will be explored later in this Introduction.
- Agni provides Increase to the worshiper to battle the enemies encountered in the spiritual journey. (RV 1.79.11.)
- Agni provides this Increase by awakening the worshiper's consciousness, driving and guiding the worshiper's thoughts, and providing expression to the worshiper's words. (RV 3.3.8.)
- Agni provides increase by bestowing spiritual endowments and benefits to the worshiper. (RV 5.10.7.)
- The worshiper indeed depends on the spiritual strength and illumination of Agni for the Increase. (RV 8.60.10.)

Agni does not simply provide the Increase to the worshiper. The Sacrificial Fire, for example, account for Brahmanaspati's own powers of Increase. (RV 2.25.2.)

The Vedic force and energy of Agni also "increases the Kine." (RV 1.93.2) This is another exercise of symbolic speech. The cow, however, represents more than an animal. The Cow is normally a very placid mammal, interested more in chewing cud than in anything else. It takes a lot to infuriate a cow, and once riled, quickly calms down. The ancients no doubt superimposed their own aspiration on the cow's demeanor. Its stoic calm indisputably indicated a deeper understanding which stood as a stark contrast to the great penchant for mischief in humans. In keeping with these aspirations, cows were subsequently interpreted as these:

- Cows represent the inner illumination of the rays of knowledge. (RV 2.24.6, 4.1.16 (glory of the cow of light discovered after meditation of the supreme name of the milch cow.)
- Cows represent consciousness as knowledge. (RV 3.30.20, 3.39.6 (Indra finding meath (empirical knowledge) in the cows), 10.92.10 (inspired knowledge), 3.31.10, 3.31.11.)
- According to Sri Aurobindo, cows represent the power of consciousness, discrimination, and discernment. (See also, RV 2.11.2, 2.15.10, 2.16.9, 2.34.15 (right-thinking), 3.31.11, 10.92.10.) In recognition of this meaning, some English translations render *gobhir*, as "Ray-Cows," signifying the rays of knowledge. (See, RV 1.7.3, 1.16.9, 1.23.15, 1.53.4, 1.62.5, 1.95.8, 1.151.8, 2.15.4, 2.30.7, 20, 2.35.8, 3.1.12, 3.50.3, 3.3.3, 4, 8.7, 2.24.6, 2.20.5, 6.19.12, 6.45.20, 24. 6.66.8, 6.64.3 (red rays), 10.92.10, 4.5.5, 4.17.11, 4.23.10, 4.27.5, 4.30.22 (Indra, lord of the ray-cows), 4.31.14, 4.32.6, 7, 18, 22, 4.40.5, 4.42.5, 4.57.1, 5.1.3, 5.2.5,5.3.2, 5.45.8, 5.80.3, 6.44.12, 6.47.27, 6.53.10, 3.55.8, 3.30.10, 21, 2.55.8, 3.35.8, 1.36.8, 9.31.5, 6.1.12 (herds of light), 6.17.2, 6.17.6, 6.43.3 (ray-cows within the rock), 6.28.1 (ray-cows bringing bliss), 6.28.3, 9.31.5 (ray cows yielding light and the milk of knowledge), 7.18.2, 7.41.3, 7.54.2, 7.90.2, 8.2.6, 8.20.8, 8.24.6, 9.62.12 (Soma pours the ray-cows and life-energies upon us), 9.67.6, 10.7.2, 10.16.7, 10.31.4, 10.68.2, 10.108.7, 10.111.2.)
- *Gobhir*, the ray-cows, figuring prominently in the Ninth Mandala, is the presiding divinity of Soma Pavamana. (RV 9.2.4, 9.6.6, 9.8.5, 9.10.3, 9.14.3, 9.32.3, 9.43.1, 9.50.5, 9.61.13, 9.66.13, 9.68.9, 9.74.8, 9.85.4, 9.85.5, 9.86.27, 9.91.2, 9.97.15, 9.103.1, 9.107.2, 2, 9, 18, 22.)
- Kine, referred to in the Vedas as the milking cow, is the source of truth, essence, and knowledge. The imagery is inescapable. Just as just as there is the milk of knowledge so is the Kine, the milking cow, its symbol.

- Kines also represent the union of heaven and earth.

The Jaiminiya Brahmana (JB 1.19.) makes the following correspondences of cows to knowledge:

- The agnihotra cow is speech.
- The calf of agnihotra cow is mind.
- The milk of the mother cow flows to her calf.
- The milk of agnihotra cow produces the speech that causes the mind to low.
- This mind of the calf is followed by speech.
- For this reason, the mother cow runs after the calf who walks in front.

The correspondence is thereby complete. Agni, the "God of Fire" moves the flame. From the flame the meaning moves to Light, from Light, the meaning moves to Knowledge. There is a link missing in these correspondences. That missing link will be discussed in the next discussion.

The Active Principle of Consciousness (The Light of Consciousness)

Close your eyes. You may see a dim, flickering light. If you are properly engaging in meditation that light may become more brilliant, more steady, dazzling, blazing. That light is a product of fire, it is the visual emissions of the flame of the fire, it is the light of consciousness. This is how Agni becomes the Light of Consciousness. The dynamic Vedic energies and force of Agni emits the effulgence which becomes the Light of Consciousness.

Agni is the divine force inhering in the active principle of Consciousness. (TB 1.2.1.58.) The big difference between the example in the preceding paragraph and the Vedic force of Agni is simple. The consciousness experienced when closing your eyes is the product of consciousness; the Vedic force of Agni is Consciousness itself. The association of fire with Agni is essentially symbolic. Fire itself, or the characteristics of Fire, contain an essential meaning. One of those meanings is that of Consciousness. The attributes of the Fire of Change as embodied in Agni inform the characteristic of Consciousness.

Consciousness is associated with light, brilliance, brightness. It is no accident that a smart person is called "bright," a person who is not so smart is called "dull." A loved one is called "Light of my life." An idea is called "brilliant," or a person has a "bright" idea, although this is often used sardonically. Those characteristics are derived from the simple root of *ang*, wherefrom these various aspects of Agni are obtained.

When we previously said "change" in association with the divine forces of Agni, we mean the most expansive application possible. Change is closely related to the Principle of Consciousness. Like the ebb and flow of water, conscious states change. One "changes" their mind or opinion. There is an art device called "stream" of consciousness. A restless, unsettled mind is one which is ever changing, changing its focus in any given moment, constantly distracted.

A simple association of Agni to fire is superficial and scratches the surface of its full meaning. The Brahmanas speak of five forms of Agni. (TB, 1.2.1.70.) There are five attributes to the Principle of Consciousness which permeate the dynamic force inherent in Agni. These attributes will be examined at length later in this book. Taken together, these five attributes form the basic components of the Principle of Consciousness. An overlooked Nineteenth Century Vedic scholar, Pandit Vidyavacaspati Madhusdan Ojha, assigns mrtyu, change or impermanence, as the defining characteristic of Consciousness (Agni). The pervasion of this active principle inherent in Agni runs across every level:

- On a material, microcosmic level Change represents the digestive fire which supports the individual and operates the material world.
- In a mental level Change represents the light of knowledge.
- On a spiritual level, Change (Agni) represents the fire which burns away impurities, sins, of the worshiper, providing the forgiveness of sins.
- On cosmic level Change (Agni) represents the Fire of Divine Will.

Agni is identified with Fire. Fire is the ultimate transformative agent. There are five attributes to this aspect of Fire:

- Common Fire is the symbol for Consciousness. Physical fire completely consumes whatever meets its path. The flames transform its object into ashes and smoke to where it is reduced to its most basic elements.
- Physical, common, fire, contains the dynamic which is translated to the gastric, digestive fire, which transform food into energy.
- This energy is characteristic of the effulgence of light, representative of the speed and impulse of light of consciousness.
- The light of consciousness is symbolizes the sacrificial fire, which is also symbolic of the cosmic life force which sustains the universe and all creatures therein.
- Placed in a sacrificial context, while the sacrificial fire is representative of other aspects, the sacrificial fire is at essence symbolic of the purification of the worshiper, his soul and body. The fire purifies and extinguishes the sins of the worshiper. The flames themselves are brilliant, glowing and constantly changing form.

The Vedas frequently call Agni the "Messenger of the gods." Taken on a surface level, this means that Agni summons the gods to participate in the sacrifice. On a deeper level, it signifies that in his capacity as the Messenger, the cosmic force of Agni seeks and consolidates other Vedic forces to provide the pervasion of consciousness. The common bond of these divinities is that they govern the Subject, consciousness, Agni, Indra, and Soma, and the divinities associated with Indra, the Asvins and Maruts, and the various permutations of these three primary divinities, Agni-Soma, Indra-Agni, Indra-Soma — all have a Fire element. There is an entire class of divinities from which originate from fire. Supreme among those gods, in fact, among all gods are Agni, Soma, Indra, and the Maruts. The names of these divinities are derived from a manifestation of fire, and all of these manifestations relate to some aspect of Consciousness, as symbolized in a ritualistic setting.

The Vedic forces and energies in the following chart all relate to some aspect of Agni as Consciousness, and by extension, to the Light of Consciousness.

Vedic Force	Sanskrit	English Meaning	Aspect of the Fire Principle
Agni	*agne*	Fire	The Light of Consciousness
Indra	*indha*	Charcoal, Ember	The Light of Consciousness transformed to its essential mental elements and function
Soma	*indhu*	Bright Spot, Spark	The flame before the kindling; the Impulse which motivates higher mental function
Agni-Soma	Agne-Soma	Fire-Spark	The Kindling, Impulsion, of the Light of Consciousness, beginning transformed itself to a more fully realized mental function
Indra-Agni	*I/ndraagnii*	Charcoal, Ember, and Fire	The Light of Consciousness transformed to its higher, fully realized mental function
Indra-Soma	*I/ndraasomaa*	Charcoal, Ember, and spark	The Impulsion transforming the Light of Consciousness to its higher, fully realized mental function

Asvins	Ashwini-Kumaras	The divine twins	The divine twins which symbolize the sunrise and sunset for ritual purposes, but in the world of consciousness represent the difference between knowledge and ignorance
Maruts	*marici*	Shining Ones	The effulgent nature of the Light of Consciousness

The salient points raised in this chart are the following:

- First, Agni represents Fire, the Light of Consciousness. The Fire Altar is the center of the Sacrifice, and fire plays a central role. As a practical matter, the fire works to train the mind to its blaze, and as the mind is transfixed on the dancing flames the fire serves to represent the effulgence of the conscious mind.
- Indra represents a different aspect of consciousness. After the flames of the Fire Altar are spent and extinguish on their own or by design, the fuel which supplied the Light of Consciousness are reduced to charcoal and embers. Indra is derived from the cognate for charcoal and embers, indha, and for this reason, Indra represents the Light of Consciousness transformed to its essential mental elements and function.
- Soma. Soma in its most purified form is *Indhu*. *Indhu* is related linguistically to Bindu, a foundational feature of mystic Tantra, and signified a bright spot, a focal point, a portal, a spark. This spark is the Impulsion of Soma. Impulsion is a defining feature of Soma. Impulsion supplies the very impetus for consciousness, Mind, thoughts, indeed, all forms of mental activity. According to the Vedas, the subtle energies which kick-start the living force of the worshiper is called, isas, translated as "impulse" or "impulsion." Not

to be confused with a related topic, "life Force," more commonly known as "breath" or "prana," isas is the ignition that starts a motor vehicle, so the impulse provides those energies required to run the many other physiological functions of the worshiper. So without the impulse, prana, breath and the other bodily functions of the worshiper would be impossible, or, so to speak, stuck in neutral. Soma is therefore the flame before the kindling of the Fire Altar (Consciousness) and thereby provides the flame before the kindling; the Impulse which motivates higher mental function.

- Agni-Soma is the combination of the qualities of Agni and Soma. It is the fire and spark to consciousness. It is the kindling, or Impulsion, of the Light of Consciousness, beginning transformed itself to a more fully realized mental function.
- Indra-Agni is the combined forces of Indra and Agni which relate to consciousness.

The Vedic force of Agni is the Charcoal, Ember, and Fire, of the Fire Altar. As such, it represents the Light of Consciousness transformed to its higher, fully realized mental function.

- Indra-Soma is the combined forces of Indra and Soma which relate to consciousness. Ritualistically, it is the Charcoal, Ember, and spark of the Fire Altar. As it relates to consciousness, it is the Impulsion transforming the Light of Consciousness to its higher, fully realized mental function.
- The Asvins is one half of the divine twins, Ashwini-Kumaras. As the divine twins, they represent the materiality of the material world. As they relate to the Vedic dharma, they represent the Two-Dimensional Universe. As they relate to consciousness, they represent the divine twins which symbolize the sunrise and sunset for ritual purposes, but in the world of consciousness represent the difference between knowledge and ignorance.
- The Maruts are the "shining ones." If the Asvins represent the Two-Dimensional Universe, the Maruts represent one step higher in the Three-Dimensional Universe. Due to their shining nature they represent the effulgence of the Light of Consciousness.

The Fire of Change and Transformation are in constant flux. Paradoxically, the impermanent nature of change creates its own permanence. This permanence is evoked by the introduction of polarity. In the fire of change, the polarized qualities are transformed into their opposites. This process of reversal is the essence of the Vedas. In the process of reversal the Fire of Change becomes an eternal, unchangeable, never-changing fire.

"The Light of Consciousness" as a broad statement and by itself and of itself can mean anything. Specific characteristics of the Light of Consciousness, how it arose and how it operates, is found in a summary of those characteristics is found in Sukta 29 in the Third Mandala. This Sukta implicates issues of the Light of Consciousness, the role of sacrifice in the creation of that light, and how the Light of Consciousness is created and others. Steeped in meaningful symbolism, it is by far the most concise exposition of this aspect of Change (Agni) found in one place. A full discussion of Jatavedas, the aspect of Agni representing the Light of Consciousness, is found later in this book.

For now, let just say that Agni is the Light of Consciousness. That means a great deal for the Vedic energies in Agni, what does that mean for us here on earth? Ever take a photograph of yourself, say a selfie in a crowded room full of objects and people? Finally you have the shot you want, and you see yourself clearly among all the surrounding clutter. When you look at the photograph later you are amazed that you can hardly see yourself, whereas before you could place yourself in the same shot immediately. Why is that? Consciousness. This is how consciousness works. It can isolate, identify, segregate, and concentrate. Without consciousness there is chaos. Consciousness is like food. As the worshiper digests food, it keeps and retains what is essential for a properly working body and discards the rest. This is what the next chapter is about.

The Active Principles of "Food" ("Feed your head." Jefferson Airplane)

The Vedas love paradox, this is known, and one of the most obscure paradoxes is the frequent references in Vedic literature to Food. Food is symbolic speech to signify, very generally, activity involving mental participation. Mostly, it is representative of the mental processing of Consciousness, both as the subject and as the object of consciousness.

It is curious that an active principle as nuanced and complicated as Consciousness, Change or Transformation implicates an action as simple and mundane as Food. Apart from the Vedas themselves, references to food can be found in the Upanishads, the Brahmanas, in the writings of Sankara, the Bhagavad Gita, and other Vedic and Hindu writings. At first blush it might be possible to dismiss these references as the preoccupation of a generally hungry, pre-Industrial population. But this is not the case.

There is probably no more obscure reference in the Vedas than that of Food. The metaphysical meaning of Agni is sometimes articulated in terms of food. What could this possibly mean? That special meaning to "food" in the Vedic world regards the give and take of sacrifice. That special relationship is succinctly described in the Bhagavad Gita (BG, 3.12-3.14 (Feuerstein, trans. 2011):

For, sustained by sacrifice, the divinities will give you the desired "food."

He who enjoys their gifts without giving something in return is but a thief.

Good men consuming the sacrificial leavings are released from all guilt,

but those who cook for their own sake are evil and "eat" the karmic fruit of Wickedness.

"From food beings come into being. Food is produced from rain.

"From sacrifice the rain comes into being. Sacrifice is born from ritual action."

Sri Adi Sankara further summarized the philosophy of Vedanta in a single stanza in his short work, *Dg-Drsya Viveka*. In the opening stanza, Sankara states, "The form is perceived, and the eye is its perceiver. The eye is perceived and the mind is its perceiver. The mind with its modification is perceived and the Witness (the Self) is verily the perceiver. But it, the Witness, is most perceived by any other." The import of the rcs and samans dealing with Food is similar. Soma is both the food, the enjoyment of food and the provider of food. In other words, it is the Self, the Mind, and the objects the Mind perceives, all wrapped up in one existential package. Agni provides the substratum by which the forms of the material existence may be presented in front of the mind, as well as providing the basis for the Mind to perceive those forms. These shapes, figures, and forms are provided by the Self and thrown in front of the Mind as rain during a rain shower. Agni the enjoyer can be read different ways. As simply the "enjoyer" Agni is also the Mind itself, enjoying the kaleidoscope of shapes, figures, and forms in front of it, as if watching a movie at the Cinema or watching TV while eating a TV dinner at home. In the Rg Veda, food is takes several forms:

- Food is associated with sustenance. (RV 5.70.2.)
- Food is life. (RV 8.3.24.)
- Soma is food. (RV 9.55.2, 9.41.4, 9.61.1, 3, 9.9.63.2, 9.64.13, 9.65.13, 9.66.4, 23, 31, 9.71.8, 9.74.2, 3, 9.85.3, 9.91.5, 9.97.5, 9.99.2, 9.101.11, 9.104. (Soma food of the gods), 10.94.6.)
- Food is associated with wealth. (RV 8.5.36.)
- Food is also associated with progeny (RV 7.96.6, 9.8.9, 9.13.3, 9.65.21), which, because a person can expect to live on after death through his or her issue, is representative of immortality.
- Water or the waters are considered food. (RV 1.30.1, 1.33.11, 1.52.2, 1.63.8; 1.100.5, 2.34.5, 2.35.1, 11, 2.41.18, 3.4.7, SPB 2.1.1.3, 13.8.1.4, 13.)

Food plays an important role in sacrifice. In the Veda references to food abound. Entreaties for food are ubiquitous. The request for food is another example of coded language signifying a much deeper meaning. The Vedic divine force of death was not Yama but Mrtyu. (Merh, *Yama, The Glorious Lord of the Other World*, p. 62.) Mrtyu, is seen as the lord over humanity, the personification of death, the Grim Reaper. Mrtyu is the consumer of mortal being. (SPB 10.1.3.1.) Hunger, indeed, *was* death. (SPB 10.6.5.1.) If hunger is death, food is life, and life of a god is eternal. Food, thus, in the coded language of the Veda, represents

- The immortal life, or the request for the life divine,
- Salvation, or the request for salvation,
- Liberation, or the request for liberation, moksa,

- The divine, eternal energy which fuels liberation, salvation or the life divine.

Food is the by-product of these Fires. In fact, the entire natural order, the Vedic dharma, is divided into two parts, the eater and the eaten. (SPB 10.6.2.1.) In the Veda, food, that which is eaten, takes several forms and has several meanings:

- Food is associated with sustenance. (RV 5.70.2.)
- Food is life. (RV 8.3.24.)
- Soma is food. (RV 9.55.2, 9.41.4, 9.61.1, 3, 9.9.63.2, 9.64.13, 9.65.13, 9.66.4, 23, 31, 9.71.8, 9.74.2, 3, 9.85.3, 9.91.5, 9.97.5, 9.99.2, 9.101.11, 9.104. (Soma food of the gods), 10.94.6.)
- Food is associated with wealth. (RV 8.5.36.)
- Food is also associated with progeny (RV 7.96.6, 9.8.9, 9.13.3,9.65.21), which, because a person can expect to live on after death through his or her issue, is representative of immortality.
- Water or the waters are considered food. (RV 1.30.1, 1.33.11, 1.52.2, 1.63.8, 1.100.5, 2.34.5, 2.35.1, 11, 2.41.18, 3.4.7, SPB 2.1.1.3, 13.8.1.4, 13.)

In the coded language of the Veda, to say something is food is to refer to the entire universe and all that exist in it. (BU 1.5.1.) Sankara, in his Commentary of this portion of the Brhadaranyakaupanishad, states that this is tantamount to saying that Food is the Object.

This is not a power reserved only to Vedic deities. The worshiper is included in this process as well. All the talk about "conquering death" or "becoming immortal" is coded language signifying that Agni, the Fire of Change, transforms the worshiper, ordinarily an object in the natural order, to the Subject. Taking food to this deeper level of meaning, once transformed into the Eater of food the worshiper is transformed:

- Is complete in Speech (SPB 3.9.1.9), meaning the worshiper is endowed with logos, the wisdom of the Vedic dharma.
- Stands in the midst of cattle (i.e., gains Knowledge, or food). (SPB 7.5.2.14.)

The worshiper takes on these characteristics once this aspect of dharma, the natural order (*rta*) is incorporated into his or her life. But dharma enlightens other aspects. The process of enlivening the earth is a reference to the Five Fires doctrine. The Five Fires is the Vedic precursor to the Hindu concept of reincarnation and transmigration of souls. The Five Fires describe the transmigrational journey as the soul travels from one body to another.

Like smoke wafting upwards, when a person departs from this world, the soul travels upwards in the air. (BU, 5.10.1.) In his commentary of this stanza of the Upanishad, Sankara states that this destination is the *Hiranyagarbha*, the "golden" seed, the cosmic egg or germ.

Whether the concept of reincarnation was recognized in the Vedic world is a topic of scholarly debate. If this mantra does not settle that debate in favor of recognizing reincarnation, it certainly provides its ideological basis. The cycle of fire can be repeated over and over forever. This entire process is characterized by Fire, but not just the physical fire. Fire is the process of the changes from the Heavenly Fire, to the Fire of Parjanya, to the Vegetative Fire, then to Digestive Fire, and finally to the Female Fire.(BU 6.2.14.) Fire, Agni, is essentially the medium of Change and Transformation from one stage to another. To any stage. This fire becomes the basis for any change and transformation, not simply the recycler of souls. This is the essence of dharma, the natural order (*rta*). The Veda makes specific application of food to this divine cosmic force of Agni:

RV 3.27.11:

The Fire of Change (Agni) is kindled with food. Read: The inner transformation which leads to salvation or liberation is powered by the Fire of Change.

RV 4.2.7, 11:

Whoever desires liberation or salvation ("brings food") to the sacrifice receives liberation or salvation ("food"). Read: Ask and yee shall receive.

RV 2.1.6, 10:

The Fire of Change (Agni) is the Lord of Immortality ("Food"). Similar rcs are found in RV 5.8.5, 6.2.8, 8.60.13, and 3.12.5. Read: Achieving liberation or salvation requires an inner transformation in the worshiper.

RV 3.27.1:

The primal nature of consciousness (*ghrta*) is the food of Change (Agni). Read: The inner change which brings liberation and salvation is fueled by the higher state of consciousness.

RV 7.3.4:

The Fire of Change is the eater of food. Also found at RV 7.4.2. Read: There is a symbiotic synergy in the principle which brings liberation and salvation. The energy of that principle must be replenished.

RV 1.130.3:

The strength of intelligence and divine grace, (Indra), after receiving food, gives food. Read: These attributes inherent in Indra, when the worshiper so requests, bestows the life divine.

RV 4.29.5:

The strength of intelligence and divine grace is the giver of food. Also found at RV 2.13.4, 8.6.23, and 8.46.2. Bala (Indra) bestows the life divine.

RV 4.23.8:

Rta, the cosmic order, has many forms of food. Read: the sanctity of life runs through its undercurrent, the cosmic order.

In the course of the sacrifice the worshiper receives food from the various Vedic divinities.

- The worshiper receives food from Agni, the Fire of Change. (RV 1.317, 11, 1.58.2, 1.65.3, 1.71.3, 7, 1.73.5, 1.140.13, 1.144.7, 2.4.8, 2.6.5, 2.9.5, 3.1.22, 3.3.71, 3.6.11, 3.7.3, 11, 3.15.7, 3.22.5, 3.23.2, 5, 5.4.2, 5.6.1, 2, 10, 5.7.1, 5.21.7, 6.1.5, 6.13.5, 6.14.1, 7.7.7, 7.8.7, 7.16.4, 7.42.6, 8.23.29, 10.2.6, 10.11.5, 10.20.10, 10.49.2, 3.) This is tantamount to the worshiper to receive the enhanced Self-awareness and find its place in the universe.
- The worshiper receives food from Bala (Indra), the principle of strength, human and divine intelligence, and divine grace. (RV 1.5.3, 1.53.3, 4, 5, 11, 1.104.7, 1.121.14, 15, 1.159.8, 1.183.13, 185.6, 1.187.7, 1.189.5, 2.13.5, 4.32.7, 5.32.4, 6.17.3, 14, 6.19.5, 6.22.3, 6.24.9, 6.39.1, 5, 7.20.10, 7.21.10, 7.24.6, 7.25.6, 7.37.6, 8.13.5, 8.81.10, 8.82.28.) In so receiving the worshiper receives those qualities inherent in Bala (Indra).
- The worshiper receives food from Indra-Agni. (RV 6.60.12, 13.) In receiving food from Indra-Agni the worshiper receives the vital strength of consciousness.
- The worshiper receives food from the Maruts. (RV 1.88.1, 1.17.16, 1.166.2, 15, 10, 8.7.3, 13, 8.20.2, 8.) In this way the worshiper receives the qualities inherent in the Maruts, strength and knowledge. Indra-Maruts. (RV 1.145.15, 1.147.15, 1.16515, 1.165.17.)
- The worshiper receives food from Asvins. (RV 1.21.11, 1.34.5 11,1.96.8, 1.116.8, 1.120.8, 9, 5.76.4, 7.65.4, 7.73.2, 8.5.9, 8.8.15, 16, 8.22.9, 12, 8.26.3, 8.35.4, 5, 6.)

The Principle of Consciousness is seen in the digestive fire of food. The thought process itself is sometimes indicated by this figurative speech. Thus we say, we say that something is "food for thought." When we are referring to the deliberative process in making a decision, that we need to "digest" the subject. In the same way, this divine force has the following qualities which exist in Agni:

- The gastric fire is symbolic of the energy released by the power of fire.
- The strength of the conflagration is representative of the awesome power fire can exhibit.
- The brilliance of the flames matches the association of light to consciousness, used so many times, not only in the Vedas, but in Vedic thought in general.
- The sacrificial fire is the icon of purification and redemption.

In the Brhadaranyakaupanishad, the "eater of food" is that which produces food again and again. (BU 1.5.2.) In his Commentary to the Brhadaranyakaupanishad, Sankara, the great Vedic thinker of Advaita Nondualism, interprets what is meant by "Food." According to his interpretation, Food is regarded as the object of the enjoyment of food (BU 1.5.2), a veiled reference of act of perceiving the manifest universe. This interplay is simply the distinction between the Subject (the Eater of Food) and the object (Food). This distinction also expounds on the function of Agni's divine force. Agni is both the head of the sacrifice (RV 1.1.1) and the sacrifice itself. (RV 1.1.4.) This is how Food is considered in the Vedas.

Agni (Change and Transformation) is the Eater of Food, both in his physical aspect of fire and in the sacrificial aspect as the fire altar. (SPB 10.6.2.2.) In all aspects, Agni (Change and Transformation) is the Eater of Food. (SPB 2.1.4.28, 2.2.1.1, 2.4.4.1, 8.6.3.5, 10.4.1.11, 11.1.6.9.) The "Eater" can mean anything from the dissolving agent of the Vedic dharma, to the perceiving subject of the Vedic dharma, to the Vedic force which superimposes the material universe, to obtaining knowledge, enlightenment, or consciousness. As the Eater, Agni produces food again and again. Agni as the eater of food which transforms the food eaten (as the digestive, gastric fire) into the vital life force, the energy of which is transformed into the force of the light of consciousness. This process, in turn, transforms simple, physical fire, into a spiritual, sacrificial fire, which represents this entire process of Change. The scope of this eternal process of Change thus encompasses the body, mind, and spirit. In the fire of producing food again and again, the entire natural order is created, recycled and re-created. Being the Eater of Food is coded language for saying that Agni is the Subject, the Absolute Self.

Agni's dominant presence in the Rg Veda arises from this aspect of Change. The digestive fire is a process of Change. Food once eaten is broken down to its nutritional elements to nourish and replenish the body. Thus, in this capacity Agni is the eater of food which transforms the food eaten (digestive, gastric fire) into the vital life force, the energy of which is transformed into the force of the light of consciousness. This process, in turn, transforms simple, physical fire, into the sacrificial fire, which represents this entire process of Change. The scope of the Eternal Law of Change thus encompasses the body, mind, and spirit.

These digestive elements of the Fire of Change (Agni) are consistent with the grammatical derivations of *ang* found in the Rg Veda. The root *"ang"* has many separate meanings, all of which inhere into the *svadha* — or essential, inherent, nature — of Agni:

- *anga*, signifying brilliance or effulgence, specifically to describe the aspect of Change in the light of consciousness. (RV 1.1.6, 1.84.7, 8, 19, 1.118.3,1.164.7, 2.41.10, 3.33.11, 3.48.5, 5.3.11, 6.44.10,6.50.10, 6.52.3, 6.72.5, 7.20.9, 7.56.2, 7.91.1, 8.6.26,8.7.2, 8.80.5, 8.96.13, 10.4.4, 10.42.3, 10.54.4, 10.64.13, 10.79.4, 10.129.7, 10.131.2, 10.149.3.)
- *Angdh*, the attribute of resplendence, again, expressed in association of consciousness. (RV 9.5.10.)
- *Angdhve*, signifying the flash of revelation. (RV 10.100.10.)
- The Angiras, the family of Vedic Rishis. (RV 1.1.6, 1.74.5, 2.23.8, 4.9.7, 5.11.1, 6.2.10, 8.60.2, 8.74.11, 8.75.5, 8.102.17.)
- Angirastama, the mystic essence of the Agniras Rishis. (RV 1.75.2, 8.43.18,8.43.27.)
- *Angiraso*, that aspect of Angiras in possession of super-human intellectual powers, a siddhi. (RV 1.62.2, 1.71.2, 3.53.7, 4.2.15,4.3.11, 5.11.6, 6.65.5,7.42.1, 10.14.6, 10.67.2, 10.78.6, 10.108.9.)
- *Angiro*, the divine reflection of Angiras imbued with the glory of Change. (RV 1.31.11, 1.112.18, 4.3.15, 5.2.8, 5.21.1, 6.16.11.)

All these qualities are inherent in Agni, the Fire of Change:

- The gastric fire is symbolic of the energy released by the power of fire.
- The strength of the conflagration in angiraso is representative of the awesome power fire can exhibit.
- The brilliance of the flames in *anga* and *Angdh* matches the association of light to consciousness, used so many times, not only in the Vedas, but in Vedic thought in general.
- The sacrificial fire is icon of purification and redemption.

In this world, there is are several manifestations of the cosmic force of Agni. (TB, 1.1.8.1.) This cosmic force of Change presides over several other divine forces, each of which possess their own power. These qualities converge together to assist the worshiper in the Vedic path to liberation and salvation. Agni as the Fire of Change transforms the worshiper bodily, mentally and spiritually.

Agni's dominant presence in the Rg Veda arises from the expansive scope of this Change. Agni is the eater of food which transforms the food eaten (digestive, gastric fire) into the vital life force, the energy of which is transformed into the force of the light of consciousness. This process, in turn, transforms simple, physical fire, into the sacrificial fire, which represents this entire process of Change. This fire of Change operates on an individual, microcosmic, level, and in a greater, macrocosmic level in the Vedic dharma. The scope of the Eternal Law of Change thus encompasses the body, mind, and spirit.

The Purifying Fire

The Fire of Agni purifies. Two cultural vignettes give the best picture of what it means to say that Fire, Agni, is an agent for purification. One is from author Ajai Bhambi. In *Planetary Meditation*, Bhambi correctly stated that there are many forms of fire, but there two of note. Fire is both a creator and a destroyer. (Bhambi, 2012, p. 39.) The other topic is from the movie, *Leon: The Professional*. In one scene, Leon and Matilda kill a drug dealer in front of his table literally covered with drugs. After the drug dealer is killed, Matilda sets fire to the drug dealer's table which is full of drugs. When asked why she is doing that, she replies, staring intently at the flames, "Now it's clean." These cultural references demonstrate some important truths about Agni, the Vedic personification of Fire. As an instrument of purification the Vedic force of Agni can either create or destroy, but even an action of destruction is results in a renewal or purification. These two cultural references give a good example of the double nature of Fire. That same power which can cleanse and purify can also reduce an object to cinders. But even when all that remains is ashes, the object is purified, reduced to its most basic physical elements. This is one of the great paradoxes of Fire.

The Fire of Agni is a purifying agent. This is one of the end-results of physical fire. It burns and consumes that which is aflame. The object which is aflame is reduced to ash, and in the process of its destruction, the object burned is purified and is renewed. Take, for example, a forest fire. Yes, this is a tragic, catastrophic event, and yes, the trees and shrubbery are burned, destroyed, charred beyond recognition. The forest, however, will grow once again in the process of regeneration. The sturdy, healthy trees will survive, the weak will not. Still, this involves a process of purification. This distinction was not lost on the ancients. The ancient Greek word for "pure," a word used today in Modern Greek, is αγνος, *agnos*. This Greek word for purity survives in the English name, Agnes. The similarity between *agnos*, Agnes and Agni cannot be coincidental. Similarly, the worshiper's soul is purified and perfected through this active principle of Transformation (Agni).

- The worshiper's soul who accepts the food offered at the sacrifice is increased and blazes while being consumed and purified by the flames fed by the fuel, and glows like a galloping steed with the sound of the worshiper's cry reverberating the very foundations of Heaven. (RV 1.58.2.) The imagery in this rc (mantra) conjures several issues. The food is the experience obtained at the sacrifice; the steed is the energy of the knowledge thereby obtained; the reverberating sound is the cosmic reach of that knowledge.
- The purifying flames of Agni are ageless, they glimmer during the night, the rays have the active force of light which diffuse like floods. (RV 1.143.1.)
- The red, blazing flames of Agni purify the Earth. (RV 1.146.2.)

- When the eternal flames of Agni purify they illumine, enlighten, the world and the worshiper. (RV 2.8.4.)
- From the very beginning the eternal purifying flames of Agni enlightened the Earth and Heaven. (RV 3.2.2.)
- The purifying fire is all-pervasive and extends everywhere like light. Agni in his capacity as the source of the purifying fires works in conjunction with his manifestation as a terrestrial fire, Grhapati, to induce the enlightenment of the worshiper. (RV 5.4.2.)
- When the worshiper receives the purifying effect of Agni's flames at the sacrifice when they are sought by the force of their impulsions. (RV 5.6.4.)

The purifying flames ravage the forest trees, *Vanaspati*. (RV 5.7.4.) The *Vanaspati*, writes R.L. Kashyap, carries a double meaning of what they literally signify, trees, but also material existence in the metaphorical sense. This is a possible interpretation. In a real sense, however, the trees in *Vanaspati* represent the presence of distracting thoughts and mental impressions. Just as an individual cannot see the "forest for the trees," the purifying fires of Agni clears the unrestrained, untrained thoughts, and allow the self-realization of the worshiper.

- The very light emitted by the purifying flames of Agni stimulate the worshiper's self-realization and awareness. (RV 6.15.5)
- Through the purifying flames of Agni, the worshiper will find the inner truth of the Vedic dharma (*rta*) if that truth is sought. (RV 5.27.4.)
- These purifying flames of Agni have the brilliance and effulgence of the Sun. (RV 6.4.3.)
- The purifying flames not only cleanse the worshiper's mind, spirit and body, but dispenses to the worshiper the full panoply of spiritual endowments possessed of Agni, including a full appreciation of the fullness of the Vedic dharma. (RV 6.5.7.)

The themes that run throughout these rcs are that the purifying flames of Agni are eternal and ageless. They permeate the reaches of Heaven and Earth, and pervades throughout the Vedic dharma, and that as a result of the purifying flames the Heaven and Earth and the worshiper are "illumined," or enlightened. In other words, the flames may but they also educate.

The worshiper's soul is purified symbolically at the sacrifice through the Sacrificial Fire. Fire is the focal point for the Sacrifice in part because fire, like the Sacrifice itself, is the agent for renewal. The fire is representative of the process of renewal and regeneration similar to the burning of the forest. The old forest is destroyed and a new one grows in its place. At the sacrifice the worshiper's soul is transformed and materially altered. A new soul emerges in its place. The new soul, the reborn soul, is generated through the agency of the sacrificial fire. Just as old timber is burned so a new growth may occur, so the worshiper's soul is transformed, reduced to ash in the fire at the sacrificial altar, and a new one appears. The process may occur once in a lifetime or several times. RV 1.140.2 describes the process of this regeneration. It is in five stages, and as the soul is able to regenerate, so the this rc (mantra) may be interpreted in several ways. Those several ways are best exemplified in RV 1.10.2.

The Many Interpretations of RV 1.140.2
(Five Methods of Purification)

The meaning of RV 1.140.2 pertains to the powers of Agni's force and energy to purify and cleanse. The Veda is a scripture amenable to many interpretation and clothed in symbols. In a scripture prone to symbolic meaning such as the Rg Veda, one rc, RV 1.140.2, is more prone to multiple interpretation than most. The levels of meaning of this rc (mantra) are region. They include interpretations based on astronomical and alchemical meanings and other methods. In this way, RV 1.140.2 specifies five methods by which the Vedic force of Agni exercises its powers of purification.

The purification powers of Agni are foundational and originate from the essential incendiary powers of Agni. The Fire of Change (Agni) blackens the forests. (RV 6.60.10.) This rc (mantra) emphasizes how the reduction to ash is above all an act of purification, a final reduction to the most essential elements. The stages of purification can be seen in RV 1.140.2. This rc (mantra) states that the Fire of Change (Agni) is "two-fold generated, devours the triple (sacrificial) food, and when the year expires renovates what has been eaten, the Showerer (of benefits) is invigorated (in one form), by eating with the tongue of another, in a different form the restrainer (of) all consumes the forest trees." (Wilson translation). According to the obscure language of this rc, the fire towards purification are made in five stages:

- Two-fold generated.
- Devours triple food.
- Renovates the food when year expires.
- The Showerer is invigorated by eating with the tongue of another.
- The restrainer consumes the forest trees.

The language of this rc (mantra) owes its obtuse meaning to the fact that it operates on so many levels. It is very possible that the "tongues of Agni" is figurative language for the flames of a fire or kindling. The phrase operates on many levels. The manner in which this phrase can be applied can be seen in a rc (mantra) found in the First Mandala, RV 140.2. According to the translation of Ralph Griffith, this rc (mantra) reads:

> Child of a double birth he grasps at triple food, in the year's course what he hath swallowed grows anew.
>
> He, by another's mouth and tongue a noble Bull, with other, as an elephant, consumes the trees

Now granted, Griffith's translation not a model of clarity, and it is notorious for being among the most antiquated and inaccurate translations available on the market today. Still, this rc (mantra) shows there are five elements to the powers of purification in Agni: (1) a two-fold birth, (2) devouring "triple food," (3) the food rejuvenates when the year expires, (4) the Showerer (i.e., the Bull) is invigorated by eating with the tongue of another, and (5) the restrainer who consumes the forest trees. Agni is the Presiding Deity of this Sukta. Sukta 140 demonstrates not only how rich the level of interpretation can take in interpreting the Veda, but also how the meaning remains relatively uniform despite the malleability of its meaning.

This brings us to the first level of meaning — Sacrifice. On a strictly ritualistic level, the meaning employed by Sayana of RV 1.140.2, the purification of fire at the sacrificial altar progresses in this manner:

First Method: Ritualistic Meaning of RV 1.140.2

Two-fold generated	Change (Agni) is kindled by rubbing two sticks
Devours triple food	The sacrificial altar consumes three different offerings: grhta, butter and Soma
Renovates the food when year expires	The ministrant recovers the oblation from the ladle
The Showerer is invigorated by eating with the tongue of another	The sacrificial fire is built with the offerings
The restrainer consumes the forest trees.	The sacrificial fire consumes, thereby purifying, the offerings

There is another level of meaning at work. There is an astronomical interpretation.

Second Method: Astronomical Meaning of RV 1.140.2

The astronomical aspect of the Vedic dharma in many ways hold more currency than others. This aspect ties in the importance of the place and timing of the Sacrifice, which were calibrated by the ascertainment of astronomical phenomena, such as equinoxes and solstices, against the larger purview of the fulness and pervasion of the Vedic dharma.

Two-fold generated	Change (Agni) represents the unity of heaven and earth, the sun and the moon
Devours triple food	Change (Agni) pervades the earth, mid-earth, and atmosphere
Renovates the food when year expires	The Winter Solstice (Mahavrata), the beginning of the new calendar year

The Showerer is invigorated by eating with the tongue of another	The Vernal Equinox, that portion of the calendar year when regeneration is in progress
The restrainer consumes the forest trees.	The Summer Solstice, the warmest portion of the calendar year

There is another level of meaning. In this interpretation it has an alchemical meaning. If the astronomical meaning looked towards the macrocosmic fulness of the Vedic dharma, the alchemical meaning shifts to the microcosm, to ascertain the subtle basis of matter. The wonderful paradox in this change of perspective is that the farther one digs into the subtle basis of matter, the more the microcosm reflects and resembles the macrocosm.

Third Method: Alchemical Meaning of RV 1.140.2

Alchemy has been defined as "the art of liberating parts of the cosmos from temporal existence to achieve Salvation." (Kalyanaraman, *Indian Alchemy Soma in the Veda* (2004), p. xviii.) Liberation is achieved by the body breaking free from the chains of material existence. The yoga of Patanjali provides, among other things, several ways to disengage from the physical attachments of the material world, ranging from deep exercises in meditation, to the move towards samadhi, the ultimate unification with the Absolute Self. One such practice is *samyama*, which combines the exercise of dharana, concentration, Dhyana, meditation, and samadhi. (YS, 3.4.) One such exercise is the *samyama* over the five elements. When *samyama* is practiced over the five elements, complete mastery over them is achieved. (TS, 3.45.) The worshiper's physical attachment to karma is derived from the elements. (YS, 2.18.) The correct exercise of *samyama* over the elements breaks this bond with the physical world. (Comm., YS, 3.45, *http:// www.swamij. com/yoga-sutras-33949.htm.*) This is the exact purpose of alchemy. In the science of alchemy, the progression of the elements were accomplished in three stages:

Elements	Alchemical Process
Earth to Water	Digestion
Water to Air	Distillation
Air to Fire	Calcination

As a result of this exercise of *samyama*, the worshiper becomes master over the elements. Having concentrated on the essence of physical matter, the worshiper breaks free from the physical confines of the material world. (YS, 3.45.) This is exactly the process exercised by legitimate doctors of the alchemical arts practiced in the Middle Ages. What the yogi in Patanjali's day would achieve through *Tapas*, intense meditation, the Medieval alchemist would achieve the same result, not only through meditation and intense mental austerity, but through the chemical and scientific processes which were then available. It is this process which is extrapolated in RV 1.140.2. The alchemical layer of meaning progress is summarized in this chart:

Two-fold generated	Agni representing the unity of heaven and earth, the sun and the moon
Devours triple food	Refers to the triple Alchemical Process. Stage One: Finding, grinding, and distilling an herb or metal in a vessel with spirits. Stage Two: Burning the product through calcination, producing a purified rasa. Stage Three: Further distillation of the purified rasa to a powder (bhasma).
Renovates the food when year expires	Refers to the powder (bhasma) which possesses the purifying powers.
The Showerer is invigorated by eating with the tongue of another	Refers to the purifying powers of the powder (bhasma), which is to invigorate the human body, confer siddhis, immorality, or to transmute base metals to gold.

The restrainer consumes the forest trees.	Refers to the powder (bhasma) of rasa, the ultimate object of the alchemical process, and the mechanical alchemical process at the furnace through the process of Fire.

Triplets abound in the alchemical process, as triplets abound in the Vedic force of Agni. The "triple food" could refer to the progression of the elements in the alchemical fire. The Vedic alchemist appreciates the role of Fire in the alchemical process. Fire is a necessary element to alchemical process. Fire is used in the alchemical process to find the Philosopher's Stone. The ultimate characteristic of the Fire of Change (Agni) is Fire itself, and this fire is used in the alchemy sciences in the progression towards spiritual renewal, which is culminated in the Philosopher's Stone itself. In Western alchemical traditions, the elements are symbolized as aspects of triangles: Fire, an upward triangle, air, an upward triangle with a line through it, water a downward triangle, and earth a downward triangle with line through it. In Western traditions, the combination of these symbols resulted in the Seal of Solomon, symbolic of the combination of all elements in a holistic unity and the Philosopher's Stone.

Similarly, triads abound in describing the constituent parts of the Vedic force in Agni. A few of these examples follow:

- RV 3.20.2 states Agni has three tongues. Sayana interprets this rc (mantra) as referring to the flame of fire originating from the three altars, the Grhapatya, Ahavaniya, and Daksinagni. These three altars were revealed in the Veda to be the "three brothers, (RV 1.164.1; 10.51.6.)
- RV 3.20.2 indicates that the three tongues of Agni emerge from their three abodes — the Grhapatya, Ahavaniya, and Daksinagni — upon which is placed three viands — *ghrta*, butter and Purification (Soma).
- The three viands create the three forms — *pavaka*, *pavama*, and *suci*. It thus becomes apparent that the Tongues of Agni is more than the flame of a fire. The tongue of the Fire of Change (Agni) is active catalyst of the fire of change in creation, the dynamic force

of evolution. The evolution of the Fire of Change (Agni) produces three forms of creation in *pavaka, pavama,* and *suci.*

- These forms refer to the three states of purification. *Pavaka* is the purifying agent, which produces the *pavamana,* an epithet for the purifying essence of Soma. Afterwards, *suci,* the highest state of purification, is reached. Coincidentally, we will later see that Suci is the highest level of Celestial Fire of the several manifestations of Agni. In later Vedic traditions, this composite of the triple nature of purification is represented in the Sri Yantra, a symbolic focal point to foster mental and spiritual purification.

The triple nature of Agni is expressed in other ways, in a simple three-sided geometrical form and triads. In Agni is reposed in the Three Goddesses. (RV 1.13.9; 2.3.8.) The Three Goddesses will appear later as a terrestrial manifestation of Agni.

- Agni as the Sacrificial Fire has three heads and seven rays. (RV 1.146.1.)
- Agni the Sacrificial Fire represents the unifying force of the three existential levels of Heaven, Mid-Earth, and Earth. (RV 10.88.3.)
- In this way, Agni in his aspect as the Fire Altar, with Stamobhaga bricks, twenty-one bricks, is used to symbolize the three worlds and the regions. (SPB 8.5.3.5, 6.)
- These three regions represent the three principal manifestations of the Fire of Change (Agni): Celestial, the "Middle" Agni, and Terrestrial Agni. (BD, 1.91, TB 1.2.1.56, 57.)

By his very nature Agni came into existence with a three-fold nature, by design, when created by the Vedic dharma. The divine fashioned the Fire of Change (Agni) to have this three-fold nature. (RV 10.88.10.)

- Indeed, there are three aspects to Agni Vaisvanara: (1) the Fire of Knowledge, (2) the force of Vital energy, and (3) the sacrificial fire. (RV 3.2.9.)
- When Agni in his aspect as the Mystic Fire is kindled, he has a triple nature. (RV 3.20.2.) The three-fold nature consists of three

houses — meant here is the physical, every-day, house, and three lunar Zodiacal, lunar, houses; the three worlds — the Earth, Mid-World (firmament), and Heaven; and the three tongues — the three levels of Vac, Speech: Madhyama, Pasyanti, and Para.

- The very name of Agni is derived from three elements. The Rishii Sakapuni reveals that the word Agni is derived from three verbs – from "going," from "shining or burning," and from "leading;" the letter "a" is from root "I" which he reveals to imply "to go," the letter "g" is from the root "anj" meaning "to shine" or "dah" meaning "to burn," and the last letter is by itself the root "ni" which means "to lead." (Nik., 7.14, cited in Wikipedia, https://en.wikipedia.org/wiki/Agni.)

The triple nature of Agni has a direct bearing on the worshiper. There is a personal element to all this.

- Maha Purana, section LXVII.202 – 203 states there are three kinds of Agni inside every human being: The first, *krodha-agni* or "fire of anger;" the second, the *kama-agni* or "fire of passion and desire;" and the third, the *udara-agni* or the "fire of digestion." (cited in Wikipedia, https://en.wikipedia.org/wiki/Agni.)

Once grounded in the person of the worshiper, the spiritual journey endeavors to allow the worshiper to transcend the bounds of material existence, either through salvation or liberation. This is the purpose of the Fourth Method of Purification.

Fourth Method: The Transcendence of Purification

There is another, ultimate, interpretation of RV 1.140.2. This process speaks simply of the purification process itself. The process of purification is accomplished in five stages. The number is significant. Five is the number of the dimension prior to liberation at the Seven-Dimensional Universe. The process is summarized in the following chart:

Two-fold generated	Polar opposites are united
Devours triple food	The internal dynamics of spiritual clarity (grhta) and inner purity (Soma) begin to operate
Renovates the food when year expires	Mental and Spiritual regeneration, the product of these internal dynamics, is received by the worshiper
The Showerer is invigorated by eating with the tongue of another	Mental and Spiritual strength arrives to the worshiper
The restrainer consumes the forest trees.	The worshiper is mentally and spiritually born again, twice-born, casting away the previous self

In this level of meaning the "trees" represent the presence of distracting thoughts and mental impressions. Just as an individual cannot see the "forest for the trees," the purifying fires of Agni clears the unrestrained, untrained thoughts, and allow the self-realization of the worshiper. As so many things in the Vedas, the similes used have their material, every-day correlate. While a forest fire is a terrible terrestrial, physical, fire, whenever Agni "burns the trees," the mind is clear, the unnecessary, irrelevant thoughts are cleared, and what remains after the conflagration is the clear, crystalline mind of self-realization, enlightenment, awareness. One may use whatever adjective one wishes; the Fire of Agni is the fire of purification.

Fifth Method: Consumption of the Trees and Rebirth

As anyone living in the State of California can attest, or, indeed, anywhere in the contemporary world, the passing of every summer sees the number, intensity, and extent of forest fires increase. The fire seasons are lasting longer and become more and more intense and destructive. While there are many man-made causes for this phenomenon, some of the causes are purely changes in atmospheric conditions. The world-wide increasing intensity and destruction of fires underscore Change and Transformation at work. All the Change and Transformation we witness in the weather conditions is yet another manifestation of the Vedic force of Agni at work. Management would hold "controlled burns" of forest and grass lands. Before the introduction of human habitation, fires would occasionally take place; the sturdier vegetation and trees would survive, and the weaker, more vulnerable would burn. Now, however, without these intermittent, controlled fires, when a fire does occur, the effect is devastating, taking strong and weak vegetation alike. With the presence of intermittent, controlled fires, the forest as a whole would thrive. These controlled fires stimulated the germination of seeds for other trees. In this way, the purification by fire assists the regeneration of life.

This is how the fifth method of purification works. We will see later that Plato compared mortal humans were compared to a plant, whose roots reached to Heaven. The Plant was sprinkled with celestial waters, "a divine semen, which enters the head." Water, with fire, is symbolic of the process of purification, and just as water is sprinkled to purify the subject, so must a fire take place to clear the dry, dead brush, and rejuvenate the forest and allow the forest to grow taller, stronger and in a more healthy manner.

Next, then there are seven tongues. The tongues of the Fire of Change (Agni), otherwise referred as the "seven flames," are the heart and soul of the fire exercised by Change to develop and edify the soul. These tongues are the primary vehicles for change. These flames are identified in RV 1.140.4, which contain the individual qualities of these flames. Change's flames contain the following characteristics as being:

- Liberating, fostering individual liberation,
- Constantly in motion,
- Quick and speedy,
- Painting a path of Black,
- All-pervading,
- Impelled by the wind, meaning containing the essence of prana, the life-force, and
- Constantly changing and modifying.

These attributes were modified somewhat and clarified in the Mundakopanishad, where at RV 1.2.4, the characteristics of the flames of Agni were described as:

- Black,
- Fierce,
- Mind-Swift,
- Red as an iron,
- Smoke-colored, and Cracking.

These benefits are not for all to see, but, as so many things in the Vedic path to Salvation, hidden and occult. Purification, bliss and illumination (wisdom) — these are the benefits the worshiper must seek to obtain from the Vedic force and energy of Agni. This is why the "hidden tongue" of the sacrifice is defined as the benefits of the divine life arriving to the worshiper.(RV 10.53.3.) It is with this hidden tongue through which the divinity communicates to the worshiper.

The Seven Tongues of Change (Agni)

The "Seven Tongues of Agni" is a one of the most colorful epithets for this Vedic force. The "tongues" of Agni refer to his flames. There is an equivalence in diction between the Seven Tongues of Agni and the Seven Flames of Agni. It is also one of the most descriptive. It is also one of the most impenetrable. This impenetrability is grounded in color and alchemy. Classical alchemical was concerned about color. Joseph Needlham, the noted scholar of Chinese science, writes that the entire purpose of traditional alchemy was to loosen the bonds of temporal existence to achieve perfection. In terms of metals, that meant turning base matter into gold, which, as we have seen here, represents liberation and salvation, but in the area in which Needham studied and wrote, represented longevity, Immortality, and finally grace and redemption. While alchemists attempted to transmute base metals into gold in their upward journey, the base metals traversed through the color chart. Each color represented a different stage of development, the final color was gold, into which indeed the base metal had been transmuted.

The different schools of Classical Alchemy differed widely. There was general consensus on the change in the color base inert metals underwent in the transmutation process. The base metals began the journey upwards on the color chart, beginning with the colors:

- Black, called Melansis or Nigreda, representing Death. A case can be made that this was the vast, indiscriminate, undefined mass of matter described in RV 10.129, wherein began the process of evolution of the Vedic dharma.
- White, called Leukosis or Albedo, representing Resurrection.
- Yellow, Gold, called Xanthosis, representing Immortality.
- Red, or Ruddy Brown, called Iosis, representing Rebirth. Other traditions include a further step. The color in this additional step is Green, or Green-tinted, called Verditas.

After the once inert material substances at work progress up this color chart, the alchemist is supposed to reach the Philosopher's Stone, the irreducible essence of physical matter, carrying within it life-giving properties, including, but not limited to, Immortality. The Mundaka Upanishad hints at this transformation in listing the seven flames of Agni. and names the flames in Mundaka Upanishad, 2.4. The seven flames are

- Kali. Kali is black. Black is the beginning stage of the transformation of the Alchemist's base, inert matter. Because it is black, Kali represents Death. Kali is the successor of Rudra, one of the manifestations of the terrestrial Agni.
- Karali, terrific.
- Manogava, swift as thought.
- Sulohita, very red.
- Sudhumravarna, purple.
- Sphuligini, sparkling.
- Visvarupi, brilliant, having all forms.

In his commentary of this portion to the Mundaka Upanishad Adi Sri Sankara interpreted the Seven Flames in a cursory manner as "[t]he seven tongues of the (flaming) fire, from *kali* down to *visvaruchi*, are intended to swallow the oblations thrown on it." Namely, the Seven Flames of Agni simply represents the Sacrificial Fire, the Fire Altar, or both. Other interpretations of this passage of the Mundaka Upanishad abound. In one interesting online post, this passage of the Mundaka Upanishad was interpreted in terms of sub-atomic particles. The interpretation in question, *www.booksfact.com/upanishads/tachyons-ultra-voilet-infra-red-bands-nuclear-energy-blacks-holes-in-mundakopanishad.html,* the Seven Flames of Agni were interpreted as different levels of electromagnetic radiation and Tachyons, theoretical sub-atomic particles traveling faster than the speed of light, all of which traverse throughout the spectrum — the ultra-violet band, the infra-red band, nuclear energy, and Black Holes. In a larger sense the Seven Flames of Agni represent this vast array of the different forms and intensities of energy. The first two flames consist of the general description of this energy contained in the Seven Tongues.

- Kali.
- Karali.

The Mundaka Upanishad then give specific qualities of the Seven Flames, or Tachyons.

- Manogava. They are "swift as thought" and is interpreted to represent the Tachyons themselves.
- Sulohita is "very red," representing infra-red rays. In an alchemical sense steeped in the esoteric traditions, red or ruddy brown represents rebirth. In the alchemical sense the color red is symbolic for the transmutation of baser metals to the Philosopher Stone. In terms of alchemical processes, red signifies the step of Separation of base matter into more rarified material.
- Sudhumaravarna, is "purple," representing Ultra-violet rays. In some alchemical traditions, the color purple represents the alchemical pro-cess of Coagulation.
- Sphuligini. Sparkling, brilliant, qualities represent cosmic rays of any kind.

- Visvarupi. Visvarupi are Black Holes in space which are able to absorb everything, including light itself, consequently, "having all forms."

This is an interesting interpretation but one which must be harmonized with the overall purpose of the Vedas — the worshiper's spiritual edification and education. If there is any one maxim that summarizes this overall philosophy of the Vedas, it is opening verse of the Emerald Tablet, "As below, so Above." Agni's Fire of Change is complete, in that it consists of the entirety of the Vedic dharma, from the imminent to the transcendent, from the body to the soul, from the profane to the divine, from the microcosm to the macrocosm. This process also expands to the greater Vedic dharma. In other words, from the bottom, up, and back again. As below, so above. This back and forth action is demonstrated in a phrase found in a couple of places in the Rg Veda — the Seven Tongues of Agni. These are references to the flames (RV 1.66.9, 10, 1.72.10, 1.76.4, 1.79.5, 1.97.5, 1.116.8), or "tongues" of Change (Agni). Change's (Agni's) tongue refers to the flame of fire (RV 8.43.8, 8.72.18, 10.4.4, 10.8.6), the active mechanism of the Fire of Change.

There is another likely interpretation, one which is more consonant with the spirit of the Vedas. Millennia later colors would come to play an important part to assist the worshiper to envisage the process of inner liberation through meditation. This process of meditation would enable the worshiper to travel up the inner chakras, the subtle energy centers in the worshiper's subtle body, to free and untangle the inner barriers to liberation. This would be accomplished by illustrating the road to liberation with the same back-and-forth movements to and from the Vedic macrocosm and Vedic microcosm. The articulation of this process found its clearest expression in a minor Upanishad, the Yoga-Tattva Upanishad. The Yoga-Tattva Upanishad is an early Upanishad which provided the philosophical basis for Hatha Yoga and Tantric traditions. The Yoga-Tattva Upanishad (*http:// merki.lv/ vedas/ Upanishadas/Yoga%20Tattva%20 Upani-shad%20-_eng_.pdf.*) has this to say about the process of liberation:

- There are the five elements: Prithvi, Apas, Agni, Vayu and Akasha. (YTU, 83(b).)

- From the feet to the knees is said to be the region of Prithvi, is four-sided in shape, is yellow in color and has the Varna (or letter) 'La'. Carrying the breath with the letter 'La' along the region of earth. (YTU, 84 – 86.)

- The region of Apas is said to extend from the knees to the anus. Apas is semi-lunar (Semi-Circle) in shape and white in color and has 'Va' for its Bija (seed) letter. Carrying up the breath with the letter 'Va' along the regions of Apas, he should contemplate on the God Narayana having four arms and a crowned head, as being of the color of pure crystal, as dressed in orange clothes and as without decay. (YTU, 88 – 89.)

- From the anus to the heart is said to be the region of Agni. Agni is triangular in shape, of red color and has the letter 'Ra' for its (Bija) seed. (YTU, 91.)

- From the heart to the middle of the eyebrows is said to be the region of Vayu. Vayu is hexangular in shape, black in color and shines with the letter 'Ya'. (YTU, 94(b).)

- From the center of the eyebrows to the top of the head is said to be the region of Akasha, is circular in the shape, smoky in color and shining with letter 'Ha'. (YTU, 98 – 98(a).)

Summarized, this information would look like this:

Element	Body Area	Geometric Shape of Element	Color	Saman
Prthvi (Earth)	Feet to Knees	Square	Yellow	La
Apas (Water)	Knees to Anus	Semi-Circle	White	Va
Agni (Fire)	Anus to Heart	Triangle	Red	Ra
Vayu (Prana)	Heart to Middle Brow	Hexangular	Black	Ya
Akasha (Aether)	Mid-Brow to Top of the Head	Circle	Smokey Black (Grey)	Ha

The progression of colors up the chakra system reflects the array of internal colors which appear during the course of meditation. There is a word for this phenomenon — *chidakasha*. These colors and images flash seemingly involuntarily. In reality the product of the mind's own internal mental activity.

These passages from the Yoga Tattva Upanishad are noteworthy in many ways. From a microcosmic perspective the colors represent the vast array of mental states during meditation. In much the same way each chakra is represented by different colors. They assign the areas of the worshiper's body to each corresponding element. These body areas correspond roughly to the chakra system later postulated in full in many Hatha Yoga texts. Variations in the color chart certainly exist among the Upanishads. There is a modern consensus as to which colors are assigned to which chakra. (*https://www.color-meanings.com/chakra-colors-the-7-chakras-and-their-mean-ings*), and that assignment looks like this:

Chakra	Location	Color
Muladhara	Base	Red
Svadhisthana	Navel	Orange
Manipura	Solar Plexus	Yellow
Anahata	Heart	Green
Vishuddha	Throat	Blue
Ajna	Mid-Brow	Brown
Shahasrara	Crown	Violet

The Seven Tongues of Agni are indeed a hidden reference to liberation. The ultimate destination of the worshiper's meditations is the Crown, the top of the head, where ultimate liberation occurs. "Sahasrara chakra is located above *Brahma randhra*, 'the cave of Brahma.' It is a hole in the crown of the head through which the soul is said to escape at death. When the Yogi separates himself from the physical body at the time of death, this *Brahma randhra* bursts open and the soul comes out through this opening (*Kapala Moksha*). This opening is also called the 'Door to Pure Consciousness' or door of liberation." (*https:// static1. Squarespace. com/ static/ 5569e-19fe4b02fd687f77b0f/t/5aad82526d2a73*

12c140f7ae/1521320558691/ Tantra kundalini. pdf.) The Sahasrara is the culmination of the worshiper's spiritual journey and includes and is the source of all the other chakras. The chart above colors the Sahasrara violet. Other sources color the Sahasrara Golden and White. The application of color to the Seven Tongues is unmistakable.

- Like Manipura, Sulohita is "very red," marching the intensity of the Kundalini snake at the navel.
- Like the Sahasrara, Sudhumaravarna, is "purple."
- Also like the Sahasrara, Sphuligini. is sparkling and brilliant, a ray catapulting the worshiper's soul to liberation.
- Like Visvarupi "having all forms" the Sahasrara subsumes all other chakras.

The Seven Tongues of Agni present Liberation in all its levels and varieties. From the microcosmic perspective the Upanishad again expounds the composition of the Vedic dharma in greater detail. These colors explain the composition of the Vedic dharma. The Vedic dharma is composed of five elements, and the Vedic force of Agni is the third element of Fire. The passage proceeds from the macrocosmic constitution to the microcosmic. The Yoga Tattva Upanishad goes on to explain the geometric shape of each element, beginning with Prthvi (Earth) to Akasha (Aether). This explanation resembles to a remarkable degree the explanation given in the *Timaeus* of Plato.

The explanation given in the Yoga Tattva Upanishad changes direction and expands to the colors of the elements to the greater Macrocosm. The expansion then continues with the mantras which should be uttered by the worshiper to achieve the desired result — liberation. These internal chants should appear familiar to you, Dear Reader. This is the Upanishadic equivalent to the Saman chant. The entire correspondences of these passages taken as a whole are viewed as another example of the expanding and contracting movements of Saman. These passages also provide further elaboration on the Seven Tongues of Agni and provide a plausible explanation. The change in color in the Seven Tongues correspond to the changes in the intensity of *Tapas* and religious austerity. The Seven Tongues of Agni are an incorporation of the elements of the universe and the path the worshiper treads in the spiritual journey. This rhythmic expansion and contraction began very early for the Vedic dharma. In the very beginning of the universe there was space, and that space was the Vedic force of Indra. (JUB, 1.28.1, 2.) That same space also consisted of the Vedic force of Agni, and Agni emitted his energy in all corners and all directions as seven rays. (JUB 1.28.3.) The Seven Tongues of Agni is one component of this process of expansion and contraction.

The purpose of the Vedas is to teach the worshiper to live in accordance with the Vedic dharma. One way in which the worshiper lives in accordance with the Vedic dharma is through purification. The Fire of Change (Agni) is the agent for purification. This aspect of the Fire of Change (Agni) is the medium by which and with which Purification (Soma) is communicated to the Divine realm, and hence, to the worshiper. (RV 3.57.5.) There is no more powerful medium for purification than the Seven Flames of Change (Agni). Change (Agni) is Fire, the quintessence of fire, and whereas Soma (Water) purifies the purified object through cleansing and pouring, Change (Agni) purifies by reducing the purified object to its most elemental components. The seven tongues of the Fire of Change (Agni) is synonymous for "purified" or "purification." It is not a quality reserved only for the Fire of Change (Agni). The Maruts (RV 1.44.14, 1.89.7), Mitra (RV 3.54.10), and Visvedevas (RV 6.21.11, 6.52.13) are all possessed of the seven tongues of Agni. The purification power of the Fire of Change (Agni) is far more expansive and extensive.

The Seven Tongues of Agni correspond to the Seven-Tiered Universe. RV 10.65.7 gives the elements that comprise the seven tongues of Agni. They are:

- Pervades Heaven.
- Promotes *Rta*.
- Supports, upholds and sustains Heaven.
- Provides the source of the Sacrifice.
- Creates the Waters.

The Fire of Change (Agni) summons the gods with his tongue. (RV 5.26.1, 6.16.2.) This is highly symbolic language to communicate many spiritual, mystical and occult functions. On one level it has the meaning that the purification fire is responsible for the inner dynamic of Divinity. Divinity receives its purified state through the Fire of Change (Agni). (RV 5.51.2.) The Fire of Change (Agni) is the tongue of Divine Grace and the Maruts in drinking Soma. (RV 3.35.9, 10.) Worded differently, this signifies that the transformative powers of Agni are the medium by which Divine Illumination (Indra) and Bliss (Soma) shepherds the worshiper in its journey to Vedic salvation. The Fire of Change (Agni) itself is infused with its purifying powers with its tongue, the agent, process, and fire of the purifying power of creation. (RV 1.46.10.) On another level it refers to the role of Agni as the "Messenger" of the gods. This can be taken to mean that the Vedic force of Agni verbally summons the other Vedic forces to the sacrifice to be infused into the worshiper. Taken on another level, it points to capacity to conjoin and unify the Vedic forces and energies into one spiritual force. In this interpretation the Vedic force and energy of Agni is a precursor to the monotheistic religions which followed much later than the mystic revelations of the Rishiis. Accepting this interpretation, of course, begs the question of whether the religion undergirding the Vedic dharma is in reality a monotheistic devotion and not polytheistic, a frequent criticism of the Hindu traditions, but this is properly the subject of another separate treatment.

Thus communicated, the Lord of Cosmic Order, Varuna, Lord Protector of the Dynamic Cosmic Order, spreads the rarified essence of purity to the four quarters of the cosmos. (RV 5.48.5.) The sanctity of the material world is thereby affirmed. Received by the divine representatives of the material world (the Adityas), they make the Fire of Change (Agni) the medium of this Fire of creation and purification. (RV 2.1.13.) A spiritual process that begins with the Fire of Change (Agni) thus returns full circle once more to the Fire of Change (Agni) to later begin the cycle of purification anew.

The Veda speaks of the tongue of the Fire of Change (Agni) either found, spreading or burning the trees. The meaning of this rc (mantra) is obscure. It is doubtful that it refers to a forest fire. Sayana interprets this rc (mantra) as a metaphor of the Fire of Change (Agni) accepting *ghrta* in the sacrificial flame. (RV 4.7.10.) *Ghrta*, the brilliance of mental and spiritual clarity, thus becomes a medium of purification. This meaning becomes clear when grhta is described as the tongue of the gods. (RV 4.58.1.)

Elsewhere, the Vedic force of Soma, the personification of purification and bliss, is the described as the tongue of the sacrifice. (RV 9.75.2.) This is due to the acceptance of the Vedic force of Soma by the worshiper's tongue (speech) at the Soma sacrifice (RV 8.17.5); this is to say that the worshiper learns to articulate divine knowledge at the Soma sacrifice. RV 4.7.10 is consistent with RV 4.58.1, which states that *ghrta* is the tongue of divinity. *Ghrta* in this instance refers to the brilliance of mental clarity and illumination, the very dynamics of the divine, added to the fire at the sacrifice. This is also consistent with RV 6.6.5, which states that the tongue of the Fire of Change (Agni) rescues the cattle, cattle here meaning the freeing the worshiper from ignorance with the knowledge (Cattle) of the divine. With this mental clarity the tongue of the Fire of Change (Agni) brings wisdom and illumination. (RV 10.46.8.)

There is another rc (mantra) in which *ghrta* can be reasonably inferred. RV 6.3.4 states that the Fire of Change (Agni) burns timber like a goldsmith fuse metal. Here an alchemical meaning is intended, but not just the alchemy of instruments and apparatuses. "Timber" here signifies inert matter, *prakrti*. The meaning is that Change (Agni) reduces inert matter to its essential components to transmute the active elements of common matter to eternal matter through the processes of internal (meditation and contemplation) and external (calcination) alchemy. But this is better explained by the Vedic alchemist.

Agni the Internal Essence of the Vedic Dharma

There is a little-known quotation from the Brhanaranyaka-Upanishad. There, at 5.15.1, it is said that "Fire is the symbol of AUM." Elsewhere, the primeval Brahman, the creator of the universe, is said to be encapsulated in the sound of AUM. Whenever the universe is dissolved and subsequently evolves, the Divine Sound, OM, resonates. (JUB 1.7.1, 1.9.1, 1.10.1.) The origins of the Vedic dharma go back very far indeed, back to that state when there was no material cosmos as we now know it, but the indeterminate mass of inert matter in which neither existence nor non-existence existed. (RV 10.129.1.) It is from this indeterminate mass that *tapas*, the practical product of Fire (Agni) emerged. From the intense internal heat of *tapas*, arose the Vedic dharma, as well as Existence itself. The terminology used

in the Veda is the functionally equivalent word for the Vedic dharma —
Rta. (RV 10.190.1.)

Agni is essence of the Vedic dharma. But what is that essence? Granted,
the Vedic dharma encompasses the totality of the material and subtle
universe. But what is the nature of that essence? Apart from those objects,
material and subtle, there is an internal energy inherent in those objects.
Delving further, what is the nature of that energy? The conclusion the
Rishiis arrive is Fire (Agni) and its by-product, *Tapas*. The *Tapas* of Indra
destroys Vrtra. (RV 1.55.1.)

- With fervent heat (*Tapasa*) Agni exterminates the demons and
  destroys the fiends with burning flames. (RV 10.87.14.)
- The Sacrificial Agni (*Agnim*) destroys all malice and ill-will with
  his burning flames. (RV 7.1.7.)

One example of the creative power of *Tapas* is its role in the creation
of the Vedic dharma. (RV 10.190.1.) *Tapas* also is the creative product
or impetus in other matters by giving birth to most of the fundamental
elements and processes in the Vedic dharma.

- *Tapas* is the internal heat contained in Soma. (RV 9.113.2.)
- From the boundless ocean, Matarisvan, the fierce flowing heat, the
  strong internal fire of *Tapas*, brings the force of life. (RV 10.109.1.)
- The life force that was covered with dark emptiness of
  indeterminateness which covered the cosmos arose through the
  internal power of *Tapas* (heat). (RV 10.129.3.)
- The *Tapas* of Indra creates the Sky (i.e., the Mid-World) after
  Vrtra's death. (RV 10.167.1.)

One could legitimately substitute "Agni" for these references to Tapas.
Tapas is the product of the inherent, internal Fire of Agni.

Enter the influence of AUM. AUM is simply the verbal articulation
of the internal friction of Fire, it is for this reason that the Brharanyaka-
Upanishad says that Fire, Agni, is the symbol of AUM. From its first
appearance AUM brings about the foundations of the Vedic dharma.
The Mandukya Upanishad millennia later concerning the divine Sound,

Aum, in relation to the Atman. the Mandukya Upanishad analytically lists the creations of AUM (i.e., Fire.) Quoting from this Upanishad, AUM, symbolized by Fire, creates the entire Vedic dharma:

- AUM is this whole of this visible universe. Its explanation is as follows: What has become, what is becoming, what will become – verily, all of this is AUM. And what is beyond these three states of the world of time. (MAU, 1.)
- All this is Brahman. The Self is Brahman. This Self has four quarters. (MAU, 2.)
- The first quarter is Vaisvanara. Its field is the waking state. Its consciousness is outward-turned. It is seven-limbed and nineteen-mouthed. It enjoys gross objects. (MAU, 3.)
- The second quarter is Taijasa. Its field is the dream state. Its consciousness is inward-turned. It is seven-limbed and nineteen-mouthed. It enjoys subtle objects. (MAU, 4.)
- The third quarter is Prajna, where one asleep neither desires anything nor beholds any dream: that is deep sleep. In this field of dreamless sleep, one becomes undivided, an undifferentiated mass of consciousness, consisting of bliss and feeding on bliss. His mouth is consciousness. (MAU, 5.)
- This is the Lord of All, the Omniscient, the Indwelling Controller, the Source of All. This is the beginning and end of all beings. (MAU, 6.)
- That is known as the fourth quarter: neither inward-turned nor outward-turned consciousness, nor the two together, not an undifferentiated mass of consciousness, neither knowing, nor unknowing, invisible, ineffable, intangible, devoid of characteristics, inconceivable, indefinable, its sole essence being the consciousness of its own Self, ... (MAU, 7.)
- This identical Atman, or Self, in the realm of sound is the syllable OM, the above described four quarters of the Self being identical with the components of the syllable, and the components of the syllable being identical with the four quarters of the Self. The components of the Syllable are A, U, M. (MAU, 8.)

- Vaisvanara, whose field is the waking state, is the first sound, A, because this encompasses all, and because it is the first. He who knows thus, encompasses all desirable objects, he becomes the first. (MAU, 9.)
- Taijasa, whose field is the dream state, is the second sound, U, because this is an excellence, and contains the qualities of the other two. He who knows thus, exalts. (MAU, 10.)
- Prajna, whose field is deep sleep, is the third sound, M, because this is the measure, and that into which all enters. He who knows thus, measures all and becomes all. (MAU, 11.)
- The fourth is soundless: unutterable, a quieting down of all relative manifestations, blissful, peaceful, non-dual. Thus, OM is the Atman, verily. He who knows thus, merges his self in the Self. (MAU, 12.)

The Vedic dharma matches the scope and breath of AUM. The Maitrayana-Brahmana Upanishad gives the extensive reach of the subtle basis of the Vedic dharma by its description of AUM. In 6.5, the Maitrayana-Brahmana Upanishad teaches that AUM is

- The combined Masculine and Feminine principles.
- Three forms of the Sacrificial Fire, which are Ghrapati, also a terrestrial manifestation of Agni; Dakshinagni, form of fire, the Sacrificial Fire in which offerings are made to the Ancestors; and the Avanayina, the consecrated fire for oblations.
- The three existential planes of the worlds, which are the Earth, Mid-World, and Heaven (Svar).
- The Past, Present, and Future.
- The internal sources of heat, which are Fire, Breath, and the Sun.
- Food, the Waters, and the Moon.
- The mental impulsions of the microcosm, the worshiper, which are intellect, mind and personality.
- The combined wisdom crystallized in the Rg Veda, Sama Veda, and Yajur Veda.

Another Upanishad, the Braham Vidya, summarizes the relation between AUM and the Vedic dharma. This is in the following chart:

Altar	Veda	World	Letter of AUM
Grhapati	Rg Veda	Earth	A
Dakshina	Yajur Veda	Mid-World	U
Ahavaniya	Sama Veda	Heaven	M

In a nutshell, this graph is the subtle foundation of the Vedic dharma. At first blush it may appear that Agni's role as the principal player of the Vedic dharma is peripheral. In reality, the role of Agni is critical, and he acts at the very heart of the Vedic dharma. The Grhapati, Dakshina and Ahavaniya are all forms of the Sacrificial Fire. The role of Agni is better demonstrated by his well-known epithet of being the "Son of the Waters."

The "Son of the Waters"

Any doubts as to the essential importance of Agni to the Vedic dharma is resolved by one of his most iconic epithets — the Son of the Waters. Any discussion about the Vedic force of Agni, his many aspects and manifestations and epithets, would not be complete without the enigmatic epithet, "Son of the Waters." "Son of the Waters" is another colorful phrase used to describe Agni. The Waters is a symbol of the Vedic dharma, representative of the essence of the Vedic dharma. Whenever this or other expressions are associated with the Vedic force of Agni, instead of the physical substance of water, what should be associated is the very subtle structure of the Vedic dharma. This expression, therefore, communicates how very intimate and interwoven is the relationship of the Vedic force of Agni with the Vedic dharma at large. The question remains, How could it be possible that the god of Fire is associated with water?

We know that the Fire of Change (Agni) is the messenger of all sentient and insentient beings to the divinities. It is therefore appropriate that the sacrificial fire should be the messenger of the wealth of divine life to all sentient and insentient beings. (RV 1.2.1.) All mendicants, including the Fire of Change, are found in the waters. (RV 1.23.20; AV 1.6.2. Yet, there is an inextricable connection between (Agni) and the waters. This is expressed in many ways:

- A well-known epithet for the Fire of Change is that he is the son of the waters, *apaalm naalpataam*. (RV 1.22.6; 1.122.4; 1.143.1; 1.145.1; 1.186.5; 2.31.6; 2.35.1, 2, 3, 7, 9, 13; 3.9.1; 5.41.10; 6.50.12, 13; 7.34.15; 7.47.2; 10.30.3; 10.92.13.) Agni lives in the waters. (RV 1.65.3, 4, 9, 10; 1.67.3, 4, 9, 10; 170.3, 4; 1.95.4, 5, 8; 1.44.2; 1.149.4; 2.4.2; 3.1.3; 3.72.2; 3.55.12.) An entire Sukta, RV 2.35, is devoted to the "Son of Waters." But more about that a little later.
- Not only is he the child of the waters, but the force of Agni is carried by the celestial waters. (RV 1.59.4; 1.71.2; 2.35.3.1.4; 9, 14; 9.92.4.)
- The active fire of Change (Agni) has been described as the kinsman of the waters (RV 1.65.7, 8) and the germ of the waters (RV 1.70.3; 1.95.4), the latter signifying the initial stages of the powers of purification.
- The Fire of Change (Agni) bestows peace through the waters. (AV 2.10.2.)

Fire is inextricably mixed with Water. All this seems counter-intuitive. It appears inconsistent according to their basic natural properties that a fire whose essence is the combustibility of matter should find its residence in the waters. Yet in the veiled language of the Vedas, there is no contradiction:

- In its many regenerative properties the Fire of Change is described as the "Bull (*vRSabha*) of the Standing Waters," (RV 7.5.2; 2.35.13) the bull representing the symbol of the creative, generative power in the universe. The active fires of Change (Agni) produces the waters. (RV 3.4.2.)
- Fire, the essential quality of Change (Agni), protects the water. (AV 11.2.8.)

Most importantly, Agni as the "Child of the Waters" is coded language signifying from whence the Vedic force of Agni arose. The Waters is symbolic language signifying the essential nature of the Vedic dharma

— the complete Vedic dharma. If Agni is the "Child of the Waters," Agni arose from the same intrinsic forces which power the Vedic dharma. Thus, the Veda states that an aspect of Agni, Vaisvanara, was born at the "highest place," *parama vyoma*, an existential plane higher than the Seven-Dimensional Universe. (RV 7.5.7.) From that high and lofty place, the Fire of Change operates as "the germ (seed) of waters, germ (seed) of woods, germ (seed) of all things that move not and that move" (RV 1.70.3.) In that capacity Agni becomes the Seed of everything in the Vedic dharma. The Fire of Change thereby represents the latent potentiality of all things, alive or inert. That latent potentiality germinates and grows when nourished by the Waters. The active principles of Change (Agni) produces the Waters. (RV 3.4.2.) Fire, the essential quality of Change (Agni) protects the Water. (AV 11.2.8.) The Fire of Change (Agni) and the Waters share a few common characteristics: Fluidity, Pervasiveness, Continuity. The Vedic force of Agni and the Waters have powers of purification. It is for this reason that when sprinkling water the priest sometimes utters the name of Agni. (SPB 1.1.3.11, 12.) On a larger level, this regenerative process is a re-enactment of the give-and-take process of Sacrifice: Agni is born from the Waters, the Vedic dharma, and thereafter becomes the Seed to perpetuate the Vedic dharma.

The Vedic force of Agni contains the internal potentiality and latency of all things in the Vedic dharma and of the Vedic forces which regulate those things. Agni contains in his belly the Vedic force of Indra, whose own belly is full of the Vedic forces and energies of Soma. (RV 3.22.1.) In the Vedic force of Agni, then, the potentialities and full latencies of the Vedic forces of Indra and Soma are subsumed and branch out in a cluster of Vedic forces. This is expressed in many ways, the most prominent of which is the shared characteristics of the Bull:

- Indra has also been called the Bull of the Standing Waters. (RV 6.44.21.) This presents no inconsistency. The Vedic forces and energies frequently share responsibilities and capabilities. Agni and the Maruts, whose active fires are several, are responsible for *arka/m*, which is interpreted by Sayana as the descending waters and is the luminous nature of Indra. (RV 1.19.4.)

- Soma is the Bull Who Fertilizes the Force of Consciousness. (Nir., 3.3.) Soma is the Bull of Earth. (RV 9.44.28.) Soma is the Bull of Heaven. (RV 9.44.28.).) Soma is the "Bull with a Thousand Seeds." (RV 9.109.17.) This means that in establishing the inner essence of the Three-Dimensional Universe, Soma is the seed of that world (RV 9.86.39), located at the "Navel," or innermost locus, of the material world. (RV 9.72.7.)

- In an interesting rc (mantra), the Vedic force of Indra is said to drink the Soma juice with the tongue of Agni. (RV 3.35.9.) This rc (mantra) continues the mutual identification of the three Vedic forces of Agni, Indra, and Soma. It also further clarifies that relationship. By drinking the Soma juice for Indra, Agni becomes the agency by which the power of Soma is conveyed to Indra. A number of levels of meaning exist when this is accomplished through Agni's "tongue." The "tongue" of Agni is commonly interpreted as flames of fire, and so the Rishiis' meaning is that the efficacy of fire is the mechanism by which the benefits of Soma are incorporated into Indra's being. The tongue is associated with speech, and so by drinking Soma for Indra's benefit, Agni is giving articulation to the purpose of the Soma juice. It also underscores a theme which will be repeated several times in this book. When fighting the serpent Vrtra, Indra acts as the incarnation of Agni, thereby effectively providing two mighty Vedic forces to fight Vrtra.

There are many examples of these shared powers and capabilities. They are originate from RV 3.22.1, and like a mighty oak, the potentiality engrained in Agni grows.

The Rg Veda explains elsewhere the Fire of Change (Agni) is kindled (*idhyase*) in the waters. (RV 3.25.5.) In the coded language of the Veda, this terminology refers to the essential paradox of the binding and equivalence of water and fire in the Fire of Change (Agni). In Ayurveda, the *dosha* of *Pitta* is the combination of the two elements of water and fire. *Dosha* is Change, and water and fire do not combine but modulate each other. (Miller, *Ayurveda and Aromatherapy* (2005), p.14.) We will see later in this book that once "kindled" Agni becomes the Sacrificial Fire, the fire capable of conveying mystic powers to the worshiper. It is from this kindling that water and fire is united. It goes without saying, then, that this coupling between the water and fire elements of Agni is a mystical process. When so coupled, water, with fire, becomes an agent for purification. (SPB 1.1.1.1.) The sacrificial grass is considered to be the cosmic primeval, Water. (Gonda, *The Ritual Functions and Significance of Grasses in the Religion of the Veda*, (1985), p. 36.) Agni as Fire is produced out of the water from which the grass is represented. (SPB 2.2.3.1; 1.2.3.9; BSS5.19.8.) This is what it means when it is said that the Fire of Change (Agni) is kindled (*idhyase*) in the waters. (RV 3.25.5.) This expression is also expressed as the active Fire of Agni: On the one hand Agni the child, germ, or "kinsman" of the waters and on the other hand Agni progenitor, the creator and purveyor of the Waters. This ambiguity is resolved when viewing the Fire of Change (Agni) as creating the purifying powers of the waters, the germination powers unleashing the latent potential of the Seed, but also providing the essential purifying properties of fire. There is no "beginning" or "end" to this process. Instead of moving in one direction, and dissipating in space, the force which creates the purifying properties of the waters returns in a circular motion. The active fires of Agni and Indra in the context of the Waters thus are viewed as an organic whole and are functionally equivalent.

It is in this context that we consider RV 2.35. As indicated earlier, an entire Sukta is devoted to the Son of the Waters as its Presiding Deity. The Presiding Deity of Sukta 35 of the Second Mandala is Agni, in his aspect of the "Son of the Waters." These rcs give the most complete treatment of Agni as the "Son of the Waters."

- RV 2.35.1:
  The Rishii Grtsamadah Bhargavah Shaunakah, who revealed this Sukta, invokes the "Son of the Waters," to learn the mysteries of the Vedic dharma's vastness. It is this vastness that the "Son of the Waters" addresses. This is the spiritual endowment the Vedic force of Agni in this manifestation discloses to the worshiper.

- RV 2.35.2:
  Agni in his manifestation as the "Son of the Waters" created all things present in the Vedic dharma.

- RV 2.35.3:
  Pure waters stand around Agni in his manifestation as the "Son of the Waters." Some of these waters flow together and others flow into the vast Ocean. This language is highly symbolic. Sri Aurobindo would interpret this rc (mantra) as saying that the vastness (ocean) is symbolic for the Absolute Self, and the other tributaries flow into the individual mind of the worshiper and others. If this interpretation is correct, the initial give-and-take process of Sacrifice from which the "Son of the Waters" was born becomes more intricate. In other words, Agni in this manifestation is the "Son of the Waters." This epithet necessarily implies Agni is born from the essence of the Vedic dharma. As continuation of the give-and-take process, therefore, Agni, gives back of itself to the Vedic dharma. The "Son of the Waters" carries forward this exchange by supplying the mental impulses to guide the worshiper either to the Absolute Self (the vast ocean) or to remain in the material world.

- RV 2.35.4:
  The rc (mantra) states that the waters surrounding Agni in his manifestation as "Son of the Waters" make him bright, and that the brilliant flames shine upon the worshiper. Agni in his manifestation as "Son of the Waters" is clothed by the light in the waters. This is symbolic simile for the sacrificial flame, but one infused with the mysteries of the Vedic dharma.

- RV 2.35.5:
  This rc (mantra) recites that Agni in his manifestation as "Son of the Waters" bestows food. We spoke of the metaphorical meaning of food earlier in this introduction. It has vast meaning, as vast as the Vedic dharma itself. "Food" can mean energy, offerings to the sacrificial altar, the worshiper's body itself. Food is a part of Agni in his manifestation as "Son of the Waters."

- RV 2.35.6:

  The Rishii reveals the steed (read, Horse) was born here in the Svar, where Agni in his manifestation as "Son of the Waters" protects the Rishiis. The eminent Vedic scholar, R.L. Kashyap, interprets "Horses" to mean "energy." In certain circumstances, yes it does. In the Vedic dharma Horses represent the senses, the mind's perception of the senses. There is no reason why these concepts are mutually exclusive. Agni in his manifestation as "Son of the Waters" represents the energy inherent in the sense perceptions.

- RV 2.35.7:

  Here, the rc (mantra) says that Agni in his manifestation as "Son of the Waters" invigorates his essential nature by consuming the milk of the Cow in his house. The Cow implicates another set of properties. The cows represent knowledge, wisdom and illumination, most likely because these are the representatives of their products: milk, butter and ghee. Because the cows produce several by-products, different cows in the Vedas represent different aspects of knowledge or the mind: A barren or immature cow is taken to mean the lack of consciousness, incomplete or faulty knowledge, because of its unripe milk. (RV 3.30.14 (unripe milk); 2.7.5; 1.112.3; 1.116.22; 1.117.20; 1.61.9 (ray cows); 6.72.4; 4.19.7; 7.68.8.) On the other hand, the ray-cows represent Aditi, the infinite consciousness. (RV 4.58.4; 4.1.6.) The Ray-Cows also represent hidden or occult knowledge. (RV 4.53; 4.58; 4.5.10.) Here, Agni in his manifestation as "Son of the Waters" supports his own intrinsic nature by consuming the milk of the Cow, *Dhenu/m* (RV 1.20.3; 1.91.20; 1.112.3; 1.118.8; 1.137.3; 1.139.7; 1.160.3; 1.164.26; 2.32.2; 2.34.6; 3.57.1; 4.33.1, 8; 4.34.9; 4.42.10; 5.1.1; 6.35.4; 6.48.11, 13; 6.63.8; 7.18.4; 8.1.10; 10.39.13; 10.61.17; 10.64.12; 10.176.1.) The precise word for "Cow" used in the rc, yields milk which is symbolic for knowledge associated with Soma, or Bliss. (RV 9.34.6; 9.61.21; 9.72.1; 9.86.2; 9.97.50.)

- RV 2.35.8:

  Present in the Waters, Agni in his manifestation as "Son of the Waters" is possessed of *rta*, the internal essence of the Vedic dharma. Born of the Waters, Agni in his manifestation as "Son of the Waters" is the very essence of the controlling principle for the Vedic dharma.

- RV 2.35.9:

  Agni in his manifestation as "Son of the Waters," while standing in the Waters, is clothed in lightning. The Rishii here mixes metaphors again, water and lightning. This is symbolic speech to convey the thought that the essence of the Vedic dharma (Waters) consists of lightning, a simile of the brilliance of Consciousness. That lightening may issue from the "Son of the Waters" is testament to the source of all Consciousness originating from the recesses of the Vedic dharma. In this state, Agni in his manifestation as "Son of the Waters" is communicated as "golden-hued." In the Vedic dharma colors matter. Gold and all things golden represent immortality and the eternal. (SPB 6.7.1.11; 6.7.2.1, 2; 7.4.1.16, 17; 7.4.2.8; 8.1.4.1; 12.5.2.6.) Consciousness, as an attribute of Agni in his manifestation as "Son of the Waters," is eternal.

- RV 2.35.10:

  Agni in his manifestation as "Son of the Waters" is golden, and every aspect of Agni in his manifestation as "Son of the Waters" is golden. Agni in his manifestation as "Son of the Waters" is eternal.

- RV 2.35.11:

  The various aspects of the "name" is explained in much greater detail later in this book. One such category is the "secret name," that name mentioned in this rc. The secret name is the occult, esoteric meaning of the subject named. This rc (mantra) makes clear that "gold," the essence of eternity, is the secret name of Agni in his manifestation as "Son of the Waters."

- RV 2.35.12:
  The worshiper surrenders its soul before Agni in his manifestation as "Son of the Waters." In the give-and-take process of Sacrifice the worshiper offers food, the worshiper's very body and soul. In return the worshiper receives an understanding and appreciation of the vastness of the Vedic dharma.

- RV2.35.13:
  Agni in his manifestation as "Son of the Waters" is the Bull. The Bull is the Showerer of Benefits is the very essence of the Rainmaker. Just as the rains bring water to renew the earth, so does the Showerer of Benefits replenish the worshiper's soul while traveling on the Vedic path to salvation and liberation. Vrsaa, the Bull, is the active Principle of Regeneration. Agni as the Bull, the Principle of Regeneration is found in RV 1.7.8; 1.140.2; 1.149.2; 3.1.8; 3.2.11; 3.27.13; 3.44.4; 4.3.10; 6.16.5; 6.3.7; 6.48.3; 7.10.1; 8.64.8; 8.93.7; 8.93.20; 10.11.1; 10.115.2, 8; and 10.187.3, and here, as Agni, the Son of the Waters.

- RV 2.35.14:
  Agni in his manifestation as "Son of the Waters" occupies "this highest place," *parame.* Cosmologically, *parame* is the highest existential plane, above even the seven layers of the Seven-Dimensional Universe. It is from this plane that this material world came to be. The undifferentiated mass which had existed (or, more exactly, did not exist) coalesced into the material world through the actions of *kama* (desire) which was present in the *parame*, melding with the essential nature (*svadha*) of the lower world. (RV 10.129.5.) If there is anything more vast than the beginning stages of this Kalpa, it is in this rc.

- RV 2.35.15:
  With these attributes, the worshiper approaches Agni in his manifestation as "Son of the Waters" to obtain purification, strength, and to learn the vastness of the Vedic dharma. These are the tools the worshiper will need for the spiritual journey.

These elements all come together to create a complex Vedic force.

—0000000—

There are many faces to Agni. The object of this book is reveal and explain as many faces as possible. This book is about Agni, but it is also about fire, the nature of fire, the many faces of fire. The object is to demonstrate that Agni is more than simply the deity of Fire but the divine personification of the various facets in the nature of fire. Agni has many fires. This present book strives to show the many permutations of Agni and, in a larger sense, define as many facets of "fire" with its many meanings and has several aspects and manifestations. Please bear with me dear Reader if certain critical concepts are repeated. There are some elements to the Vedic dharma which are critical. If these concepts are repeated, they are an important part of the Vedic dharma. This book attempts to be as complete as possible, but, of course, with a scripture like the Rg Veda, this is impossible. The Rg Veda is an unfathomable, incredible scripture. The deeper you delve into its "meaning," other meanings and interpretations appear. Like a Matryoshka doll, one sentence, one word, may have multiple layers of meaning. Once one shell of the doll is revealed, you discover there are other shells and layers beneath. This book is a personal view, culled after years of study and reflection. The footnotes and doctrinal are not included to intimidate or annoy. They are as much for the reader's benefit as it is for the author's own assurance that he is not falling into error. If the interpretation is incorrect, outlandish, audacious, unfounded, unorthodox, or simply mistaken, or if there is some other inadequacy — or if just plain wrong — the fault lies not in the rcs (chants from the Rg Veda) in this marvelous, moving, piece of wisdom called the Vedas, but belongs solely to this author. Let us begin.

ALL ABOUT AGNI

The Aspects Of Agni

THE FIRE ALTAR

The Fire Altar is the centerpiece of Vedic sacrifice. The purpose of the Agnicayana ritual, the fire ritual, is to actualize the rcs (mantras) contained in the Rg Veda and to make flesh the deep principles contained therein. The Fire Altar is the focal means by which the worshiper realizes and understands the teachings of the rcs (mantras) and implement them in the worshiper's life to assist the worshiper during the spiritual journey. The fire altar is so constructed in every way to facilitate this purpose — to increase the worshiper's understanding, to implement those lessons in the Vedas and the secrets of the Vedic dharma into the worshiper's life and spiritual journey, and to enable the worshiper to surrender its Soul utterly to the fire which contain these spiritual endowments.

The Fire Altar is so constructed in order to enable the worshiper to inculcate the eternal body of the Vedic dharma into the life of the worshiper or sacrificer. The entire purpose of the Fire Altar is to provide a focal point to the worshiper's awareness and wherein the worshiper may discard the errors of previous ways of thinking, believing. and conducting one's life, and become spiritually renewed, whether that is acquiring new insights, committing to new behaviors, or achieving liberation or salvation. The mystery of how this is accomplished is as ancient as fire itself:

> "The gods then established that (fire) in their innermost soul; and having established that immortal element in their innermost soul, and become immortal and unconquerable, they overcame their mortal, conquerable enemies. And so this one now establishes that immortal element in his innermost soul; and–though there is for him no hope of immortality–he obtains the full measure of life; for, indeed, he becomes unconquerable, and his enemy, though striving to conquer, conquers him not. And, accordingly, when one who has established his fires and one who has not established his fires, vie with each other, he who has established his fires overcomes the other, for, verily, he thereby becomes unconquerable, he thereby becomes immortal." (SPB 2.2.2.14.)

Then:

> "Now, when, on that occasion, they produce that (fire) by churning, then he (the sacrificer) breathes (blows) upon it, when produced; for fire indeed is breath: he thereby produces the one thus produced. He again draws in his breath: thereby he establishes that (fire) in his innermost soul; and that fire thus becomes established in his innermost soul." (SPB 2.2.15.)

The worshiper understands, of course, that Agni alone is immortal. (SPB, 1.9.2.20.) But from there, the worshiper follows a charted course. Through participation in the construction or ceremony glorifying the fire altar the worshipers place that immortal element in their innermost souls. (SPB, 2.2.2.10.)

By setting up the fire altar, the worshipers therefore dispels the evil from themselves. The gods are immortal; he therefore, though there is for him no prospect of immortality, attains the (full measure of) life, whosoever sets up his fires during that time. (SPB, 2.1.3.4.)

A fire altar for the Agnicayana ritual must be built in order for this to take place. The Agnicayana is ideally suited for the many fires of Agni. One of the attributes of the Agni, the Fire of Change, is Prakasa, the Force of the Light of Consciousness. The following rcs (mantras) not only explain the aspect of the Agni Eternal Law which pertains to the Force of the Light of Consciousness but also informs all aspects of Vedic philosophy and religion.

Yet this fire of Change harbors a fundamental contradiction. It will represent, as we will see, celestial, transcendental, heavenly forms of fire. Yet, at the same time, it will represent the terrestrial fires. These terrestrial fires are basically responsible for Ignorance, *maya* or *mula vidya*, and are responsible for

- The projection of multiplicity in the world;
- Responsible for the body, and ego with the five elements;
- Covers the Self-luminous Self; and

- Creates the everyday, rough and tumble, material, transactional world.

The Fire Altar is the symbol not only for the greater Vedic dharma, but the inner source of the worshiper's being. The source of the fundamental contradiction is that these attributes are the source of the light of consciousness, which according to later doctrine in Advaita Vedanta, is the main tool for destroying Ignorance and attaining liberation from the transmigrational, transactional world. Vedanta resolved this dilemma by asserting Brahman's role as the Lord, or creator, of Maya. The Fire of Change alludes to this ultimate contradiction as well, as the Vedic force of Agni is repeatedly revealed to represent both Heaven and Earth. The Vedas resolved this contradictory role of the Fire of Change in the Veda world with Agni Vaisnavara, and that resolution is stated in the language of Fire. Vaisnavara is the great fire of knowledge. (Yoga Yajnavalkya 9.23.) Since its operation is that of fire, it works to burn away the impurities of ignorance. This aspect of Agni (the Fire of Change) is described at length in RV Mandalas III and IV, which can be read as a veritable textbook of the aspect of Agni Visvanara which pertains to the Fire of Knowledge.

- RV 3.2.1:
  Agni Vaisnavara has two aspects — it has the Force of the Light of Consciousness and is possessed of the digestive, gastric fire, which is \the vital energy of life.

- RV 3.2.2:
  In the beginning Agni Vaisvanara sparked the flame which illumined the Heaven and Earth. This particular language points to the capacity of Agni which is supplanted by the Purusa in the Samkhya philosophy. This rc (mantra) is quick to add that in this action Agni is the sustainer of life.

- RV 3.2.3:
  The collective attributes of god, endowed with Consciousness (*daksa*), created Agni Vaisnavara through the vital force of life and power.

- RV 3.2.4:
  Desiring its strengths, the worshiper solicits the gifts from Agni Vaisvanara. The most significant spiritual gift is the force of Knowledge which shines on all.

- RV 3.2.5:
  Agni Vaisvanara bestows vitality and power, and its resplendent Fire of Knowledge removes sorrow, pain, and sin.

- RV 3.2.6:
  The luster of this self-luminating Fire of Knowledge purifies the worshipers' soul.

- RV 3.2.7:
  The self-luminous light of Vaisvanara provides the spark of light to the body and should of all creatures.

- RV 3.2.8:
  Agni Vaisvanara — the fire of Knowledge and Vital energy of life — is the focus of the sacrifice.

- RV 3.2.9:
  Indeed, there are three aspects to Agni Vaisvanara: (1) the Fire of Knowledge, (2) the force of Vital energy, and (3) the sacrificial fire. The Vital force is found in and maintain the sensible universe, the bhuvah, and the Fire of Knowledge and sacrificial fire is found in and emanates from the higher world, the svar.

- RV 3.2.10:
  The Knowledge of Agni Vaisvanara shines everywhere.

- RV 3.2.11:
  As the sacrificial fire Agni Vaisvanara gives the benefits of the sacrifice (*ratna*, the waters), which is the purification of the worshiper.

- RV 3.2.12:

Agni Vaisvanara ascends to heaven and purifies the soul of the worshiper while traveling the sun's path.

- RV 3.2.13:
  The worshiper seeks the direction of the cosmic order (*rta*) which emanates from Agni Vaisvanara

- RV 3.2.14:
  Agni Vaisvanara is the sustainer and preserver of life and shines down upon the sacrifice and the worshiper seeking his own self-awareness and spark of higher consciousness.

- RV 3.3.2:
  Agni Vaisvanara is the mediator between heaven and earth, mind and body.

- RV 3.3.3:
  Agni Vaisvanara represents the sacrifice, from which the worshiper hopes to attain divine bliss and happiness

- RV 3.3.4:
  Agni Vaisvanara is the inspiration of the sacrifice and the source of the vital force of the worshipers; it pervades the body and mind of the worshiper and heaven and earth.

- RV 3.3.5:
  Agni, the Fire of Change, is incarnated into the world as Agni Vaisvanara, where he purifies, is immanent, all-pervading and all Powerful.

- RV 3.3.6:
  Agni Vaisvanara mediates between heaven and earth, and the mind and body.

- RV 3.3.8:
  Jatavedas, the "Knower of All Things," is a manifestation of Agni Vaisvanara, possessing the vital life-force.

- RV 3.3.9:

  Agni Vaisvanara is the first cause of the material world by virtue of its powers of Agni's vital life-force.

- RV 3.3.10:

  Agni Vaisvanara is responsible for the manifestation and multiplicity in the material world through his all-perceiving comprehension.

- RV 4.5.1:

  Agni Vaisvanara sustains the higher, cosmic Consciousness and vital life-force of the highest realm of Consciousness (bhrad), which is its product.

Agni (Change and Transformation) as Agni Vaisnavara is the Fire of Consciousness and Knowledge. There are preconditions for achieving this state. As Agni (Change and Transformation) is the process by which the digestive fire digests and process food, so is the mental aspect of Agni (Change and Transformation) is the methodology by which the information obtained from the sensory organs (*indriyam* = Indra) are processed, evaluated and from that information conclusions made. This is the occult meaning of the epithet of Agni (Change and Transformation) as "the eater of food." Agni (Change and Transformation) is the eater. So say the Vedas and the Brahmanas.

The world is divided into two parts, the eater and the eaten. (SPB 10.6.2.1.) The fire of Change (Agni) is not alone in its capacity as the eater of food. Knowledge, which, as we saw in the last chapter, is a by-product of the sacrifice. Thus, the successful initiate of the sacrifice gains knowledge, or, in the words of the Veda, is the eater of food.

- The worshiper who is incomplete in Speech becomes the eater of food. (SPB 3.9.1.9.)
- The worshiper who is in the midst of cattle (Knowledge) becomes the eater of food. (SPB 7.5.2.14.)
- The worshiper becomes the eater of food during and as a result of the sacrifice. (SPB 1.3.2.11, 12, 14, 15; 1.8.3.5, 6; 4.2.1.9.)

- The worshiper that reaches the end of the sacrifice becomes the eater of food. (SPB 10.3.5.8.)
- The worshiper who fasts at the time of the full moon is the eater of food. (SPB 1.6.3.37.)
- Agni (Change and Transformation) is the Eater, both in his aspect of fire and the fire altar. (SPB 10.6.2.2.)

In all other aspects, Agni (Change and Transformation) is the eater. (SPB 2.1.4.28; 2.2.1.1; 2.4.4.1; 8.6.3.5; 10.4.1.11; 11.1.6.9.) The pervasive character of Vaishnava, the Fire of Knowledge, is reflected in concrete terms in the construction of the Fire Altar. On a microcosmic, physiological, level Vaisnavara represents the fire which charges the synapses of the brain. On a macrocosmic level Vaisnavara represents the Fire Altar. The Altar is constructed with bricks. The bricks of the Fire Altar represent the individual monads, units of knowledge. The bricks are so arraigned to construct the altar, and the specific arrangements represent different levels of the universe, much as the mental synapses of the brain Fire to create the conscious activity of the mind to make the thinking, knowing Manu. The Fire-Altar indeed, represents the entire Vedic dharma. (SPB 10.5.4.1.):

- The Fire-Altar represents the air. (SPB 10.5.4.2.)
- The Fire-Altar represents the Sky. (SPB 10.5.4.3.)
- The Fire-Altar represents the Sun. (SPB 10.5.4.4.)
- The Fire-Altar represents the asterisms, the Nakshatras. (SPB 10.5.4.5.)
- The Fire-Altar represents Metres of the Saman. (SPB 10.5.4.7.)
- The Fire-Altar represents Year. (SPB 10.5.4.10.)
- The Fire-Altar represents the Body of Manu. (SPB 10.5.4.12.)
- The Fire-Altar represents all Beings in the universe. (SPB 10.5.4.14.)

These correspondences relate to the construction of the Fire Altar. The connectedness of the cosmos with the construction of the fire altars are very precisely practiced and honored during the Agnicayana ritual. (Weiland, (2010.) There are seven levels to the macrocosm and microcosm, and three different fuels impelling each level. (AV 19.6.15.) On one level it provides a cosmological framework for the transcendent Seven-Dimensional Universe where each level contains three different subdivisions. On another level it provides a mechanism whereby the worshiper can jump start from the material world to the transcendent world. This process is symbolized in the construction of the Fire Altar. The Fire Altar represents the whole world and the bricks the regions (SPB 7.3.1.1) and the vedi, the entire sacrificial enclosure, represents the earth. (SPB 7.3.1.15.)

So in constructing the fifth layer of the Fire Altar with Stamobhaga bricks, twenty-one bricks are used to symbolize the three worlds and the regions. (SPB, 8.5.3.5, 6.) Each level of the fifth layer contains three layers and represents a different, progressively elevated, layer of the cosmic order:

- The first three layers, one through three, is symbolic of the world;
- The second three layers, four through six, is symbolic of the mid-earth;
- The third three layers, seven through nine, is symbolic of the heavens;
- The fourth three layers, ten through twelve, is symbolic of the eastern quarter;
- The fifth three layers, thirteen through fifteen, is symbolic of the southern quarter;
- The sixth three layers, sixteen through eighteen, is symbolic of the western quarter; and
- The seventh three layers, nineteen through twenty-one, is symbolic of the northern quarter.

Most of all, the fire altar is Light, the flame of the fire blazing therein. Later, when Vedanta would much later associate light with consciousness, it followed a tradition which began in the Veda, where the key words signifying consciousness are "light," Splendor," "effulgent," "resplendent," "brilliant," and the like. Consciousness which is other than "light," and described as "effulgent," "resplendent," "brilliant," representing gradations higher than simple illumination. These gradations are referred to as "the Light of Consciousness" or "the Force of the Light of Consciousness." Thus Transformation (Agni) is known as being "light" or "the Light of Consciousness" or "the Force of the Light of Consciousness," and thus is known as Agni Vaisnavara or simply Agni. All encompass the overriding

Principle of Transformation, represented by the divinity Agni. On a ritualistic level "the Light of Consciousness" or "the Force of the Light of Consciousness," is represented by the Fire Altar which represents the consciousness that pervades the universe.

Later in this book, Agni Vasivanara, reappears. Agni Vaisvanara reappears as the Fire of the Light of Consciousness and reappears as a celestial manifestation of Agni Suci. It had already in fact been discussed as the Light of Consciousness in the Introduction. Agni Vaisvanara is a multifaceted part of the Vedic force of Agni. Before the worshiper may introduce this Fire to use on the spiritual journey, the worshiper must first fully understand and implement the fire inhered in the surrender of the Soul.

THE FIRE OF
SELF-SURRENDER

It is here in the Fire of Self-Surrender, that the worshiper finds the spiritual basis from which spring all fires. The Fire Altar is the centerpiece of the Vedic sacrifice on an exoteric level; the Fire of Self-Sacrifice is the centerpiece on an esoteric, personal level. It is here that the worshiper sits before the Fire Altar and opens the mind and heart to allow the consecrating Vedic forces and energies take possession of the Soul and mold it to their liking. It is here that the worshiper surrenders mind, body and soul. It is here that spiritual renewal is situated, and it is under these circumstances that the worshiper is reborn. This is where the worshiper's spiritual journey begins. The worshiper places complete trust in the Vedic forces and energies. The worshiper's soul and body is like putty, the Vedic forces and energies are the artisan, and the finished product is the reborn Soul of the worshiper. Thereafter, as far as the worshiper is able, the worshiper lives consistent with the Vedic forces and energies and according to the Vedic dharma. This is the fire of self-surrender.

There is an intricate exchange involved when the worshiper surrenders to the Vedic forces and energies. Self-Surrender arises from the very nature of worship. Whenever the worship invokes a Vedic force or energy, the worshiper goes to that Vedic force or energy which is channeled to the worshiper. (BG, 7.23.) Agni in its aspect as the Fire Altar is the starting point in this process.

- The worshiper begins by approaching the Fire Altar with thoughts of Self-Surrender. (RV 1.1.7.)
- The worshiper surrenders before the Fire Altar. In this context the Fire Altar represents the fire of the Vedic dharma, its natural laws and processes. (RV 10.92.4.) The Fire Altar also represents the fire of the Word. (RV 10.115.4.)
- The Fire Altar also presents the fire of impulsions and Knowledge. (RV 10.165.5.) As we learned earlier, impulsions are anything which propel the communication of the essential qualities of the Vedic divine forces to the worshiper. They are bursts of energy which power the mind, body and soul.
- The worshiper then send the "streams" — thoughts, prayers, meditative austerities — to the Fire Altar, seeking its protection. (RV 7.94.4.) The worshiper's self-surrender may be for different

purposes. The worshiper may self-surrender, conscious of the worshiper's sins, but seeking expiation from there, the Visvedevas and the One provide their expiation."

- Agni in its aspect as the Fire Altar accepts the worshiper's self-surrender. (RV 1.65.1.)
- Agni in its aspect as the Fire Altar thereupon surrenders to the worshiper. (RV 1.71.6.)
- From that point forward, the worshiper follows and surrenders to the Vedic force or energy, the force and energy of Agni, or of any other Vedic force or energy before which the worshiper prostrates. These include any one from the vast array of Vedic forces, such as Rudra, the fire of the firmament (RV 3.54.3; 7.36.5); Heaven and Earth (RV 3.54.3); the Angirasa Seers (RV 1.62.2); Indra, the supporter of the Vedic dharma (RV 4.21.5; 4.23.4); the ancestors, *ptrs* (RV 10.15.2); and Rudra, the fire of the firmament, and the Maruts, Mitra, Varuna, Aditi, Sindhu, Earth and Heaven. (RV 3.51.4.)

It has been said many times that the essence of the Sacrifice is the give and take between the worshiper, the Sacrifice, and God. The fire of Self-Surrender is perhaps one of the best demonstrations of this process. There are many forms of fire, and Self-Surrender is one of them, providing the desire and motivation to the worshiper to give totally of the Soul.

The fire of Self-Surrender is vast and comprehensive and is involved in complicated relationships between the worshiper, Vedic forces and energies, and the vast Vedic dharma. The mystery of the fire of Self-Surrender begins in its role to "kindle" the Sacrificial Fire. It bears repeating that the Kindling is not a simple ignition of the flame but the release of hidden, transformative powers. The kindled Sacrificial Fire conveys all those qualities and energies from the universe and channels those qualities and energies into the Fire and from there to the worshiper.

The kindled Agni is the alter ego — although not always — to the Sacrificial Fire. Once kindled, Sacrificial Fire works hand-in-hand with the fire of Self-Surrender to transform the previous life of the worshiper, out of which a new worshiper emerges. These combined fires power this transformation and it is to these fires that the worshiper surrenders the

Soul. There is a direct and inexorable relationship between the kindled Agni and self-surrender.

The worshiper understands the essential nature of the kindled Agni. This is a precondition to successfully surrendering the soul to the kindled Agni.

- The kindled arrives from Heaven with Indra. (RV 3.4.11; 7.2.11.)
- The kindled Agni bestows spiritual welfare, here, in the form of illumination and enlightenment and Bliss. (RV 10.25.3.)
- The Kindled Agni is the Bull. (RV 4.5.15.) The Bull represents the Regenerative Principle. This holds more than one meaning. It signifies, doubtless, that subtle principle, the physical seed, which perpetuates the physical regeneration of all life on in the material world. It also is taken to mean the divine as well as physical seed. Like rain from the firmaments, the Bull rains down the divine seed which contains the spiritual endowments required by the worshiper during the spiritual journey for liberation and salvation.
- The Kindled Agni destroys enemies. (RV 4.4.4.) What is meant here, of course, is that once kindled Agni combats and opposes Evil.
- When kindled, Agni unites Heaven and Earth. (RV 2.2.6.)
- When kindled, Agni has a triple nature. (RV 3.20.2.) The three-fold nature consists of three houses — meant here is the physical, every-day, house, and three lunar Zodiacal, lunar, houses; the three worlds — the Earth, Mid-World (firmament), and Heaven; and the three tongues — the three levels of Vac, Speech: Madhyama, Pasyanti, and Para.
- When kindled, Agni, becomes the Godhead, Jatadevas. (RV 2.2.1.) Jatavedas is a manifestation of Agni in the firmament. This represents one element in Agni's triple nature.

These endowments are conveyed to the worshiper when there is Self-Surrender. These spiritual endowments are more perfectly accomplished by the fire of Self-Surrender. It is this fire which cooks and distils Soma Pavamana, the purified Soma juice. (RV 3.30.2; 4.25.1.) Once purified, the Soma juice is offered and consumed by Agni in his manifestation as the fire of Self-Surrender. (RV 10.88.1.) This fire then creates the light of the Svar and reaches to the Heavens on high. (RV 10.88.1.) The successful worshiper understands the dynamics of Self-Surrender when releasing the Soul to utilize the energies of the Kindled Agni:

- The Vedic force of Agni is kindled by the vast laws of the Vedic dharma. (*bRha/dbhir*). (RV 6.48.7.)
- The worshiper self-surrenders to the kindled Agni, the Sacrificial Fire. (RV 2.16.1.)
- The worshiper surrenders to the kindled Agni at Dawn to ward off Evil. (RV 10.35.4.) Here Dawn carries a double meaning. It can mean daybreak when the Morning Sacrifices take place. It can also mean the worshiper's hope-for desire to obtain the illumination and enlightenment which shines from Dawn's appearance.
- A continuation of sorts from the preceding rc. The worshiper surrenders to the bath of light present at Dawn with the purpose of attaining enlightenment. (RV 10.35.5.)
- The worshiper surrenders to the kindled Sacrificial Fire to maintain physical and spiritual health and to combat every form of sickness, spiritual or bodily. (RV 10.35.6.)
- The worshiper surrenders to the kindled Agni to gain spiritual wealth. (RV 10.35.7.)
- The worshiper surrenders to the kindled Agni to learn the inner essence of the Vedic dharma. (RV 10.35.8.)
- The worshiper surrenders to the kindled Agni, the Sacrificial Fire, to channel the Vedic forces and energies of Varuna, Indra, Mitra, and of the Seven Priests. (RV 10.35.10.) A double meaning is implicated here. On one level the rc (mantra) may mean exactly what is said. Namely, that the worshiper seeks to channel energy of the named Vedic forces. A hidden meaning lurks underneath. The Seven Priests could be taken to mean the Seven-Dimensional Universe, a likely meaning given that the worshiper's channeling is done at a Sacrificial setting. Another interpretation is clearly implicated. Varuna, Indra, and Mitra are all members of the Adityas, the lunar mansions of the Zodiac. The stars of the Big Dipper are called the Seven Priests or Rishiis. (JB, 2.218 – 221; GB

1.2.8; BU 2.2.6.) This gives a new dimension to the give-and-take in the sacrifice. The worshiper surrenders to the kindled Agni, the Sacrificial Fire, to channel the energy of the Stars.

- Once surrendered, the kindled Agni kindles the worshiper, and the worshiper awakens, channeling the intuitive energies of Usas (Dawn). (RV 7.67.2.) The worshiper is delivered from ignorance and gains Knowledge. (RV 8.44.9.)
- The worshiper surrenders to the kindled Agni, the Sacrificial Fire, to learn the mysteries of Aditya. (RV 10.35.11.) Aditya has an inner meaning. Aditya and the other Adityas are the lunar houses of the Zodiac.
- The worshiper surrenders to the kindled Agni, the Sacrificial Fire, to obtain cattle. (RV 10.35.12.) Cattle or cows are codewords in the Vedic dharma for knowledge.
- The worshiper surrenders to the kindled Agni, the Sacrificial Fire, to be free of sin. (RV 10.35.13.)
- After the worshiper surrenders to the fire of Self-Surrender, all obstacles and impediments to liberation are burnt by the fire. (RV 2.15.4.)

The worshiper then approaches the fire of Self-Surrender:

- The worshiper surrenders to the fire to find food. (RV 1.198.8.)
- The worshiper is illumined by the light of the Svar in the surrender to the fire of Self-Surrender. (RV 4.3.11.)
- The worshiper channels the perfect minded state of the fire of Self-Surrender. (RV 5.1.2.)
- The ignorance which had enveloped the worshiper's mind and soul is then lifted, and the darkness is dispelled; the worshiper is enlightened. (RV 10.88.2.)

While the subject of the worshiper's self-surrender is always the same — it is the soul and very being of the worshiper — the object of this self-surrender differs. Early on that object was protection, which the worshiper hoped to obtain as a result of the fire of self-surrender. This involved a series of meditations, some involving the Vedic force of Agni, and other prominent Vedic forces. That protection was dispensed through the dynamic between the asterisms, Nakshatras, the zodiacal houses and the Vedic forces which were presiding over selected members from the stellar population:

- From the Vedic force of Agni, the Sun, with the energy emitted from the forging of the forces of Heaven and Earth, through self-surrender protection to the worshiper from the enemies in the Western quarter is dispensed by the lunar house of Krittika, in conjunction with the zodiacal houses of Mesa (Aries) and Vrsabha (Taurus). (AV, 19.17.6; 19.18.5.)
- The Vedic force of Agni also works in alignment with the Vasus, protection to the worshiper from the enemies in the Southern and Mid-Eastern quarters are dispensed through the worshiper's self-surrender by the lunar house of Krittika, in conjunction with the zodiacal houses of Mesa (Aries) and Vrsabha (Taurus) and the zodiacal houses of Makara (Capricorn) and Kumba (Aquarius). (AV 19.17.2; 19.18.2.)
- From Prajapati, in conjunction with the Regenerative Principle, through self-surrender protection to the worshiper from the enemies present in the "fixed" quarter is dispensed from the lunar mansion of Rohini, in conjunction with the zodiacal house of Vrsabha (Taurus). (AV 19.17.9; 19.18.9.)
- From Soma in conjunction with the Rudras, through self-surrender protection to the worshiper is provided from the enemies present in the Southern quarter is dispensed by two lunar houses: Mrgashirsha (Soma) and Ardra (Rudra), in conjunction with their respective zodiacal houses of Vrsabha (Taurus) and Mithuna (Gemini). (AV 19.17.3; 19.18.3.)
- From Brhaspati and the visible material world protection to the worshiper through self-surrender from the enemies present in the "highest quarter" is dispensed by the lunar mansion of Pushya, in conjunction with the zodiacal house of Karkata (Cancer). (AV 19.17.9; 19.18.10.)
- From the Grand Architect, Tvastr, in conjunction with the Seven Rishiis (the Stars of the Big Dipper), protection to the worshiper

through self-surrender from enemies in the Northern quarter is dispensed by the lunar mansion of Chitra, in conjunction with the zodiacal house of Kanya (Virgo) and Tula (Libra). (AV 19.17.7.; 19.18.7.)

- From Vayu and the Mid-World, through self-surrender the worshiper is protected from the enemies in the Southern and Mid-Eastern quarters through the dispensing powers of the lunar mansion

- From the lunar mansion of Dhanistha. (AV 19.17.2; 19.18.2.)

- From the Waters (Apas), the subtle basis for the Vedic dharma, through self-surrender protection to the worshiper from the enemies in the Mid-Western and Northern quarters is dispensed through the lunar house of Purva Ashada, in conjunction with the zodiacal house of Dhanus (Saggitarius). (AV 19.17.6; 19.18.6.)

- From Indra and the Maruts, through self-surrender protection to the worshiper from the enemies present in the Mid-Northern and Easter quarters are dispensed by the lunar mansion of Jyestra in conjunction with the zodiacal house of Vrscika (Scorpio). (AV 19.17.8; 19.18.8.)

- From Varuna, the Lord Protector of the Vedic dharma (rta), in alignment with the "Suns from the twelve months," in other words, the Adityas, the zodiacal houses, through self-surrender protection is provided to the worshiper from the enemies in the Mid-Southern and Western quarters by the lunar house of Shatabhisha and presided over by the zodiacal house of Kumba (Aquarius). (AV 19.17.4; 19.18.4.)

More specific and varied meditations of self-surrender were later revealed by the Rishiis. Those meditations were based on the invocation of "Svaha!" Svaha is defined by Monier Williams as that, an invocation, but also as an oblation, an offering to the Vedic force of Agni. Svaha thereby summarizes the most basic act of self-surrender, a formal sacrificial act of giving at the *yajna*. Those specific acts of giving were revealed as including the following:

- Self-surrender, sacrificial giving of the worshiper's being to the Rishiis. (AV 19.23.14.)
- Self-surrender, sacrificial giving of the worshiper's being to a sadhaka, a seeker of liberation and salvation. (AV 19.23.15.)
- Self-surrender, sacrificial giving of the worshiper's being to the *ganas*, the assemblage of Rishiis. (AV 19.23.16.)
- Self-surrender, sacrificial giving of the worshiper's being to the learned ganas. (AV 19.23.17.)
- Self-surrender, sacrificial giving of the worshiper's being to the Divine Supreme. (AV 19.23.20.)
- Self-surrender, sacrificial giving of the worshiper's being to the verses of the Atharva Veda. (AV 19.23.22.)
- Self-surrender, sacrificial giving of the worshiper's being to Rohita, the Sun. (AV 19.23.23.)
- Self-surrender, sacrificial giving of the worshiper's being to Surya. (AV 19.23.24.)
- Self-surrender, sacrificial giving of the worshiper's being to Prajapati. (AV 19.23.26.)

The worshiper's self-surrender is personal to the worshiper but is conducted in a very public setting. This is where the Sacrificial Fire comes into operation.

AGNI THE
SACRIFICIAL FIRE

The image and repercussions of Indra slaying Vrtra is one of the most enduring and indelible symbols in the Veda. No one image better symbolizes the Vedic world-view. The world-view according to the Rg Veda was strictly Manichean, divided between lightness and darkness, truth and falsity. The struggle between Indra and Vrtra was indeed cosmic, epic, and summarized this struggle between good and evil, light and dark, truth and falsity. As a result of Vrtra's death,

- Indra released the streams after slaying Vrtra. (RV 1.33.13, 1.51.11, 1.80.10, 2.28.4, 3.31.11, 16, 4.18.7, 4.19.8, 5.30.10.) In the language of the Veda, this means Indra allowed the worshiper's stream of consciousness to flow.
- Indra released the seven rivers. (RV 1.32.12, 2.12.3, 10.67.12.) In the language of the Veda, this is code for meaning that Indra provides to push the worshiper to elevate the consciousness to transcendent proportions.
- Converted asat into sat. (RV 6.24.5.) In Vedic astrophysics, this means that Indra commenced the formation of shape after the Big Bang.
- *Rta* was born at the request of Varuna (Lord Protector of the Dynamic Cosmic Order). (RV 1.105.15.) This means Indra was instrumental in creating the Vedic dharma.

Officially, Indra was the ultimate victor over Vrtra. Despite the conventional wisdom of the Vedas to the contrary, Agni is the initial killer of Vrtra. (RV 3.14.7; 10.80.2.) Indra is the incarnation of Agni as he commits those actions to overcome Vrtra. (Mikhailov, (2001) *RgVedic Studies*, p. 14.) Among the many results of Vrtra's death is the emergence of the Sacrificial Fire. Agni in the form of the Sacrificial Fire is the result of the Vedic forces of Indra/Agni slaying Vrtra. (RV 2.12.4.) This result is perfect in its symmetry. From the epic and violent cosmic struggle between Indra and Vrtra, Agni, the Sacrificial Fire, the center of the ritual, itself the center of Vedic spiritual life, is born. From its initial birth, the Sacrificial Fire is kindled, illumined, and its continued existence perpetuated by the worshiper, either from the worshiper's offerings, the worshiper's words (chants), or by the total self-surrender to the fire by the worshiper. (RV

8.19.13.) Once kindled, the worshiper sits around Agni as the Sacrificial Fire on the sacred grass to channel the illumination and understanding of the Vedic forces. (RV 8.45.1.) From there, if all goes well, Agni and the endowments from the Sacrificial Fire, and all in its possession is integrated into the life of the worshiper (RV 8.44.15), such that Agni becomes the worshiper's father, ally, brother and constant companion. (RV 10.7.3.)

Agni in its manifestation as the Sacrificial Fire is the Ancient Fire. (RV 8.23.7.) In the very beginnings of the universe, when all was an indiscriminate, undefined mass of neither existence of non-existence, the Waters which enveloped all bore a child and gave birth to Agni as the Sacrificial Fire. (RV 10.121.7.) This is the scriptural origin of Agni's epithet as "Child of the Waters." Agni in its manifestation as the Sacrificial Fire is supreme among all other flames (RV 10.46.9), both the first principle in the Fire concept and superior to all other forms. (RV 8.23.22.) It is a bundle of many concepts, bundles of concepts, ideas and aspects all dealing at describing the Vedic dharma. So what does the Sacrificial Fire represent in this regard? Agni as the Sacrificial Fire is representative of establishing the internal laws (*rta*) that run the Vedic dharma. (RV 8. 103.1.)

As with the other Vedic energies, Agni, the Sacrificial Fire is a force, an energy which emits rays pregnant with the qualities revealed in the Veda (and here) throughout the Vedic dharma. (RV 8.103.1.) The Veda in quick summary describes Agni in its manifestation as the Sacrificial Fire:

- It is the virtual center of the sacrifice, the fire altar placed in the center of the sacrificial ground.
- It represents the center of the subtle universe.

The Sacrificial Fire is as complex as the Vedic force of Agni itself. It is the centerpiece of the rituals in the Vedic world. It is the centerpiece in the worshiper's spiritual journey. While constantly present, the fires and embers of the Sacrificial Fire are not simply in front of the worshiper. (RV 2.24.7.) They are so engrained in the spiritual life of the worshiper that it becomes part of the worshiper's constitution. Agni the Sacrificial Fire is all-consuming. (RV 8.44.26.) They power the worshiper's constitution, physical, mental, and spiritual. As testimony to the importance of the Spiritual Fire, Agni, its source, is the first deity to whom the hymns in the

Rg Veda are directed. Agni's special standing is indicated in the very first stanza of the Rg Veda. RV 1.1.1 introduces us to the Sacrificial Fire. This rc (mantra) presents the main components of the Sacrificial Fire. In this form the divine Vedic force of Agni presents his power in many manners. These are the most prominent characteristics:

- The Sacrificial Fire consists of yajna devam, the God of the Sacrifice. One element of the sacrifice is fire or heat. The sacrificial fire is representative as providing the spark to elevation of the worshiper's consciousness. (RV 1.36.7.) The worshiper's consciousness is so raised conferring inner perfection when the sacrificial fire is kindled. Upon the kindling of the sacrificial fire, Jatavedas, the Vital Force of Knowledge, is created and conferred upon the worshiper. (RV 3.1.2, 3.5.4, 3.23.1.)
- The Sacrificial Fire consists of the *purohitram*, the Summoning Priest.
- The Sacrificial Fire is the Presiding Deity of rtvik. There is a mystic component to the Sacrificial Fire. This is the predominate characteristic which endows Agnim with its cosmic powers. Rtvik is the principle which guides the sequencing of events. This is an integral Vedic power of Agni with far reaching implications. To every event in the universe there is a preceding event which results in that event, which, in its turn, causes another event. This is what is called the "sequence of events." It is the flow which dictates the movement of the universe and every object in that universe. On a deep, esoteric level *Rta*, the sacrifice, is the representation of the universe, with its own movement and sequence of events. *Rta*, the dynamic energy of cosmic order, is sacrifice. *Rta* is also the saman, the hymns and chanting recited during the sacrifice. (RV 1.147.1.) There is a mutual equivalence between *Rta*, which is in the nature of sacrifice, yagna, and saman. (RV 8.25.4.) These equivalences are accordingly reflected in the presence of causation, motion and movement in the cosmos. The divine cosmic power of Agni accordingly is the Lord and determines the changes effected by the causation, motion and movement present in the cosmos. Rtvik is therefore a concept which runs through the most primal

processes in operation in the Vedic dharma. Sacrifice, yagna, and saman run together. These elements converge, and they all meet with Sacrifice, these powers thereby are conveyed to the worshiper through Agni.

- The summoning priest of the sacrifice (*hotra*). The hotra, the summoning Priest, is a further convergence. The function of the hotra is the call the worshipers together to the Sacrifice. This epithet reflects Agni's role as the "messenger," the divine agency responsible for summoning the other divine forces (deities). This is an important role, as the divine power of Agni serves as a binding agent to keep the other divine forces acting in unison.

It is no surprise that the Sacrificial Fire figures so prominently. At its very core, the Sacrificial Fire is an idea, the holiest and most spiritual of ideas, yet an idea, nonetheless. (RV 4.6.11.) What are those ideas? The vast array of aspects, manifestations and appearances discussed here and from the Rg Veda. Once the mantras of the ritual are uttered, once the worshiper is there with sufficient mind and willingness to accept them, those ideas are communicated and indoctrinated (in the best meaning of the word) into the worshiper. (RV 4.6.11.)

Agni in his aspect as the Sacrificial Fire is vast and far-reaching. Agni the Sacrificial Fire is not easily captured in definition. Many rcs give a list of characteristics. According to RV 3.3.5, the Sacrificial Fire has the following characteristics.

- The Sacrificial Fire is the chariot of delight.
- By nature the Sacrificial Fire is luminous.
- The Sacrificial Fire is the godhead (vaisvanaram).
- The Sacrificial Fire resides in the Waters (apsusadam).
- The Sacrificial Fire discovered the Sunworld (svarvidam).
- The Sacrificial Fire is forceful.

We will see these discreet aspects in this treatment time and again. What does it mean when we say Agni, the Sacrificial Fire, is "forceful"? RV 3.11.4 provides an answer. "Force" in the Sacrificial Fire is

- Possessing those things which are eternal.
- Possessed of the Truth.
- The embodiment of Fire, physical, subtle and sacrificial.

Truth is another critical element. The law governing the Sacrificial Fire is Truth, Satya. (RV 1.12.7.) The precise word used in this rc (mantra) is *Satyadharmanam*. More specifically, the Sacrificial Fire holds the truth (Satya) of the Vedic dharma (*dharmanam*). The Vedic dharma is a vast concept and the subject of its own treatment in this series. Suffice it to say here that the dharma, the natural order, is great enough to give birth to the Vedic force of Agni, the Principle of Transformation and Change. (RV 10.5.7.)

Agni, the Sacrificial Fire, involves the intricate interplay between the worshiper, the Vedic force and energies, and the flame of Agni, to give the worshiper the vastness of the Vedic dharma. (RV 3.13.3.) Once obtained, the joint Vedic forces of Mitra and Varuna, divine Vedic forces specifically charged with the maintenance and operation of the Vedic dharma, move in to regulate the sacrifice and edify and regulate the life of the worshiper during the spiritual journey. (RV 1.35.1.) In the course of the spiritual journey, the worshiper receives the light. "Light" here should be understood in its subtle, symbolic meaning. Light in RV 1.35.1 and elsewhere in the Veda means Grace, Illumination of Mind, the Absence of Evil. Once having obtained the light, the worshiper then kindles the Sacrificial Fire to be enlightened by the flame, which is ever present in Agni the Sacrificial Fire.

The Vedic force of Agni as the Sacrificial Fire was brought down from the highest levels of existence. (RV 1.36.11.) Once the kindled Sacrificial Fire is brought to the sacrificial ritual, the flames bringing Increase to the worshiper. (RV 1.36.11.)

Increase is one of the most esoteric, yet important, block to build the spiritual aspect of the Vedic dharma. There can be no spiritual development without Increase. The idea of increase is expressed in the fact that the spiritual development of the worshiper admits to the addition of qualities not present before of characteristics not previously exhibited. In many cases, previous views are modified, some are outright discarded. It is the very essence of sacrifice.

Sacrifice is basically a process involving giving and taking. The giving and taking goes both ways. At times the worshiper gives, offers, to the Vedic force or energy, in the expectation of receiving blessings in return. Sometimes, what the worshiper hopes to receive is a simple blessing, other times it is something deeper, channeling the energy or force of the deity, or receiving some deeper understanding about the worshiper, at what stage the worshiper is in terms of the spiritual journey, where the worshiper needs to go, what the worshiper needs to do to accomplish the goal. And in other times it is the Vedic energy or force which gives to the worshiper. We will see a demonstration of this dynamic with the Mystic Fire. Agni, in his aspect as the Mystic Fire sacrifices itself to produce the Transcendent Human. This is the result in part from self-interest, in order that the humans may perpetuate the fire in future sacrificial rituals. However, it is due in greater part from the inherent power of the Mystic Fire, a trait common to most Vedic forces and energies. Through the force and energy of its own power the Transcendent Human is born, so that all sentient beings may benefit from the spiritual blessings of the Vedic dharma as a whole.

As was stated earlier, the giving and taking process is grounded in the Two-Dimensional Universe. The rising of the Sun gives rise to the appearance of the Moon, Day rises to bring in the night, Hot is the flip side of Cold. This dynamic was not unknown in Vedic literature. The Chandogya Upanishad recognizes the dichotomy of pleasant and unpleasant smells, Truth and Falsity, pleasant and unpleasant sounds, and even pleasant and unpleasant thoughts. This dichotomy is grounded on the existence of Good and Evil. But even with these polar opposites there comes a point where there is unification. These are the purposes furthered by Increase.

Agni in the aspect of the Sacrificial Fire, RV 3.2.13:

- Is possessed of the natural order, the Vedic dharma, *rtanam*.
- Is the Master of the Yajna, Sacrifice, *yagniyam*.

Agni as the Sacrificial Fire is the "Son of Energy." (RV 3.27.12.) Energy is an important, necessary element to the Vedic dharma, and the fuel that powers the Sacrificial Fire. The Sacrifice is a communication between

Agni as the Sacrificial Fire and the worshiper. That communication runs on many levels. One level is the communication of the Energy present in the universe. There is a spiritual side to this energy. It informs the very means by which liberation and salvation is achieved in Increase. By the communication of this energy to the worshiper by the Agni's manifestation as the Sacrificial Fire, Agni supplies Increase in the worshiper in the spiritual journey. (RV 2.2.1.) Agni in this aspect supplies the impulsion in the worshiper to embark on the spiritual journey. (RV 3.2.14.) Increase is one of the most prominent features of the Sacrificial Fire. The elements of Agni the Sacrificial Fire have been summarized in RV 2.4.4 as consisting of the following:

- The inspirational power of Increase. (RV 3.1.2.)
- The powerful rush of ecstasy.
- The purifying power of fire.
- Purposeful restraint of mind.

Agni as the Sacrificial Fire accomplishes the worshiper's liberation and salvation in three ways.

- With the worshiper willing and capable to engage a change and transformation. This willingness and capability is supplied by Agni as the Sacrificial Fire.
- By supplying the worshiper with Speech to articulate the spiritual search.
- Through the restraint in deed and in thought, again provided by Agni as the Sacrificial Fire. Sometimes rendered as "yoking the chariots," the imagery could not be more clear. The Katha Upanishad (Kath. U., 3.3 – 10) engages in an extended comparison between the charioteer and the horse to the mind and the sense perceptions. The "yoking" of a horse is seen as the mental restraint obtained through meditation and enlightenment. As a general matter, Agni, the dynamic Vedic Fire of Change and Transformation, plays its own role in yoking the unruly horse. (RV 3.27.14, 3.29.6, 6.3.4, 8.22, 4.2.8, 1.36.8, 1.27.1, 1.6.53, 1.66.2,

1.69.3, 1.73.9, 10, 1.74.7, 1.149.3, 1.58.2, 2.1.16, 2.2.10, 3.2.3, 3.26.3, 4.1.3, 4.2.4.4.39.6, 4.2.11, 4.10.1, 4.15.1, 5.6.3, 5.18.5.)

The Veda provides its own version of the metaphor articulated later in the Katha Upanishad. In RV 7.3.5,

- The worshipers groom the flames of Agni as the Sacrificial Fire like a horse.
- The worshipers place Agni, the Sacrificial Fire, in its "native seat." Agni, the Sacrificial Fire, shines when the worshipers give offerings.

There can be no more vivid image of a turbulent mind that is out of control than a bucking bronco. This chaotic push and pull of the Two-Dimensional Universe is resolved with the worshiper's spiritual awakening. In the fire of spiritual awakening, the world and its perception are different because the worshiper is different. The old worshiper is discharged in exchange of the new. This awakening is accomplished through the processes of Increase. The sacrifice of the higher element produces an increase of the lower is called an out-and-out increase: it indicates the spirit that alone has power to help the world. In this setting sacrifice thus becomes a prominent feature of increase through the agency of the divine Vedic force of Soma. The worshiper's awakening is increased by the chanting of samans during the ritual. (RV 9.17.6.)

It is not simply a case that the worshiper will receive enlightenment or awakening if offerings are given. Nor is it the case that the Vedic force of Agni —or any other Vedic force —will act upon the worshiper's spiritual well-being if offerings are made. Once the worshiper surrenders to the Vedic power of Agni in its aspect as the Sacrificial Fire, the worshiper channel's the characteristics and qualities forward and treats Agni as the worshiper's personal horse. (RV 7.7.1.) In so channeling the qualities of Agni, the worshiper becomes itself a messenger like Agni, using these skills for the worshiper's spiritual journey. (RV 7.7.1.)

Agni in its aspect as the Sacrificial Fire combines with the divine Vedic force of Soma to power the Principle of Increase in the worshiper. (RV 1.1.8.) Increase is the most critical element to the operation of the Fire of Change. Increase is what it appears to be — that fire which augments

Increase: progression, procession, movement, or magnitude, not only to the worshiper, the microcosmic world, but in the vast expanse of the universe, the macrocosm. Increase may take any form whatsoever and may involve a progression in any direction. Whenever a subject or sentient being increases, it changes. "Increase" might as well be another word for "spiritual development" or "spiritual journey." The characteristics of Increase constitute the very pith and marrow of the divine Vedic force of Agni as the Sacrificial Fire and show themselves in these actions:

- The active Fire of Change and Transformation. The overarching principle. Every Increase is guided and informed by Change and Transformation, the divine Vedic force of Agni.
- The active principle of the Vedic Field. Next in rank, Increase accounts for the different levels of Existence — from the material, to the mid-world, to the different levels of Heaven — and regulate the over-lain, subtle levels consisting of the Two-Dimensional Universe, Three-Dimensional Universe, the Five-Dimensional Universe, and Seven-Dimensional Universe. The Vedic Field extends over these two distinct planes of Existence.
- The active principle of Consciousness. The Awakening is the first step in the journey towards salvation and liberation. From the Awakening, or Enlightenment, the worshiper acquires Knowledge. From Knowledge, he worshiper gains Consciousness. From Consciousness, the worshiper has the capacity to be engaged in Contemplation or Deliberation. From the act of Contemplation or Deliberation the worshiper gains Insightful Knowledge. From this Insightful Knowledge, the worshiper obtains Discernment. From Discernment, the worshiper obtains Divine Vision. In the second stage, the worshiper experiences rapture and bliss. From Divine Vision, the worshiper experiences Joy. From Joy, the worshiper is completely overcome by Rapture. From there, Rapture, the worshiper gets a taste of Liberation.
- The active principle of Food. Increase works in many ways. It may work as the nutritional sustenance the worshiper receives, and through the Digestive Fire, the Food is increased to supply energy and nutrition to the worshiper. It may work as the parade

of images the worshiper receives through the sensory organs. Once that information is consumed, Increase utilizes those perceptions to impel the energy required to process that information internally. Increase operates on a deeper level to properly interpret the overall process. With the proper exercise of Consciousness, the worshiper realizes that Agni alone is the Eater of Food. Agni (Change and Transformation) is the Eater, both in his aspect of fire and the fire altar. (SPB 10.6.2.2.) In all other aspects, Agni (Change and Transformation) is the eater. (SPB 2.1.4.28, 2.2.1.1, 2.4.4.1, 8.6.3.5, 10.4.1.11, 11.1.6.9.)

The Sacrificial Fire is the "Lord of Speech." (RV 1.38.13.) The Sacrificial Fire does not exercise lordship over Speech as the articulation of form. The precise word in this rc (mantra) is "Brahmanaspati." Agni as the Sacrificial Fire exercises his lordship over the Speech rituals at religious ceremonies, the Speech which governs the Increase of Food that we just discussed (Naig, 2.7), the Speech uttering the Sacred Word. The permutations of this Speech are varied, yet they are unified by the Fire which purifies the words chanted at the Sacrifice:

- The worshiper praises the Sacrificial Fire by the chants. (RV 1.12.7.)
- The worshiper grows spiritually by channeling the body and speech of the Sacrificial Fire. (RV 2.2.3.)

The Sacrificial Fire is the glory of the sacrifice. (RV 1.44.3) That glory is not simply reflected in the blazing flames, but in the effect those flames have on the worshiper. Quite frankly, part of the ritual experience is being drawn into another place by concentration of the flames of the fire. The rc (mantra) recognizes that on concentration on the luster and vibration of the dancing flames the consciousness of the worshiper is elevated (dhumaketum). This type of concentration has been incorporated into specific Tantric practices in Kriya Yoga to assist in meditation, specifically, Tratata, and others. In this aspect of the Sacrificial Fire, the divine force of Agni acts as a Messenger (dutam) for the other divine Vedic forces, meaning that during the worshiper's concentration of the Sacrificial Fire, their energies and qualities are merged, intermixed by the Vedic force of Agni and channeled to the worshiper. RV 3.17.4 describes Agni in the aspect of the Messenger. As the Messenger, Agni in his aspect as the Sacrificial Fire, as established:

- Resides in the center of Immortality (*amĀtasya nÀbhim*).
- Protects the worshiper during the spiritual journey.
- Receives and carries the offerings of the worshiper.

Agni, when in his aspect of the Sacrificial Fire, also acts as the Messenger, has two purposes (RV 8.44.3):

- Carries the worshiper's offerings to the other divine Vedic forces.
- Brings the other Vedic forces to the Sacrifice.

These are the three ingredients needed for the spiritual journey. In its primary purpose of illumination and understanding, Usas reveals to the true underlying nature of the Sun, Agni, the Sacrificial Fire, and the Sacrificial rite. (RV 7.80.3.) When these three elements are understood together, Usas gives the worshiper the light required for the worshiper to implement these natures in the spiritual journey. The light emanated by Usas is not that from a GE globe. It is jyotis, the mystic light of understanding and illumination. In the spiritual journey, the object of the worshiper's meditation is on the inner structure of matter. In the most amazing of paradoxes, it is through the meditation of the inner nature of matter that the worshiper understands both the wisdom of the stellar population and the worshiper's place in the universe. This is the purpose of the Nakshatras with Agni's actions to summon the members of the Adityas to the Sacrifice.

The qualities brought to the Sacrifice are consolidated by the divine Vedic energy of Agni. There, the worshiper seeks the truth and wisdom of the Sacrificial Fire. (RV 7.2.3.) Through Agni's capacity to grant the Increase, these qualities are channeled to the worshiper as a result of the ritual of the sacrifice. There, the worshipers, through the guidance of Agni as the Sacrificial Fire, creates their own individual meaning of the rite that can be used in the future in the spiritual journey. (RV 7.3.1.) That journey is formed and informed by the Increase in the worshiper spurred by the Sacrificial Fire.

The capacity of Agni as the Sacrificial Fire for Increase of the worshiper was explored in RV 1.106.1. There the Agni, the Sacrificial Fire, harkens other Vedic energies, Mitra and Varuna, to grant Increase to the worshiper. Mitra and Varuna are also divine energies which often work together. The laws regulating the Two-Dimensional, material, universe the worshiper inhabits is implemented by Mitra-Varuna. (RV 5.13.7.) Along with the Vedic energies of Agni, as manifested in the Sacrificial Fire, Mitra and Varuna are the "Showerers of Benefits." (RV 6.68.11, 7.60.9, 7.82.2, 7.83.9.) Also, with the Vedic energies of Agni, with many others, Mitra and Varuna contribute to the Principle of Regeneration which is responsible for the continued generation and regeneration of life. (RV 1.176.2.) Specifically, Agni as the Sacrificial Fire, represents the agency responsible for the possible spiritual birth and re-birth of the worshiper's soul. In so doing as this rc (mantra) reveals, Agni works in unison with the divine energies of Mitra and Varuna.

Specific benefits accrue to the worshiper when Agni the Sacrificial Fire is kindled. The Sacrificial Fire summons the other Vedic energies and forces and once summoned communicates those energies and forces to the worshiper. (RV 6.14.2.) The Sacrificial Fire is the spark which ignites the spiritual awakening of the worshiper. (RV 3.19.5.) The Sacrificial Fire gives the spiritual impulsions to the worshiper. (RV 3.23.2.) The impulsions are anything which propel the communication of the essential qualities of the Vedic divine forces to the worshiper. When the Sacrificial Fire is kindled. RV 1.143.7 specifies that Agni the Sacrificial Fire produces other consequences to the worshiper's spiritual development:

- The worshiper wins the friendship of the energies of Agni the Sacrificial Fire. "Friendship" here should be understood in its precise Vedic meaning. The Swami Paramhansa Yogananda says of Friendship the following: "Friendship is the universal Spiritual attraction which unites Souls in the hand of the Divine love and may manifest itself in either two or in many [ways]. The Spirit was One. By the Law of Duality it became two[,] positive and negative. Then, by the Law of Infinity applied to the Law of Relativity, it became many. Now the One in the many is endeavoring to unite the many and make it one. ... When Divine Friendship reigns supreme in the temple of your heart, your Soul will merge with the one vast Cosmic Soul." So once Agni the Sacrificial Fire is ignited the soul of the worshiper is united with the divine world.

- Another consequence of the igniting of Agni the Sacrificial Fire is that *Rta*, the underlying Vedic concept of the Vedic dharma, is promoted and sustained.

- The worshiper's consciousness glistens with the radiance of *ghrta*. This may appear to be poetic language, but the Rishiis chose the words of their revelation carefully, because "*ghrta*" carries a specific meaning in the Vedic dharma. Grhta represents the clarity of illumination gained by the worshiper while on the spiritual journey to Liberation and Salvation. Cows produce the milk which yields clarified butter, *ghrta*, the clarity of illumination or knowledge. It is as if that because cows produce the milk (knowledge) that can also be made in butter and ghee (illumination), there must be something inherent in the animal-symbol itself which is capable of producing these attributes. For this reason, cows are said to be symbolic of the primal light (RV 4.36.4), because they produce ghee, or *ghrta*. So one aspect of the primal Light of Knowledge is the knowledge produced, symbolized by both the cow and the milk and ghee the cow produces. There are four aspects to *ghrta*. Thus, it is said that there are four aspects to *ghrta* discussed in RV 4.58.1: (1) *Ghrta* is the highest form of offering to the divine, (2) *Ghrta* is that which is recovered by Indra when battling Vala, (3) *Ghrta* is the inspired speech from the Rishis, and (4) represents the guidance and grace of the divine and humankind's attainment of divine speech and wisdom. These benefits are made available through Agni the Sacrificial Fire.

- More importantly, the flames of the Sacrificial Fire, through the agency of the Vedic energies of Agni, lift the prayer of the worshiper to heaven.

It is at this point that the spiritual powers of Agni in his aspect as the Sacrificial Fire converge from the microcosmic world of the worshiper to the greater macrocosm. Agni as the Sacrificial Fire represents the Vedic dharma in its totality. On an existential level, the Sacrificial Fire represents:

- The Svar, the highest place of Heaven. (RV 2.1.1.)
- The Mid-World. (RV 2.1.3.)

RV 2.10.4 gives specific characteristics to the Sacrificial Fire which match those of the Vedic dharma. Agni in the manifestation of the Sacrificial Fire includes "all worlds" is "expansive" and is "vast." It is imbued with "force." Not only does the Sacrificial Fire include all worlds, it is in front of all worlds, meaning it exists prior to the creation of all worlds. This plane is partly subtle, partly material. The subtle portion is represented materially and ritualistically as the Fire Altar.

The Sacrificial Fire is conducted in the Fire Altar. The Fire Altar is the physical representation of the subtle nature of the Vedic dharma. The Fire Altar with Stamobhaga bricks, twenty-one bricks are used to symbolize the three worlds and the regions. (SPB 8.5.3.5, 6.) As indicated earlier, each level of the fifth layer contains three layers and represents a different, progressively elevated, layer of the cosmic order:

- The first three layers, one through three, is symbolic of the world.
- The second three layers, four through six, is symbolic of the mid-earth.
- The third three layers, seven through nine, is symbolic of the heavens.
- The fourth three layers, ten through twelve, is symbolic of the eastern quarter.
- The fifth three layers, thirteen through fifteen, is symbolic of the southern quarter.
- The sixth three layers, sixteen through eighteen, is symbolic of the western quarter, and
- The seventh three layers, nineteen through twenty-one, is symbolic of the northern quarter.

Agni as the Sacrificial Fire has three heads and seven rays. (RV 1.146.1.) This harkens to the "Thrice Seven" paradox mentioned in the

112

introduction. Nothing can be taken literally in the Vedas. Suffice it to say here that Agni the Sacrificial Fire does not have three heads out of which emit seven rays. This rc (mantra) engages in highly symbolic speech to describe the inner processes of the Vedic dharma. The three heads signify the three different levels of Existence — from the material, to the mid-world, to the different levels of Heaven — and the seven rays are representative of the Seven-Dimensional Universe. The Rishiis reveal that Agni as the Sacrificial Fire is both the sevenfold human and the triple abode. (RV 8.39.8.) Agni, the Sacrificial Fire, also represents the unifying agent to the Seven Rivers, representative of the seven layers of existence. (RV 3.1.4.) Agni the Sacrificial Fire represents the unifying force of the three existential levels of Heaven, Mid-Earth, and Earth. (RV 10.88.3.) On a subtle level the Vedic Field extends over these two distinct planes of Existence. On a material, gross, level, Agni as the Sacrificial Fire is the overlay of these two plains of existence. Agni the Sacrificial Fire in this respect is the ultimate Vedic paradox. In the Vedic dharma water and fire are not mutually exclusive. On the contrary, Agni the Sacrificial Fire seeks out the Vedic field. (RV 3.31.15.) Fire and Water are two aspects of the same subtle substance. The Seven Rivers increases the flame of Agni the Sacrificial Fire. (RV 3.1.4.) The Waters feed the flame. (RV 3.1.11.) Decoded, this reads that the Vedic dharma informs the Sacrificial Fire. This distinction is not lost on the worshiper. The realized, enlightened worshiper sees the fire within the waters. (RV 3.13.) The Vedic Field is of the nature of water, yet on the material level, at the sacrificial level itself, the Vedic field is represented in the Sacrificial Fire. The two, Fire and Water, exist together in unity. What this cryptic statement means, therefore, is that Agni the Sacrificial Fire is representative of and consists of elements in the entire spectrum of the Vedic dharma and yet, there are twenty-one primary Vedic forces presented in the Veda. It is tempting to believe that Agni as "thrice-seven" represents all these Vedic forces.

This exchange between Water and Fire is played out on the subtle level. The Sacrificial Fire however does not simply represent the subtle basis of the Vedic dharma. RV 1.72.6 states that there are three different classes of sacrifice — one in which food is being offered, two, one in which grhta, which is symbolic of mental clarity and acuity, is being offered, and three, in which Soma is being offered — all of which correspond to every level of the Seven-Dimensional Universe, the understanding of which results in the Salvation of the worshiper through the fire of inner transformation brought about by the process initiated by Agni as the Sacrificial Fire. As the centerpiece of the sacrifice, Agni, in this aspect as the Sacrificial Fire, promotes the spiritual benefits the worshiper hopes to acquire during the spiritual journey. RV 2.10.6 names a few of those hoped-for benefits:

- The power and light of Knowledge.
- Enjoyment, Bhaga, in all its Vedic form: (1) Lordship, (2) Righteousness, (3) Glory, (4) Wealth, (5) Wisdom, and (6) Detachment.
- The Power of Speech, Vak, logos.
- Bliss and spiritual joy, madhu. The Sacrificial Fire is responsible for the worshiper's happiness. (RV 1.35.1.)

The worshiper channels the energies from the divine Vedic energies and forces, Agni, the Sacrificial Fire, at dawn. (RV 7.41.1.) Dawn, Usas, serves its own special function to the worshiper's spiritual journey in RV 7.78.3. Dawn, Usas gives birth to:

- The Sun (Surya).
- Agni, in its aspect of the Sacrificial Fire.
- The Sacrificial rite itself.

These are the spiritual attributes taken from the Spiritual Fire. These attributes fuel and inform the worshiper's spiritual journey. (RV 6.10.1.) In a manner of speech relatively common in the Rg Veda, these spiritual endowments are the "treasures" obtained by Agni in his manifestation of the Sacrificial Fire. The Veda speaks of "benefits," and "riches." These references are not to taken literally to mean material wealth. It is to obtain these spiritual benefits that the worshipers seek the guidance of the Sacrificial Fire. (RV 7.10.3.) The worshiper receives these riches once the worshiper serves the Sacrificial Fire. (RV 8. 44.15.) These riches are interpreted to mean the specific characteristics of the spiritual increase experienced by the worshiper. The Spiritual Fire of Agni creates and instills in the worshiper to seek the same during the spiritual journey. (RV 6.1.3.)

The Spiritual Fire of Agni casts the light on the path the worshiper should tread, (RV 6.1.3), although not completely.

These rcs (mantras) speak of three different spiritual faces of Agni's spiritual powers. There is Agni, in the aspect of the Spiritual Fire, Agni Vaisvanara, and Agni. While areas exist in which Agni, Agni the Spiritual Fire, and Agni Vaisvanara definitely converge, they ultimately serve their own spiritual purposes. Agni Vaisvanara is a specialized Manifestation of the Spiritual Fire. Vaisvanara represents the Godhead, the head of the spiritual powers of the Vedic forces. Vaisvanara is also a Manifestation of the Vedic powers of Agni. Vaisvanara is, represents, relates, or belongs to all men, omnipresent, known or worshipped, everywhere, universally, generally, and in common. Vaisvanara is the manifestation of Agni's Universal Power to the worshiper. We just learned that Agni the Spiritual Fire creates and instills in the worshiper the desire to seek the spiritual rituals during the spiritual journey, making the spiritual path of the worshiper "perfect." (RV 6.15.4.) Agni Vaisvanara is ideally suited precisely for this function because it is itself the "Traveler." (RV 6.15.4.) Agni as the Sacrificial Fire is also the Traveler. Agni, the Sacrificial Fire, is the Traveler of Ways for the worshiper. (RV 7.10.3.) The Sacrificial Fire is the traveler most awake to the spiritual needs of the worshiper. (RV 7.16.1.) Agni the Sacrificial Fire guides the other divine Vedic forces and sentient beings on earth during the spiritual journey. (RV 6.49.2.) This, in turn, is because Agni as the Sacrificial Fire, is the "intuition" of the Sacrifice. (RV 6.49.2.) "Intuition" should be interpreted in its most expansive meaning as the fundamental subtle basis of Sacrifice. Agni as the Sacrificial Fire also guides the worshiper, the guidance is primarily in the performance of the sacrificial ritual, as well as the spiritual journey which follows afterwards. (RV 6.16.40.) Agni Vaisvanara, the Manifestation of Agni, then internally acts upon itself on Agni, the Spiritual Fire. (RV 6.15.6.) The product of this intra-convergence is a spiritual light that not only illuminates the path the worshiper should take during the spiritual search, but afterwards, when the worshiper's body expires, as when the soul travels father above to the transcendent world. (RV 6.1.8.) While this is the function of Agni in its manifestation as Vaisvanara, it is also the function of Agni in its aspect as the Sacrificial Fire. RV 7.1.14.) The ultimate paradox is that they are all Agni from different vantage points.

The Sacrificial Fire holds the future of the spiritual well-being of the worshiper:

- The Sacrificial Fire expiates, forgives, the sin of the worshiper. (RV 2.4.1.)
- The Sacrificial Fire removes evil from the spiritual life of the worshiper. (RV 8.71.15.)
- The Sacrificial Fire grants peace in the spiritual movement of the worshiper. (RV 8.71.15.) This can be taken to mean the Sacrificial Fire is a means to the worshiper's liberation.
- The Sacrificial Fire protects the spiritual endowments for the worshiper. (RV 8.73.8.)
- The Sacrificial Fire assumes the sins of the worshiper, later giving those sins to Yama. (RV 10.16.9.)
- By the Grace of the Sacrificial Fire, the worshiper acquires the spiritual endowments of the Vedic dharma. (RV 10.150.4.)
- The worshiper receives this Grace at the ritual where Agni, the Sacrificial Fire sits. (RV 10.150.5.)
- Agni the Sacrificial Fire wards off Evil. (RV 8.23.13.)

The Sacrificial Fire is an instrument of unification. There is an aspect of the Sacrificial Fire where it is repeated twice and known in the Veda as *agnim-agnim*. While *agnim* ordinarily is the Sacrificial Fire, *agnim-agnim* implicates the Terrestrial Fire. *Agnim-agnim* is physical fire. (RV 8.60.17.) Yet it is also the fuel of the Sacrificial Fire. (RV 6.15.6.) Saunaka reconciles the apparent inconsistency between physical fire on the one hand and fire in a sacrificial setting on the other. He says that agnim-agnim addresses two deities, Nirmathya and Ahaniya. (BD, 2.148.) The former refers the friction which produces the fire and the second deity refers to the oblation presented to the fire. By extension, agnim-agnim represents the friction which is produced as a Terrestrial Fire and the oblation represents the offering being presented to the Celestial Fire. In this way, both Heaven and Earth are represented as one in agnim-agnim.

Agni as the Sacrificial Fire is, as we said, vast and all-encompassing. It is Supreme among the Fires in the Veda. In its vastness it subsumes qualities found in the other fires, as we shall see.

AGNI THE MYSTIC FIRE

The Sacrificial Fire is vast and all-encompassing. That is how it should be, because of the great importance the sacrifice holds in the Vedic life. While as a consequence some aspects of the Sacrificial Fire bleeds to the Mystic Fire, there are definitive characteristics that can be exhibited only by the Mystic Fire.

The Pervasion of the Mystic Fire of Agni

One, is the vastness and pervasiveness of the Mystic Fire.

*   The Mystic Fire pervades Heaven, pervades the Earth and pervades all plants. (RV 1.98.2.)
*   The blazing flame of the Mystic Fire of Agni is vast and covers the Earth. (RV 2.4.7.)
*   The flaming light of the Mystic Fire of Agni is the life of the universe. (RV 2.38.5.)
*   This vastness is communicated to the sacrifice when the Mystic Fire appears. (RV 3.4.2.)
*   Agni the Mystic Fire is the Lord of the Vastness of the Vedic dharma. (RV 8.75.4.)

This quality of the Mystic Fire segues nicely into the next.

The Mystic Fire of Agni is the Subtle Basis of the Vedic Dharma

Two, the Mystic Fire of Agni is the foundation of the subtle basis of the Vedic dharma. The Mystic Fire is associated with some of the most fundamental elements of the Vedic dharma. RV 7.36.1 lists some of those elements:

*   The Mystic Fire is located at the heart of the inner truths (rta) of the Vedic dharma.
*   The Mystic Fire is the Word, the logos, the inner articulation of sentient beings and physical objects in the universe.
*   The Mystic Fire kindles, provides for, the inner workings of the Sun and Earth.

Providing as it does the subtle basis of the Vedic dharma, it supplies the very impetus for consciousness, Mind, thoughts, indeed, all forms of mental activity. The capacity of Agni the Mystic Fire to provide for Consciousness in the universe is of ancient origin. (RV 8.44.12.) Thus, when this cycle of the universe began from the indiscriminate mass of Existence and Non-Existence, according to the Vedas, the subtle energies which kick-start the living force of the worshiper is called, isas, translated as "impulse" or "impulsion." An impulse is a very small, but very intense, burst of energy, small enough to be experienced but large enough to allow the processes which follow to occur. The impulse or impulsions provide the spark of all life in the universe. Not to be confused with a related topic, "life Force," more commonly known as "breath" or "prana," as the ignition starts a motor vehicle, so is isas the impulse which provides those energies required to run the many other physiological functions of the worshiper. So without the impulse, prana, breath and the other bodily functions of the worshiper would be impossible, or, so to speak, stuck in neutral. The bodily function focused in the Vedas concern Consciousness and mental activity. The Mystic Fire is the Lord of Impulsions (isas patim). (RV 4.55.4.) The following rcs give the specific mental activities for which the Mystic Fire is responsible.

- Agni the Mystic Fire gives birth to Mental Cognition, the Mind. (RV1.70.1.)
- Agni the Mystic Fire has a Mind of Wisdom. (RV 2.9.1.)
- Agni the Mystic Fire is perfect in Judgment. (RV 2.9.1.)
- Agni the Mystic Fire provides the knowledge required to follow the austerities practiced at the sacrifice. (RV 3.14.1.)
- Agni the Mystic Fire, with other Vedic forces and energies, provide the spark or impulsion, of all actions. (RV 10.124.5.)

One element of the Vedic dharma is Consciousness. On the one hand, the Mystic Fire is the Universal Mind, the aspect of Agni which carries in his consciousness the discovery of all knowledge of the universe. (RV 10.46.8.) In this capacity Agni the Mystic Fire is what was called the Atman centuries later by Sri Adi Sankara. Indeed, Agni the Mystic Fire is called the "tmanyo" (RV 10.110.10), the Self, the forerunner of Atman, the

Universal Self. Agni as the Mystic Fire knows all things. (RV 10.162.1.) Much like the Atman, Agni as the Mystic Fire superimposes the remainder of the universe for the enjoyment (and perception) of the worshiper. In the coded language of the Veda, the Mystic Fire is the Lord of the Rivers, or in other words, the Lord of the stream of consciousness. (RV 7.5.2.) Since the Atman is the superimposition of the individual consciousness, the Mystic Fire also accounts for the worshiper's consciousness.

In the symbolic language of the Veda, Consciousness is depicted as the River. The simile can be easily seen. Just as thoughts, emotions and other mental phenomena appear and disappear, only to appear once again, so the water of the rivers gently, effortlessly and seemingly without beginning or end, ebb and flow on its course.

Agni as the Mystic Fire resides in the Rivers. (RV 8.39.8) This is symbolic speech to mean the power, energy and grace of the Mystic Fire resides in the Mind of the worshiper. The Mystic Fire presides over the flow of consciousness, the Rivers. (RV 1.65.6, 7, 1.66.10, 1.94.16, 1.96.9, 1.97.8, 1.98.3, 1.146.4, 3.5.4, 5.4.9, 5.11.5.) By channeling the energy of Agni the Mystic Fire, the worshiper gains consciousness in the spiritual journey. (RV 7.42.3.) The journey is defined as traveling on the path to discover the inner truths of the Vedic dharma (rtasya pantham). (RV 7.44.3.)

There are generic references of the flow of rivers and waters symbolizing the Law of Consciousness. (RV 1.22.6, 1.32.2 10, 14, 1.33.11, 1.52.4, 8, 1.54.7, 10, 1.55.6, 1.57.6, 1.62.6, 1.72.10, 1.80.4, 1.101.3, 1.105.12, 1.116.9, 1.125.5, 1.140.13, 1.144.3, 1.145.8, 1.171.9, 1.178.2, 2.11.1, 2.12.2, 2.24.4, 3.1.6, 3.5.6, 3.33.7, 11, 3.36.1, 4.3.12, 4.17.2, 3, 4.18.6, 4.30.12, 4.42.4, 4.58.7, 5.45.2, 6.7.6, 6.13.1, 7.18.24, 7.34.2, 7.103.4, 8.7.19, J.B. 2.6.7, SPB 13.8.4.6, 4.4.5.1, 20, 7.2.1.17, 5.3.4.1, 5.3.4.3-7, 5.3.4.8-17, 20, 22, 23, 12.8.3.12, 15.) As a river which ebbs and flows along its course (RV 1.32.12 (the seven rivers), 1.52.7 (rivulets), 1.72.8 (seven rivers flowing from heaven), 1.73.6, 1.83.1, 2.11.1, 2.38.2, 2.28.4, 3.1.3, 3.7.1, 4, 3.33.4, 6, 12, 13, 4.22.6, 3.46.4, 4.22.6, 7 (Indra setting the rivers to flow freely), 4.22.6, 7 (same), 5.49.4, 5.62.4, 5.83.8, 6.19.5, 6.20.12, 9.31.3), this simile resembles the thoughts which flow one after another in the conscious mind much like water flowing through a waterway. This is the Law of individual Consciousness. The thoughts and sensations flow one after the other, seemingly and hopefully to and with a specific goal. The transformative nature of Consciousness then is its malleability, its constantly changing nature. This quality of transformation is captured in sindhavah, the Eternal Law of the flow of the rivers, Sindhava, representative of Consciousness.

The movement of consciousness shares the attributes of Flow. This is exhibited in the individual mind's consciousness. One Vedic energy in which the flowing aspect of consciousness is prominent is found in Soma. Soma Is like Agni. (RV 9.22.2.) Soma is the Vedic force of liberation and salvation achieved through religious ecstasy. It is also found in the Flow to divine union, bliss, and joy, symbolized with the flow of Soma during the Agnistoma ritual. (RV 9.1.1, 9.2.1, 9.3.9, 9.3.10 (producing food) 9.4.6, 9.5.1-4, 6, 7, 9, 9.6.1, 7, 8, 9.7.1, 5, 8, 9.8.2, 3, 7, 9.12.8, 9.13.1, 3, 6, 7, 9.14.1, 9.16.4, 5, 9.17.2-4, 9.18.1, 9.19.6, 9.20.2, 3 (producing food), 9.21.1, 6,9.23.1, 4, 5, 6, 9.24.1, 2, 4-6, 9.25.1, 5, 6, 9.27.5, 9.28.1, 2, 9.29.1, 4, 9.30.1, 4, 9.31.1, 9.36.2, 4, 9.41.5, 6, 9.42.2, 3, 9.43.3, 6, 9.44.4, 9.46.1, 2, 5, 6, 9.49.2, 5.) The flowing of Soma is found elsewhere in other Mandalas in the Rg Veda. (RV 1.84.4, 1.91.8, 1.135.2, 1.151.2, 3.32.15, 3.44.5, 3.45.3, 3.52.2, 4.22.8, 4.28.1, 4.47.2, 4.50.3, 4.58.9, 5.51.7, 6.37.2, 6.41.1, 6.42.3.)

Another element of the Vedic dharma is Knowledge. Agni the Mystic Fire is full of knowledge. (RV 2.9.1.) Knowledge is symbolized by The Cow. Agni the Mystic Fire is the Lord of Wealth and the Shining Herds. (RV 3.16.1.) As the "shining herds" the Cows represent the inner illumination of the rays of knowledge transmitted by the Nakshatras, the lunar mansions or asterisms in the sky. (RV 2.24.6, 4.1.16 (glory of the cow of light discovered after meditation of the supreme name of the milch cow). They also represent consciousness as knowledge. (RV 3.30.20, 3.39.6 (Indra finding meath (empirical knowledge) in the cows), 10.92.10 (inspired knowledge), 3.31.10, 3.31.11.) According to Sri Aurobindo, the great Indian philosopher and Vedic commentator, cows represent the power of consciousness, discrimination, and discernment. (See also, RV 2.11.2, 2.15.10, 2.16.9, 2.34.15 (right-thinking), 3.31.11, 10.92.10.) The association of cows with knowledge is far-reaching:

- Cows represent the inner illumination of the rays of knowledge. (RV 2.24.6, 4.1.16 (glory of the cow of light discovered after meditation of the supreme name of the milch cow).

- Cows represent consciousness as knowledge. In RV 3.30.20, 3.39.6 Indra finds Meath, a fermented drink of honeyed water which includes milk as an ingredient. Meath when referred to signifies the empirical knowledge contained in the cows. (RV 10.92.10 (inspired knowledge), 3.31.10, 3.31.11.)
- According to Sri Aurobindo, cows represent the power of consciousness, discrimination, and discernment. (See also, RV 2.11.2, 2.15.10, 2.16.9, 2.34.15 (right-thinking), 3.31.11, 10.92.10.) In recognition of this meaning, some English translations render gobhir, as "Ray-Cows," signifying the rays of knowledge.(See, RV 1.7.3, 1.16.9, 1.23.15, 1.53.4, 1.62.5, 1.95.8, 1.151.8, 2.15.4, 2.30.7, 20, 2.35.8, 3.1.12, 3.50.3, 3.3.3, 4, 8.7, 2.24.6, 2.20.5, 6.19.12, 6.45.20, 24. 6.66.8, 6.64.3 (red rays), 10.92.10, 4.5.5, 4.17.11, 4.23.10, 4.27.5, 4.30.22 (Indra, lord of the ray-cows), 4.31.14, 4.32.6, 7, 18, 22, 4.40.5, 4.42.5, 4.57.1, 5.1.3, 5.2.5,5.3.2, 5.45.8, 5.80.3, 6.44.12, 6.47.27, 6.53.10, 3.55.8, 3.30.10, 21, 2.55.8, 3.35.8, 1.36.8, 9.31.5, 6.1.12 (herds of light), 6.17.2, 6.17.6, 6.43.3 (ray-cows within the rock), 6.28.1 (ray-cows bringing bliss), 6.28.3, 9.31.5 (ray cows yielding light and the milk of knowledge), 7.18.2, 7.41.3, 7.54.2, 7.90.2, 8.2.6, 8.20.8, 8.24.6, 9.62.12 (Soma pours the ray-cows and life-energies upon us), 9.67.6, 10.7.2, 10.16.7, 10.31.4, 10.68.2, 10.108.7, 10.111.2.)
- Kine, generally referred to in the Vedas as the milking cow, is the source of truth essence, and knowledge. The imagery is inescapable. Just as just as there is the milk of knowledge, so is the Kine, the milking cow, its symbol.
- Kines are also representative of the union of heaven and earth.

The Jaiminiya Brahmana (JB 1.19.) makes the following correspondences of cows to knowledge:

- The agnihotra cow is speech.
- Her calf is mind.
- They milk speech that causes the mind to flow.
- They milk the mother cow whose milk has been caused to flow to her calf.

- This mind (the calf) is followed by speech.
- For this reason the mother cow runs after the calf who walks in front.

Another element of the Vedic dharma is Regeneration. The Principle of Regeneration is that principle which guarantees the perpetuity of the world. It is seen as active agent guaranteeing the continued existence of the Vedic dharma and everything and individual living in it; it is the source of life:

- The Sun is the germ, the source, of the waters, the cherisher of the lakes and the replenisher of the rain. (RV 1.164.52.
- The smoke from burning fires raises to the heavens so that rain may return to replenish the earth. (RV 1.164.52, TS 3.2.9.7, AB 4.27, SPB 9.3.3.15.)
- The exchange between smoke and rain establishes the reflexive point uniting heaven and earth, forming an organic whole. (SPB 11.6.2.9, 5.3.5.17, 7.4.2.22.)

As the sun replenishes the rain, and the rain establishes the exchange between the heaven and earth, the worshiper should channel this energy in the Vedic path to salvation and liberation. The Bull is the Rainmaker, not just because the Bull's seed, the rain, is rain, bringing water to renew the earth, but because the Rainmaker replenishes the worshiper's soul, replenishing the soul with strength, vigor, and other benefits, while traveling on the Vedic path to salvation and liberation. Agni, as the Mystic Fire, provides the foundation for the Principle Regeneration. The Mystic Fire inundates the Bull, the Masculine Seed, with fire and inner Truths of the Vedic dharma. (RV 4.3.10.) Thereupon the Bull impregnates the Earth to begin once again the cycle of life.

The Mystic Fire as Agni the Messenger

Three, is the association the Mystic Fire holds with Agni the Messenger. In the beginning rcs (mantras) of the Veda the Mystic Fire is defined in terms of Agni the Messenger. (RV 1.1.2.) RV 3.17.4 provides a general description of Agni in the aspect of the Messenger. As the Messenger, Agni in his aspect as the Mystic Fire, carries out these services for the worshiper and resides in the center of Immortality (*amAtasya nAbhim.*) Agni, the Mystic Fire:

- Protects the worshiper during the spiritual journey
- Receives and carries the offerings of the worshiper.

When Agni also acts as the Messenger in his aspect of the Sacrificial Fire, there are two purposes (RV 8.44.3):

- Carries the worshiper's offerings to the other divine Vedic forces.
- Brings the other Vedic forces to the Sacrifice.

This capacity as the "Messenger" is explored at length in RV 1.44.5. In this rc (mantra) Agni summons the Vedic forces of Savitr, Usa, Asvins, and Bhaga to the sacrificial grounds. These Vedic energies, and the principles they encompass, are:

- Savitr, the so-called Sun deity, represents the Principle of the continual Perpetuality of Creation.
- Usas, sure enough, is the deity representing the Dawn, and she does. Her divine reach is not limited to the time of day occurring at daybreak, but to the spiritual awakening of the worshiper. Thus, for the purposes of this treatment, this is the spiritual energy represented by Usas — spiritual awakening.
- The Asvins, Principle of Duality, are the constant companions of Indra, and these spiritual energies do converge.
- Like Usas, Bhaga is a mixture of divine and mortal manifestations. On the one hand, Bhaga is Enjoyment — but the full spectrum of enjoyment. Bhaga is the divine Vedic force which consists of six distinct qualities. According to the Mahabharata, those qualities are (1) Lordship, (2) Righteousness, (3) Glory, (4) Wealth, (5) Wisdom, and (6) Detachment. A mixed bag to be sure, but Bhaga serves an important function in representing these qualities on a divine level.
- Mitra and Varuna are also summoned by Agni the Sacrificial Fire. (RV 1.136.6.)

- Aryaman, Aditi, and Vishnu. (RV 7.39.5.)
- Agni. (RV 7.39.5.)

It is clear to what purpose Agni, the Messenger, serves. As the Messenger the divine Vedic force of Agni conjoins and converges the other Vedic forces and energies together. In keeping with the aspect of Agni which makes this conjoining possible, this conjoining is the result of a mystical fire.

But what is Agni doing on this list? How can the Messenger bring himself in any meaningful way? Is this another example of Vedic paradox? The answer is that Agni's presence is logical and that no real paradox is taking place. The Sacrificial Fire takes a brief astronomical, astrological, turn. A close examination of the list of these Vedic forces and energies reveal they are none other than the Adityas, astral Vedic gods associated with atmospheric phenomena, and more closely associated with the houses of the zodiac. Agni is one of the Adityas and a presiding deity for zodiacal houses, planets and constellations. As the Sacrificial Fire, as the Messenger, brings the spiritual endowments of physical heavens to the worshiper. So in RV 7.10.4, the Sacrificial Fire brings the following members of the stellar population to the Sacrifice:

- The Shining vasus (Stars).
- Indra, the presiding deity of Chitta, the Vedic counterpart to Alpha Virginis (α Virginis, abbreviated Alpha Vir, α Vir), is the brightest star in the constellation of Virgo, the 16th brightest star in the night sky, and Jyestha, the Vedic counterpart to constellation Scorpii, and the stars α (Antares), σ, and τ.
- Rudra, the presiding deity for Ardra, the Vedic counterpart to Betelgeuse, the portal constellation in Orion. Orion holds special significance. Orion itself is an astral portal body. Orion is the stellar gateway marking the beginning of the Devayana, the Path of the Gods, and the termination point of the Piriyana, the Path of the Fathers.
- Bhraspati, the presiding deity for Tishya, or Pushya, the Vedic counterpart to the cluster of stars s to γ, δ and θ Cancri, in the Cancer constellation.

The Mystic Fire as the Unification of Opposites

Significantly, as the messenger, Agni, the Sacrificial Fire, is the spiritual go-between these and other Vedic forces and energies, including Heaven and the worshiper, symbolically called "Earth." (RV 7.2.3.) At that point, Agni the Mystic Fire presides over and unites Heaven and the center of the Earth. (RV 1.59.2.) The Mystic Fire carries the powers of unification, and the Mystic Fire is united by the heat of forced fusion of opposites. The fusion occurs when Agni as the Mystic Fire enters into the worshiper and other Vedic energies and forces. (RV 7.49.4.) Just as the Sacrificial Fire is kindled by the heat produced by the rubbing of two sticks, whenever two polar opposites are united, heat is produced. This is the basis of the Mystic Fire. On a macrocosmic level, the Mystic Fire as the Messenger is indeed a fearsome force. RV 4.7.11 describes the Mystic Messenger as "swift," roaring in the wind, consuming all and everything with its blazing fire. The convergence of these Vedic energies is indeed mystic. It is the result of a mystical fire. The results of this fusion of forces yields tangible results. On a microcosmic level, this mystic convergences produce the following treasures to be discovered and utilized by the worshiper during the spiritual journey:

- Protects the spiritual endowments for the worshiper. Agni as the Mystic Fire protects the prosperity for the worshiper. (RV 1.36.17.)
- Agni the Mystic Fire provides the path of liberation and salvation from Earth to Heaven. (RV 1.59.2.
- Agni the Mystic Fire becomes Agni Vaisvanara, the Universal Self, the Master of the Sacrifice. (RV 1.59.7.)
- Agni the Mystic Fire gives birth to Mental Cognition, the Mind. (RV 1.70.1.)
- Agni the Mystic Fire formulates and conveys the details of religious austerities and practices (vrata) to the worshiper. (RV 1.70.2.)
- Agni the Mystic Fire provides the impelling energies which operate the worshiper's mental function and acuity. (RV 1.71.8.)
- Through the redemptive properties of Agni the Mystic Fire, the worshiper acquires Bliss, and overcomes grief and sin. (RV 1.99.1.)

- The aspect of Agni as the Mystic Fire wipes away the sin and guilt of the worshiper. (RV 10.36.12.)
- Agni the Mystic Fire gives the worshiper the life-energies (vajambharam) needed to pursue the spiritual journey. (RV 10.80.1.)
- Agni the Mystic Fire makes the entire Vedic dharma available to the worshiper to pursue the spiritual journey. (RV 10.80.1.)
- The Mystic Fire relieves the inner demons of the worshiper. (RV 10.115.5.)

There will be much more about Agni Vaisvanara later.

The cumulative effect of these mystic convergences and fusions results in the most wonderous convergence of all. The cumulative effect of Agni as the Messenger bringing the other Vedic forces and energies, where the worshiper channels these forces and energies, at the sacrifice, is that Agni becomes the Seven-fold Human (saptamanusah). (RV 8.39.8.) At this point the reader should recognize the significance of this moniker. The seventh existential level is the Seven-Dimensional Universe, the subtle, intangible transcendent world. It is one thing for the worshiper to assume the qualities and natures of the divine during the spiritual journey. It is another for the deity to assume human qualities, even if on a symbolic level. When the Agni the Mystic Fire becomes the "Seven-fold Human" this is a role-reversal of the highest order. It signifies a complex fire of rejuvenation. Therefore at the sacrifice the nature of the Mystic Fire changes, and in an exercise of self-sacrifice the Mystic Fire passes only to be recast as a Seven-fold Human. The Seven-Fold Human is the Divine in our mortal life. Viewed in this way, it is a complex example of the give-and-take of the sacrifice, the Mystic Fire sacrificing itself to produce the Transcendent Human, a virtual representation of the basic truth in the Vedic dharma.

The Mystic Fire of Agni and Agni Vaisvanara

Four, the Mystic Fire of Agni is closely associated with Agni Vaisvanara.

- Agni the Mystic Fire is a thinker and knower. (RV 2.10.3.)
- Agni Vaisvanara is imbued with the Mystic Fire, such that Agni becomes the Master of the Sacrifice. (RV 1.59.7.)
- The Mystic Fire provides with the grace of Vaisvanara and auspicious Mind to rule the entire Vedic dharma. (RV 1.98.1.)
- Agni Vaisvanara when acting with the Mystic Fire provides the subtle basis for the capacity of Increase in the worshiper. (RV 7.5.2.)

Protection to the Worshiper

Five, is the capacity of the Mystic Fire to protect the worshiper. Agni the Mystic Fire is a Protector. (RV 4.25.6.) The extent of that protection is vast and seeping. In RV 3.5.5, Agni the Mystic Fire

- Protects the worshiper from hurt and pain.
- "Protects" the Sun by guiding it along its course.
- Guards, in an expression open to interpretation, the "Seven-Headed Thought." Given the many associations of the number Seven to the transcendent level of existence, the upper existential level is likely referred herein.
- Gives the worshiper the spiritual endowments required for the spiritual journey. (RV 7.40.3.)

The extent of the protection offered by Agni the Mystic Fire is vast. Agni the Mystic Fire protects the Waters. (RV 3.5.8.) Water is material cause of the universe. Water is the First Principle, the underlying foundation of all. Water is the root (i.e., the cause) and the shoot sprouted (the result) therefrom. (AA, 8.1.) Water is the agent for creation and generation. (SPB 3.7.4.4.) It is the Vedic Field, that subtle web that binds all objects, sentient beings, and ideas together.

The Mystic Fire is also associated with Vanaspati, "Lord of the Plants." (RV 10.110.10.) This is ordinarily an epithet belonging to another dynamic

Vedic force, Soma. For Agni the Mystic Fire is not an epithet but a power. In the Mystic Fire, Vanaspati is the power of Vegetation. Vegetation is a complex, intricate esoteric process, which cuts through the very heart of an important aspect of the Vedic dharma. Here, the matters become esoteric; Vanaspati is not just about plants. Commentators, among them Kashyap and others, have noted that "vana" means both "plant" and "delight." They note that "vana" connotes "delight" in the Upanishads. The double meaning is an appropriate use of wordplay which is so often found in the Veda. This particular epithet emphasizes how Soma is spoken of as a deity. and of the plant from which the juice is extracted at the sacrifice. On the surface, then, this category speaks on a simple sacrificial level to represent the plant from which the Soma juice is extracted and to say that the Soma juice is lord of them all.

Here is where the discussion becomes more esoteric. "Vegetation" was a concept frequently used by that greatest modern alchemist, Sir Isaac Newton. Yes, the same Isaac Newton. In his alchemical writings, the same Newton who uncovered the physical laws of optics, motion and gravity, was a notorious alchemist. In fact, he was far more preoccupied with discovering the link between the physical and subtle worlds through alchemy than he was with mechanical physics. Newton's discovery the mechanical laws of nature was only half of his endeavors. He considered the discovery of the physical laws of nature ancillary to his alchemical preoccupations. His main investigations sought to discover how those physical laws complemented the purpose of God's influence on the world. It was through the alchemical arts that he thought the link between the physical and subtle existed. His alchemical writings, in fact, far outnumber his scientific dissertations, and their page count number literally in the hundreds of thousands. It was through his writings that he developed Vegetation. It is a broad concept, extensively employed, and he sometimes changed the parameters of this idea. But in Newton's alchemical writings, Vegetation was a major concept and major link between the physical and subtle worlds. According to Newton, there were three kingdoms of nature — animal, mineral, and vegetable. These kingdoms operated under two sets of laws: The physical, mechanical laws of nature, and the "Chemical Laws" of God. It was Newton's job to find the link between these two worlds. Newton found this link in the Vegetative Principle, which had these characteristics:

- The vegetable spirit is identified with Light and Illumination, representing the power of God.
- The congealed aether that pervades everything, "interwoven with the grosser texture of sensible matter."
- The "subtle spirit," or "nature's universal agent, her secret fire" or "material soul of all matter." According to Newton the Earth and all matter was a breathing, living organism, "draw[ing] in aethereal breadth for its daily refreshment and transpires again with gross exhalations."
- The Vegetative spirit was the agent which activated inert, dead, matter into living, breathing material.

If all this sounds very familiar, you are right. This all sounds very close to the psychic, subtle powers of Vayu, the Vedic divine force of Prana, the Life-Force and the radiance and effulgence of Soma. Where at one point in his book about Newton and alchemy, The Janus Faces of Genius, B.J.T. Dobbs wondered where Newton's ideas about Vegetation originated, it is very tempting to believe that the inspiration came from Soma. While tempting, it is hardly likely. The first English translation of the Vedas did not occur until one hundred years after Newton engaged in his alchemical ruminations. Further, what Newton was attempting to achieve was very different than a spiritual journey of a worshiper to liberation and salvation. Newton tried to integrate alchemy and the mechanical philosophy with his concept of Vegetation, which operates under the premise that metals "vegetate" — that is, grow — in the earth, being changed over time from one substance into another.

Still, with Vegetation both Newton and the Vedas tap into a very basic truth. Both concern the very essence of the material world and its link with the divine, psychic, and subtle. Both affirm that there is a link and essential sameness between these two worlds. In the case of Agni as the Mystic Fire, Vanaspati is associated with the fire of the creation of the forms in the universe. The Mystic Fire presupposes a feature of Vanaspati that recognizes the malleability of matter. The gross matter in the Vedic dharma is much like silly putty and can be formed and transformed from one form to another, like Sri Sankara's potter's clay. This ability relies on another, albeit lesser, power of the Mystic Fire. Agni the Mystic Fire is the Bull, the Craftsman, the demiurge, the Creator of Forms. (RV 10.69.7.) This power emanates from the Mystic Fire's association of Vanaspati. As Vanaspati provides the subtle basis for the material world, Agni the Mystic Fire builds on this foundation — connects the dots, as it were — from this underlying basis. The rc (mantra) states that this power is initiated by the worshiper's actions making the Mystic Flame bright. What follows thereafter is another Vedic paradox akin to the chicken and the egg: The Mystic Fire is responsible for giving the breath of life to the worshiper, but it is the actions of the worshiper kindles the flame of the Mystic Fire. What, or who, came first?

THE FIRE OF DIVINE WILL

The fire of Divine Will is one of the foundational powers of Agni. It is mentioned in the opening rcs of the Rg Veda, where the Fire of Agni is summoned as the *kavikratu*. (RV 1.1.5.) *Kavikratu* consists of two separate words: *Kavi*, connoting a Seer, a Rishii, the Revealer of the mysteries of the Vedas. The Angirasas do not signify a simple Seer or Rishii. Once Vala, Vrtra's alter ego, was dead, Indra, while acting as the incarnation of Agni, usurped the radiance of Usas (Dawn) though the powers of the Sun to provide illumination for the Angirasas to search the dharma for the truth of their revelations. (RV 2.20.5.) Once found these revelations were given to humans. (RV 3.53.7.) In addition, once the revelations were discovered the Angirasas acquired vast powers.

- They acquired the vast powers of Agni and allowed that greatness to increase. (RV 1.71.3.)
- They acquired the fire of luminous thought. (RV 1.71.3.)
- They became the offspring of Agni. (RV 10.62.5.)
- They became the "sons of heaven" and possessed the power of illuminated knowledge (*diva putra*)(4.2.15; RV 10.67.2), emphasizing their divine origin and power.

This Fire indeed represents a symbiotic relationship between the Angirasas and the Fire of Agni. The Angirasas found Agni who had been hidden in an eternal flow of water and once released Agni became the formidable Vedic force that he is today. (RV 5.11.6.)

A Rishii possessing such powers implicate much more; *kavi* implies that which inspires, possessing intuition, capable of revealing deep mysteries of the Vedic dharma. That force or energy possessing *kavi* protects while revealing inner secrets. This fire also consists of kratu. Kratu contains an array of powers, including intelligence, persistence, resilience, all of which are subsumed under the umbrella of unshakeable, strong, will. The combination of these two powers are formidable, and together they form the Fire of Divine Will.

True to the internal constitution of this aspect of Agni, *kavi* pertains to the Fire of Revelation. It is the fire which powers the Rishiis to guide humankind. In addition, it also acts to kindle the other internal fires of Agni. In his aspect of *Kavi*, Agni is the voice of Revelation and Divine

Knowledge. His fire is the quintessence which is the conduit of divinity to the worshiper:

- In his aspect of *Kavi*, Agni kindles the Fire of Light. (RV 1.12.6.)
- In his aspect of *Kavi*, Agni is the guiding force which inspires the worshiper in the spiritual journey. (RV 3.23.1.)
- In his aspect of *Kavi*, Agni is the Lord of the vastness in the Vedic dharma. (RV 4.25.3.)
- In his aspect of *Kavi*, Agni reveals the divine qualities of the Vedic forces and energies to the worshiper. (RV 8.39.1.)

In his aspect of *Kavi*, Agni provides the inspiration to the worshiper and especially to the Rishiis who reveal the inner truths found in the Vedas.

- In his aspect of *Kavi*, Agni is the first among the Angirasas. (RV 1.31.1.) This group of Rishiis who revealed the mysteries found in portions of the First, Second, Fifth, Ninth and Tenth Mandalas. (*https://en.wikipedia.org/wiki/Angiras_(sage).*) As with many things in the Vedas, there is a double meaning to this group of Rishiis. "Angirasa" is derived from the root ang from which the word for "charcoal," *angara*, is found. (Tilak, *The Arctic Home in the Vedas*, p. 147.) The Angirasas come from the latter stage of purification, after the cleansing Fire of Agni is applied. This latter, higher, stage of purification points to the effect the knowledge they reveal makes upon the worshiper. In this sense, therefore, the Fire of Agni is, indeed, first among the Angirasas.
- In his capacity as *Kavi*, Agni is narasamsah, which is the spokesman and leader for the Vedic forces and energies. (RV 5.5.2.) We will see Narasamsah again when we learn the terrestrial fires of Agni.
- In his aspect of *Kavi*, Agni reveals the innermost secrets of the Vedas to each Rishii, and each group of Rishiis, not simply the Angirasas, and the internal heat generated thereby is increased with each revelation. (RV 8.44.12.)
- In this sense, in his aspect of *Kavi*, Agni is the Seer, the flame, the purifier, the ecstacy enjoyed during the sacrifice. (RV 8.60.3.)

This aspect of Agni, the Fire of Divine Will, has a special part to play in the epic struggle with Vrtra. While nominally Indra works with Agni in the fight with Vrtra, Indra does so as the incarnation of Agni. The Angirasas as well contribute in this struggle to assist Indra, accepting Indra as their commander. (RV 1.100.4.) The Angirasas also fight Vrtra as Agni's divine incarnation of Agni. (RV 1.33.6.) The Angirasas accomplishes all those things which are attributed to Indra alone:

- Find and release the cattle, which symbolize knowledge. (RV 1.130.3.)
- Break open the mountains through the power of the inner essence of the Vedic dharma (rta), thereby releasing the Waters. (RV 4.2.15.)
- Once the mountains were torn asunder the Angirasas allow a torrent of divine, immortal, ageless Understanding pour out, for all, including the worshiper, to enjoy. (RV 4.3.11.)
- The Angirasas see that there is a fountain of *goh*, cattle, Cattle in their representation as the foundation of divine, illuminated Knowledge, and release that Cattle for humans. (RV 5.45.8.)
- The Words transmitting the mantras and revelations of the Angirasas smash the mighty mountain releasing the gobhir, representative of the combined wisdom of the asterisms and Nakshatras in the Vedic dharma. (RV 6.65.5.)
- The Angirasas release the Waters, the fundamental essence of the Vedic dharma, and the Cattle (in all of its permutations and meanings). (RV 7.42.1.)

The importance of this fire cannot be underestimated. Not only is *Kavi* the leader of the worshiper's spiritual journey but plays an important role in the sacrifice. The Vedic sacrifice ritual is intended to demonstrate a fundamental truth of the universe: that there is a give-and-take between the Microcosm (humankind) and the Macrocosm (the universe), of every object therein, encompassing the process from creation to dissolution. This give-and-take is the essence of how the natural order (rta) operates. This give-and-take is an outgrowth of the binary, dualistic Two-Dimensional Universe. On the one hand, the worshiper seeks and offers obligations to the chosen Vedic force or energy. On the other hand, the force and energy of the chosen Vedic force is channeled to the worshiper. On a rudimentary level, this give-and-take is the bargained for exchange for the condition of life in the universe: One being dies so another may live. The dynamics of the exchange takes many forms and is premised on a fundamental assumption that if it is accurately performed sacrifice has a secret power to produce the desired effect. The dynamics in this new level demonstrates the give-and-take process which has been operating every moment in the material universe for eons. In his aspect of *Kavi*, Agni is the "give" in this equation of the Vedic sacrifice. (RV 8.102.1.)

The fire of Divine Will is the wisdom of the ages. It has the clarity of vision to reveal the innermost secrets of the universe and the incendiary power to convey that vision to the Seers and worshipers. This vision is for the worshiper's spiritual benefits to use during the spiritual journey. It is one of a host of spiritual endowments that the Veda calls "benefits," "treasures," or "wealth." The brevity of its mention belies the importance of this fire.

The give-and-take of sacrifice is straddled with an inherent contradiction. While it is grounded in the Two-Dimensional Universe, the material world in which we all live, the goal of the worshiper is to transcend this world, to achieve a higher level of existence. This process of transcendence is achieved either through the grace of salvation or through internal liberation. The worshiper achieves this personal goal through the next fire of Agni.

AGNI THE
TRANSCENDENT FIRE

No fire is more important than an another; all are equal in importance to and in the eyes of Agni. However, the Transcendent Fire occupies a special place. The Rg Veda asserts that the Transcendent Fire is the greatest of all fires and provides the spark which propels the mental and spiritual impulses of the worshiper. (RV 5.6.6.) Transcendence is the goal of the worshiper's spiritual journey, just as the Seven-Dimensional Universe is the place the worshiper seeks to arrive. It is through the Transcendent Fire that the worshiper is elevated upwards towards liberation and salvation. (RV 3.6.1.) The Transcendent Fire is the perfect vehicle for the worshiper's spiritual journey. (RV 8.19.5.) The Transcendent Fire offers much to enable that journey. The Veda offers a string of epithets describing this aspect of Agni:

- The Transcendent Fire of Agni is the possessor of the Rta, the inner essence of the Vedic dharma. (RV 8.103.8.)
- The Transcendent Fire is pure light, the increaser of the truth, Rta, the inner essence of the Vedic dharma. (RV 3.21.)

After these general characterizations, the Veda give a string of identifications which bring the Transcendent Fire closer in focus:

- The Transcendent Fire is Vaisvanara, the Godhead. (RV 3.21.) As representing the Godhead, the Transcendent Fire is the accumulation of all Vedic forces and energies in powerful, focused force.
- The Transcendent Fire is Agni Jatavedas, the Knower of All Things. (RV 5.5.1.) As the "Knower of All Things," the Transcendent Fire is represents Knowledge itself. In this capacity the Transcendent Fire represents a host of characteristics. As the Knower of all Things, Agni in its manifestation in Jatavedas gives strength to the worshiper during the spiritual journey. As the Knower of all Things Born, Agni in its manifestation as Jatavedas is strengthened as a result of the Sacrifice for the benefit of the other Vedic forces and energies and the worshiper. The "knowing" power of Jatadevas has more to do with providing the subtle essence of the material universe in which the worshiper and we all live. Significantly, as

the Knower of all Things Born, Jatavedas, like Agni Vaisvanara, is the Godhead, the accumulation of all Vedic forces and energies in One.

• The Transcendent Fire is Shyena, the Hawk from Heaven which brings Soma to the human beings below. (RV 7.15.4.)

The Transcendent Fire is closely related to the fire of self-surrender. As with all fires, the worshiper surrenders to the Transcendent Fire. (RV 1.78.5.) When the worshiper surrenders completely, the worshiper is imbued with luminous strengths. (RV 1.78.5.) The "luminous strengths" refer to the guidance the worshiper needs during the spiritual search, much like a flashlight shining on a dark path. Further, light and luminosity is associated with consciousness, and luminosity — consciousness — is the essential nature of the Transcendent Fire. (RV 7.1.4.) In language uncharacteristic even to other manifestations and aspects of Agni which are closely related to light, the Transcendent Fire blazes with intense light. (RV 10.35.6.) True to its essential nature of the Transcendent Fire, the worshiper is literally enlightened as to where to tread during the spiritual path. In this way, the Transcendent Fire guides the worshiper in the spiritual journey, a function for which the Transcendent Fire is perfectly suited. (RV 8.19.5.) In a sense, Self-Surrender is a necessary precondition to obtain spiritual endowments from any Fire of Agni. In order to obtain these spiritual and other endowments from the fires of Agni the worshiper must first surrender to the Fire Altar in which all other fires are subsumed and from which the energies inherent therein are conveyed to the worshiper. With the Transcendent Fire that relationship is more pronounced and most clearly manifested.

This fire emphasizes the necessity of the surrender of the worshiper. When surrendering to the Transcendent Fire, the worshiper offers, surrenders, horses, Bulls, and Cows. (RV 10.91.4.) You should understand by this time these offerings are coded language for much deeper objects.

• When the worshiper surrenders his horses, the worshiper relinquishes the capacity for sight, hearing, etc., the worshiper's means for sensory perception. By surrendering the capacity for sensory perception, the worshiper relinquishes the old methods of perception to exchange for another, more enlightened, approach.

- The Bull is related to the Principle of Regeneration. Thus the worshiper's Bull is the very pith and marrow of the worshiper's ability to procreate. The procreation is not, of course, for offspring, but for a spiritually rejuvenated life.
- The Cow is symbolic of Knowledge, inspired, divine or mortal.

RV 10.91.4, then, contemplates the total surrender of the worshiper's body, mind and spirit. All of which are exchanged for a better model.

Transcendence is its own entity and moves with its own power. To move with the wave of Transcendent Fire the worshiper must surrender the mind, body, and soul completely, jump on board, and travel upwards. After the surrendering of the mind, body and soul, the worshiper creates an understanding of Rta, the inner essence of, and receives the vastness and fullness of, the Vedic dharma. (RV 3.6.1.) On a ritualistic level, the process begins with enticements on the part of the worshiper. The rcs describe these enticements, offerings really, but the underlying meaning is couched, as in most things Vedic, in coded language.

- The worshiper offers food to receive the Transcendental Fire. (RV 1.127.10.) Here, "food" can be taken to mean that which was ascribed in the Introduction, namely, the forms and objects of the material existence presented in front of the worshiper's perceiving mind, as well as the basis of the Mind to perceive those forms. In other words, in this general sense, food may have the meaning of the worshiper's entire personal world-view. The basis of the worshiper's sacrifice then becomes in this rc (mantra) the worshiper surrendering the previous life in place of the spiritually renewed one.
- The worshiper offers luminous light to receive the Transcendental Fire. (RV 5.5.1.) The "luminous light" in this rc (mantra) is ghrta, ghee, which carries a deeper meaning. According to RV 4.58.1 there are three aspects to ghrta: (1) the highest form of offering to the divine; (2) that which is recovered by Indra when battling Vala; and (3) the inspired speech from the Rishis. Ghrta was recovered

from the Panis, released by Indra typically with Vajra (RV 1.11.5; 2.24.6; 8.3.4; 1.93.4; 4.58.4) and when Indra released the waters after slaying Vrtra. (RV 5.29.3; 1.52.8; 1.61.10; 1.32.2 (releasing the waters to the ocean); 1.32.12 (seven rivers); RV 2.12.12 (same); 1.61.10; 3.31.1 (releasing the Vipas and Sutudri Rivers); RV 3.34.9; 3.31.21; 3.34.4; 3.44.5; 4.16.8; 3.54.15; 2.19.2; 8.63.3.) Ghrta represents the guidance and grace of the divine and humankind's attainment of divine speech and wisdom. (RV 8.100.10, 11; 10.71.5; 4.1.16.) Ghrta is the primal light of knowledge. (RV 4.36.4.) Thus, in the give-and-take of the sacrifice, the worshiper surrenders that inner luminosity encompassing the state of knowledge possessed in the exchange for the guidance of the Transcendental Fire.

There is an elaborate dynamic involved with Vac, the Word, the Transcendental Fire, and the worshiper. In the beginning the Word arose to give birth to of the Transcendental Fire at the moment of his birth. (RV 7.8.6.) Vac, the Word, includes both spoken speech and the logos, the subtle articulation of the subtle meaning of the word spoken. Without the Word no form could exist. (SB, 2.5.) Without speech, any form could not be known and the worshiper would be bereft of intelligence (SA, 5.7.) Having obtained information from the sensory organs, the worshiper obtains (SA, 5.3; 5.6): through speech with intelligence all names, through smell all odors; through sight with intelligence all forms, through hearing with intelligence all sounds; through the tongue with intelligence all taste; through the hands with intelligence all feeling, through the body with intelligence all pleasure and pain; through the generative organ with intelligence all "dalliance" and joy; through the feet with intelligence all motion; through the mind with intelligence all thoughts. Without the Word, the worshiper would not know these odors, sounds, tastes, pleasure or pain, joy, motion or thoughts. (SA, 5.8.) Much like the Tommy character in the Who's rock opera, the worshiper is "deaf, dumb, and blind."

- The Transcendent Fire is the Word that is infused into Agni at the time of his birth. (R 7.8.6.)
- In the sacrificial setting the worshiper offers the Word to the Transcendental Fire and surrenders to the Transcendent Fire

which gives to the worshiper the impulsions, the mental stamina, needed to sustain the Word. (RV 6.10.3.)

- Having found the Word, the Transcendent Fire illumines the worshiper's mind with knowledge of the Rta, the inner essence of the Vedic dharma, along with the vastness and fullness contained therein. (RV 3.6.1.)
- In addition, as part and parcel of the tools needed for the spiritual search, the Transcendent Fire gives the worshiper the means to ward off Evil. (RV 6.10.3.)

The Transcendent Fire does not only benefit the worshiper. Luminosity, the light of consciousness, is the essential nature of the Transcendent Fire, and pursuant to its essential nature it enlightens both the Vedic dharma and the Vedic forces and energies which inhabit it. The Transcendent Fire is intended for all peoples, not just the worshipers. (RV 1.50.3.) This is how it affects both the worshiper and the forces and energies of the Vedic dharma:

- The Transcendent Fire provides the light to the Vedic force of Indra. (RV 10.35.1.)
- Indra obtains the blazing light of the Transcendent Fire after consuming Soma. (RV 8.3.20.)
- The Maruts, while an energy closely related to Indra, is powered by the fires of Agni. The brilliance of the Transcendent Fire is imbued to the Maruts. (RV 6.66.2.) Once received from Agni, the Transcendent Fire illumines the Maruts who emit its brilliance. (RV 2.34.1.) The Maruts rely on this source of power for their being and continued efficacy. (RV 5.87.3, 7.)
- The Transcendent Fire illumines the entire expanse of the Vedic dharma. (RV 1.127.5.)

The Transcendent Fire moves the worshiper upwards the existential levels, with the eventual destination being the Seven-Dimensional Universe, Heaven. It does not take much for the worshiper to realize just what the Transcendent Fire consists of — indeed, what is the essential nature of any fire. Thus, it is not a great leap to move to the next fire — the Fire of Light.

THE FIRE OF LIGHT

"These concepts reduce the whole universe to a world of light, potential or existent, so that the whole story of its creation can be told with perfect accuracy and completeness in the six words, 'God said, "Let there be light." '"

—Sir James Jeans.

Agni as the Fire of Light is another foundational fire, mentioned in the opening rcs (mantras) of the Rg Veda. (RV 1.1.3.) In its own way, while all fires are equal in the domain of Agni, the Fire of Light is one of the most foundational, because all fires consist of Light, that effulgence of *Rta*, the natural order. The Fire of Light kindles the full panoply of powers inherent in Agni. (RV 8.43.14.) In RV 1.1.3, the Fire of Light illumines the entire inner vastness of the Vedic dharma and increases day after day. This "day after day" portion of the rc (mantra) is a multiple entendre. Unraveling the hidden meaning of this phrase involves a meditative/religious practice which is found in other fires of Agni and is a crucial exercise in elevating the worshiper's consciousness away from this material world. It is an exercise important enough to bear repeating in these other fires.

The phrase, *dive-dive*, "day after day," occurs in several places in the Veda. (RV 1.1.7; 1.31.7; 1.34.7; 1.89.1; 1.123.4; 1.136.3; 2.9.5; 2.30.2, 11; 2.34.7; 3.4.2; 3.35.3; 3.51.2; 2.52.8; 4.8.7; 4.15.6; 5.20.4; 6.15.2; 6.30.2; 6.32.5; 6.47.21; 6.71.6; 7.98.2;.12.28; 8.98.8; 9.1.; 9.75.4; 9.101.6; 9.107.19; 10.37.7; 10.92.8.) On one level this "day after day" refers to how this fire supplies the light of the Sun to shine on the material world. The repetition of "day after day" is increased by this fire. It does not mean that the day becomes brighter and brighter, say, as a form of global warming. The power of increasement signifies temporal duration. "Day after day" is a code word for eternity. That "day after day" means eternity was confirmed millennia later in the Bhagavad Gita. There, Krishna associated the "day" with the waxing moon and the six-month period of the Sun's path to the Northern hemisphere. (BG, 8.24.) It is there, Krishna said, that the worshiper finds Brahman, or, in Vedic terms, liberation and salvation. "Day after day" is that which is increased and has nothing to do with temperature, or, for that matter, brightness, although these are the appointed meanings on a superficial level. It is eternity grounded in the material level. The function of that phrase, "day after day," is related to the terrestrial fire of Usasanakta. The fire of Usasanakta, a manifestation of the terrestrial Fire of Agni regulates the operation of Time in that Two-Dimensional Universe. That regulation is not a simple perpetuation of the running of time, although that regularity of Time places a part. The Pythagoreans believed that the meditation of the passage of days, nights, weeks, etc., forces the worshiper to conclude there is no difference between the future and the past. In arriving at this conclusion the worshiper pierces through time to eternity and dwells in the eternal present. (Weil, *Imitations of Christianity*, p. 96.) This is a result of intense meditation or austerities, and therefrom conjoins the days together and liberates the worshiper from the host of other dichotomies which bedevil the worshiper's mind and impede the spiritual journey. "Day after day," then, is that mental state wherein the worshiper is freed from the temporal constraints of the material world while remaining within its boundaries. It is with this meaning that "day after day" should be understood, and it is with this power that the Fire of Light shines the inner secrets of the Vedic dharma upon the worshiper.

There should be no surprise why these secrets should be communicated by the Fire of Light. This fire originates from the innermost recesses of the Vedic dharma, that most subtle plane of existence wherefrom resides, *Rta*, the natural order itself. (RV 1.36.11.) The Fire of Light sits in the seat of all Being. (RV 3.5.6.) From this existential level, the Fire of Light:

- Is the source of Knowledge in all manner.
- Is a skilled craftsman, the maker of forms, that which gives form to all objects.
- Is the articulation of Speech, that which assigns a name to these forms.

Given the importance of the Fire Altar, the Fire of Light plays a significant role in the Vedic sacrifices.

The Fire of Light is instrumental in one of the more controversial aspects of Vedic sacrifice, the Asvlayana, or Horse Sacrifice. It is upon the Fire of Light that the horse is roasted for the enjoyment of the Vedic forces and energies. (RV 1.162.11.) Whether a real horse was roasted or not is immaterial; this rc (mantra) must be considered in its symbolic meaning. The Horse is symbolic for the sense perceptions; a trained horse, senses which are restrained and steady, is the object of enlightenment and one of the goals of the worshiper's spiritual journey. To have the horse roasted is akin to having the past vasanas, mental impressions from past incarnations, burnt by intense and austere yogic practice, releasing the mind to proceed towards the path towards samadhi, or liberation. This is the function of the Fire of Light. It literally enlightens the worshiper's mind. (RV 1.70.5.) In the Vedic context, when the mind is awakened, the Fire of Light delivers the worshiper's mind from confusion and ignorance and lightens the darkness of evil. (RV 1.70.12.)

In keeping with this quality, the Fire of Light is compared to the Horse in other rcs:

* Agni in his aspect as the Fire of Light is indeed the Horse, that which is "given" in the give and take of the sacrifice. (RV 3.29.7.)
* Agni in his aspect as the Fire of Light is the chariot which carries the worshiper in the spiritual journey. (RV 4.15.2.)
* Agni in his aspect as the Fire of Light is the "steed" carrying the vastness of the Vedic dharma to the worshiper. (RV 5.6.3; 10.80.1.)

The Fire of Light does not accomplish these tasks alone. The Maruts assist Agni in his aspect as the Fire of Light. This should also come as no surprise. Both the Fire of Light and the Maruts are radiant. (RV 1.19.5.) Both reside in Heaven to shine down on the worshiper. (RV 1.19.6.)

* Together the Maruts and Agni in his aspect as the Fire of Light move mountains, cross oceans, and acquire the essence of the Vedic dharma, the Waters. (RV 1.19.7.)
* The Maruts are described as the caretakers of the Fire of Light. (RV 1.19.1.)
* The Maruts work with Agni to sustain his aspect as the Fire of Light.(RV 1.19.2.)
* The Maruts and Agni in his aspect as the Fire of Light are the Knowers of the All-Gods, the Visvedevas, the collective forces and energies of the Vedic dharma. (RV 1.19.3.)

They work together to bestow spiritual gifts upon the worshiper:

* The Maruts and Agni in his aspect as the Fire of Light spread knowledge. (RV 1.19.9.)
* The Maruts and Agni in his aspect as the Fire of Light bathe the worshiper in Light (RV 1.23.23), thereby heaping Increase upon the worshiper. (RV 1.22.10.)

"Let There Be Light"

By now you have probably asked yourself, "Wait a minute, isn't it a bit self-evident that fire is light? After all, Agni, Fire, is light. Why is there a separate aspect of Agni as "light?" This is a legitimate question. Light is a very important component to the Vedic dharma. The Rg Veda is replete with light, in all its permutations. It is a religious and esoteric doctrine based on light. There are upwards to five hundred different words expressing this very important concept. At a very basic level the Veda is a world divided between light and darkness, good and evil, us and them. At its most general overview, life is a battle between the agents of light and the forces of darkness. The final destination for the worshiper, what would be called millennia later "liberation," is the luminous region of light, to conquer darkness. And, yes, fire is in the nature of Light and Agni is fire; however, just as there are many aspects and manifestations of Agni, there are many varieties of light. The amazing ability of the Vedas is clearly demonstrated in Agni's aspect as the Fire of Light. It is in this Fire that the astrological and astronomical level of meaning becomes clear. The Vedic astrologer, the person assigned to know these things, knows that Agni receives its power and in turn presides over several members of the stellar population:

- Agni is the presiding deity with Prajapati and Soma ruling the zodiacal houses of Mesa (Aries) and Vrsabha (Taurus).
- Agni is the presiding deity representing the Sun. (SPB 10.5.4.4.)
- Agni represents the asterism of Krittika. (AV 19.7.2.)
- In his capacity of ruling the Krittika asterism, Agni dispenses the spiritual endowment of Divine Response and the inner secret of *yajna* (Sacrifice). (AV 19.7.2.)
- In his capacity of ruling and representing the asterism of Tula (Libra), Agni, with Indra, dispenses the spiritual endowment of *radha* (Spiritual Increase, Great Achievements).
- Agni, in alignment and conjunction with Indra, rules and represents the zodiacal house of Tula (Libra).

In conjunction with these stellar players Agni dispenses three important, interrelated, spiritual endowments.

- From the asterism of Krittika, through his powers as its presiding deity, Agni dispenses the secrets of yajna (Sacrifice).
- From the asterism of Krittika, through his powers as its presiding deity, Agni dispenses the spiritual endowment of Divine Response.
- From and in conjunction with the asterism of Tula (Libra), through his shared powers as its presiding deity in alignment with the Lunar house of Indra, the lunar house of Agni dispenses *radha* (Spiritual Increase, Great Achievements).

The Vedic force of Agni is communicated through the Fire of Light. There are many forms of the Fire of Light. This portion describes the most important. What follows are just very few of the most prominent examples of light.

Go, Gobhir

We have seen this type of light earlier. Kashyap renders *go* or *gobhir* as "rays of light." Indeed, in most situations they are. This is exactly the conventional interpretation of go or gobhir. Kashyap and other scholars follow this meaning first ascribed by Sri Aurobindo, and render go or gobhir "ray-cow," "rays of intuition," "rays of knowledge," or the like. The ancients ascribed a variety of meanings to the general, collective, plural word for "Cows."

- Cows, *gobhir*, signify the winds that blow rain clouds to different areas of the sky. (RV 1.7.3.)
- Cows represent dawn's light which disperse the darkness of light. (RV 1.62.5; 5.74.4; 6.64.3.)
- Cows are invoked to welcome the Asvins, the twin Vedic forces which represent the Divine Duad of the Two-Dimension Universe. (RV 10.61.4.)
- Cows are likened to the rain which replenishes the Earth, symbolizing the spiritual endowment of nourishment. (RV 10.99.4.)

- Cow also symbolize the water used to be mixed with the Soma juice at the Soma Sacrifice, which is later consumed by the worshiper. (RV 9.86.47.)
- Cows are mentioned to represent the heat of the Sun which creates the water vapors which eventually rises up to the clouds. (RV 7.36.1.)
- The Cows represent clarified butter, ghee, or ghrta, which, as we will see, contains a host of its own meanings. (RV 5.3.2.)
- In another sacrificial setting, the Cows represent the milk which is infused with barley flour to prepare mead. (RV 8.2.3.)

The Cows, not surprisingly, represent various items made out of leather. While there is a pedestrian meaning to this aspect of Cows, they all refer to items like the leather straps and joists used in chariots in the chariot simile used in the Katha Upanishad. (RV 6.47.11.) The Cows also refer to the leather used for the leather string for the bow. (RV 8.20.8.)

Monier Williams offers a more specific definition. If the contest is between the general and specific definition of the word, the specific meaning prevails. One specific definition Monier Williams gives for *go or gobhir* is "herds of the sky," or skylight or the light from the collective stellar population, from stars, planets, or other apparent astronomical phenomena or events. It really isn't difficult to understand why it would take this meaning, "herds of the sky." The "herd" implicates the group of physical cattle, but the collective grouping implicates the vastness of the esoteric knowledge to be found in the stellar population. It is difficult for the contemporary who lives in an industrial urban environment, where the firmament is covered in a perpetual hazy of smoke and particulates, to appreciate the splendor of the evening light. But go outside the city limits, to the mountains, and look at the sky without the cover of pollution. The evening sky is positively alive and lustrous with light, with tiny, discreet, drops of light punctuating the inky darkness of the background. These glittering flecks of light do not even flicker. A star which flickers indicates the presence of an environmental obstruction, blocking the image of the starlight above. In the evening sky unimpeded, the Milky Way is a clear, distinct band of milky blue traversing one end of the horizon to the other. The worshiper will gain a greater appreciation of the ancient Greek explanation of how the Milky Way was created. It was created when Hercules was violently pushed away while he was suckling Hera's breast, spilling her milk across the sky, giving rise to its milky name. In the same way witnessing the stellar population and this band of light creates a profound experience from which the worshiper gains a greater appreciate the Vedic dharma and its lessons. This more specific definition adds a greater understanding to both Agni and the Fire of Light. For example, it was earlier revealed that Agni the Mystic Fire is the Lord of Wealth and the Shining Herds. (RV 3.16.1.) Monier Williams would change this to say that Agni is the Lord of the light, the fire, the energy emitting from the stellar population. In a deep, esoteric sense this is exactly how go or gobhir should be applied to the Fire of Light. While cows represent this Bovine Knowledge, it is the knowledge obtained, derived, and learned from the stellar population. And what better way to communicate the Fire of Agni than though go or gobhir, starlight? We see the stellar population in the cool of the evening as a flicker of light. In reality that faint light is millions of miles away. That tiny speck is as hot and massive as our own Sun, many times greater in bulk and heat. They are fire in the most pure, emblematic form.

So is it with the other passages in the Veda which reveal their mysteries of the fire of *go* and *gobhir*. It is upon the Rishiis to reveal these mysteries.

- RV 1.23.15: Pusan, who endows the worshiper with the spiritual benefit of Bhaga (enjoyment) through the asterism of Revati and zodiacal house of Mina (Pisces), brings the worshiper the happiness and bliss of Soma at the spring season. The Rishii expresses the phrase "spring" in a highly stylized, cryptic manner. The rc (mantra) reveals that the pleasures of the Soma experience occurs when "the farmer tends his fields" and when he feeds his livestock. In other words, spring. The season has a special significance. Spring is the season when Sacrifices begin, it is the season of renewal of the earth and the worshiper. It is the time of year when the Vernal Equinox occurs, itself pregnant with meaning in the Vedic dharma. Pusan, as opposed to Surya, Sun gods both, confers the benefits to the worshiper. Both are associated with the Sun.

- RV 1.95.8. The Fire of Agni assumes his effulgent, celestial form from the starlight emitted from the evening sky, from the zodiacal houses of Mesa (Aries) and Vrsabha (Taurus), and from the asterism of Krittika.
- RV 3.1.12. The Fire of Agni "gives birth" to the "herds of the sky," *go or gobhir*. This is the way of the Rishiis have in saying the Fire of Agni supplies the material and subtle basis for the power that brightens the starlight appearing in the evening sky. This rc (mantra) highlights another reason Krittika holds so much significance to the Vedic astrologer. It is from this asterism that the subtle power of Agni is concentrated. That subtle power makes its physical appearance collectively in the "herds of the sky," *go or gobhir*. This subtle power is conveyed to the worshiper through the auspices of Indra, the incarnation of the Fire of Agni. (RV 3.50.3.)

Indra, the incarnation of the Fire of Agni, is instrumental in conveying knowledge obtained, derived, and learned from the stellar population:

- RV 1.7.3: So, in a Sukta in which Indra, as the incarnation of the Fire of Agni, presides, Indra destroys the mountain, releasing the cattle, *gobhir*, which, in the fire of the zodiacal house of Vrscika (Scorpio), release not simply cattle, but happiness and bliss.
- RV 1.16.9: For these same reasons, Indra, as the incarnation of the Fire of Agni, provides happiness and bliss to the worshiper.
- RV 1.53.4: Indra, as the incarnation of the Fire of Agni, in conjunction with the fire of the zodiacal house of Vrscika (Scorpio), releases happiness and bliss held by Vrtra.
- RV 1.62.5: Indra, as the incarnation of the Fire of Agni, dispels the darkness with the light shining from the planet of Jupiter and the asterisms of Jyestra.

This astronomical application is found in other rcs (mantras). In this context, Vrtra concealed, and Indra released, the "shining cows," the "herds of the sky," *go or gobhir*. (RV 3.31.10, 11; 4.3.11; 4.19.7; 6.17.7; 6.38.3, 5; 6.60.2; 9.87.3; 9.89.3.) Recall, in the struggle with Vrtra, Indra is acting as an incarnation of the Fire of Agni and are thus functionally identical. In RV 1.36.8, as the creation of the energies inhered in starlight, the Bull as Agni reveal the "herds of starlight" after Vrtr is felled. Exactly what is the fuller implications of this rc (mantra) is clarified in RV 5.45.8. There, these "herds of starlight" lead the worshiper down the path of *Rta*, the inner essence of the Vedic dharma. We will be hearing more about Vrtra a little later.

Ghrta

Related to *go* or *gobhir* is *ghrta*. *Ghrta* is light, but specifically the Light of Knowledge derived from the Nakshatras. *Ghrta* is derived from the Sanskrit root, *gh*, meaning, to go, to hasten towards, + *Rta*. *Ghrta*, ghee, is "that which hastens towards or go to *Rta*," anything which supports the Vedic dharma. There are four aspects to *ghrta* discussed in RV 4.58.1:

*   *Ghrta* is the highest form of offering to the divine.
*   *Ghrta* is that which is recovered by Indra when battling Vala.
*   *Ghrta* includes the cows recovered from the Panis, released by Indra typically with Vajra, and the waters released when Indra slew Vrtra.
*   *Ghrta* is the inspired speech from the Rishis.

From these elements *ghrta* represents the primal light of knowledge. This is but another way of saying that *ghrta* is an aspect of Consciousness which is yet another way of saying "the Vedic dharma."

Ghrta also refers to the cows recovered from the Panis, released by Indra typically with Vajra. (RV 1.11.5; 2.24.6; 8.3.4; 1.93.4; 4.58.4.) The imagery is not difficult to imagine. The cow is a figurative symbol for light and for representative for knowledge and illumination. Cows came to be symbolic of these two word-concepts for a variety of reasons. One reason offered is their revered status in Indian society. A more likely reason is the simple fact that they are the animals who produce the milk which yields clarified butter, Ghee, *grhta*, which has its own special meaning. Cows produce the milk which yields clarified butter, *ghrta*, the clarity of illumination or knowledge. It is as if that because cows produce the milk (read, "knowledge") that can also be made in butter and ghee (read, "illumination" or "awakening"), there must be something inherent in the animal-symbol itself which is capable of producing these attributes. For this reason, cows are said to be symbolic of the primal light. (RV 4.36.4.) As anyone who has cooked with ghee knows, it is practically impossible to clean ghee off a countertop, due to its oily, dense composition. There is an element of permanence to the substance, a permanence shared with knowledge once attained. But as anyone who has seen a clear bottle of ghee on the deli shelf can attest to, the oil portion of ghee, *ghrta*, has the ability to separate from the whey, such that the upper portion, the oil, is a crystal clear golden color, and the lower portion containing the congealed whey, is cloudy and bilious. This is also the nature of Consciousness: Clear at one moment, cloudy the next. The clear portion, however, is so brilliant, so crystalline, that this provides the metaphorical meaning for *ghrta*: Mental acuity, clarity and brilliance. In this state the mind is receptive; in its cloudy state, blocked in its own cloudy fog. The cloudy fog is created by Vrtra, the clear brilliant state of mental acuity and consciousness is removed by Indra, who with Tvastr, grants the Bliss which accompanies this state of consciousness through the power of the asterism of Chitra in conjunction with the zodiac house of Vrscika (Libra). *Ghrta* is associated with several Vedic forces and energies.

- The lunar house of Agni, the Sun, who dispenses the secrets of *yajna* and Divine Response from the power of the Krittika asterism, in conjunction with the zodiacal houses of Mesa (Aries) and Vrsabha (Taurus).
- The lunar house of Soma, the Moon, who dispenses Bliss through the asterism of Mrgashirsha, in conjunction with the zodiacal houses of Vrsabha (Taurus) and Mithuna (Gemini).
- Vrtra is the concealer of the Vedic dharma, covers the essence of the pervasion of the universe.

There will be more about this synergy later in this book. For now, the next light from the Nakshatras is *Jyotis*.

Jyotis

Jyotis is an aspect of Agni and perhaps is the best known to the general public, for all the wrong reasons. There is and has always been an astrological component to the Vedic dharma. In the post-Vedic periods, after the influence of Hellenism to the Indian sub-continent, Jyotis became associated with predictive astrology. To the worshiper and to the Vedic astrologer, there is indeed a wisdom to the stellar population. That wisdom is not associated with the prediction of modern events or happenings. There is indeed a measure of prognostication from the stellar population. But just as the efforts at achieving siddhis, or supernatural powers, to the yoga practitioner is possible but to be avoided, so is milking the stars to tell the future in present time is considered a waste of other valuable lessons that may be learned. The yogi masters advise that the achievement of the siddhis are to avoided because they are an unnecessary distraction. In the same way the Vedic astrologer cautions that attempting to tell the future is vulnerable to all manner of quackery and ignores the real lessons that can be obtained from the stellar population.

Jyotis is not simply light. To the Vedic astrologer the wisdom of the stars is contained in AV 19.7.2 – 5. That wisdom is filtered through the light from the stellar population and heavenly bodies, and as that light is seen by the worshiper influences not only the worshiper but all sentient and non-sentient beings. Further, Jyotis carries specialized meanings. A subset of jyotis is *jyotir*. *Jyotir* carries specific meaning to the powers of Agni. Instead of the Fire of Agni subsuming the principles of the Light of Consciousness, Increase, the Waters, Purification — all those aspects discussed in the Introduction — *Jyotir* imbues the Fire of Agni with these specific astrological meaning:

- Generally, as for the Fire of Agni, *Jyotis* is the light of the Sun.
- As to the Lunar house of Indra in his incarnation as Agni *Jyotis* is the light of the moon.
- As to the Lunar houses of the Asvins, applicable to Agni through the incarnation of Indra, *Jyotis* is the inner eyesight, the source of the "twinkle" in the eye.
- *Jyotis* is the light of heaven.

- *Jyotis* is that light which achieves for the worshiper freedom and liberation, the "guiding light."

These specific characteristics are united in the astrological position Agni occupies. The astrological/astronomical identification of Agni thus encompasses these capacities:

- Agni is the presiding deity ruling and presiding over the zodiacal house of Mesa (Aries) and Vrsabha (Taurus).
- Agni is the presiding deity representing and presiding over the Sun.
- The lunar house of Agni represents the asterism of Krittika.
- In his capacity of ruling over the Krittika asterism, Agni dispenses the spiritual endowment of Divine Response.
- The lunar house of Agni, in conjunction with Indra, rules and represents the asterism of Vasakra.
- In his capacity of ruling and representing the asterism of Vasakra, the lunar house of Agni, with Indra, dispenses the spiritual endowment of radha (Spiritual Increase, Great Achievements).
- The lunar house of Agni, in conjunction with Indra, rules and represents the zodiacal house of Vrscika (Scorpio).

The important portion of these capacities is the dispensation of spiritual endowments. The Fire of Agni dispenses the endowments of Divine Response and radha (Spiritual Increase, Great Achievements) both to the Vedic astrologer and to the worshiper. We already know that these capacities refer to two specific functions of the Fire of Agni. One, Divine Response refers to Agni's role as the Messenger and everything that role entails; two, radha refers to Agni's prime representation as the Principle of Increase and everything that means for the worshiper. What is different with the Fire of Jyotis is the agency through which these endowments are dispensed. Agni dispenses these endowments through the agencies of the Sun, the zodiacal house of Mesa (Aries) and Vrsabha (Taurus), and through the asterisms of Krittika. Thus, through the study, learning, and consequent meditational and religious austerities of the Sun, Krittika and Vasakra, the receipt, appreciation and integration of these spiritual endowments may be achieved.

This is generally how the Fire of Jyotis generally operates. For every Lunar house, the spiritual endowments associated with the Lunar house is conveyed to the worshiper through their astrological and astronomical portals. In other words, Jyotis is the course and movement of the heavenly bodies which exert influence on earth. It answers the question of just what is that influence on beings and events on this material world. It carrier of the light of sun and all the qualities therein. It is the light of the moon and all the inherent qualities of that light. It is the source of that mental capacity which supplies the spark of awareness to sentient beings. It is the edifying light of heaven. It guides the worshiper during the spiritual journey. By contrast it does not necessarily guide the worshiper to inform him what will happen next Tuesday, or any other related question posed in a natal chart.

For the specialized member of *jyotir*, Monier Williams assigns the following meanings:

- The light of the Moon.
- The light representing the divine principle of life or intelligence and/or the source of intelligence.

The creation of *jyotir* has an ancient history welled up in the beginnings of the Vedic dharma.

- The lunar house of Agni, as the presiding deity of the Krittika asterism and in conjunction with the zodiacal houses of Mesa (Aries) and Vrsabha (Taurus), set the Sun (Surya) in its place to bestow the light of *jyotir* to all sentient beings. (RV 10.156.4.)
- The light of *jyotir* was created by Surya for the spiritual benefit of all sentient beings. (RV 7.76.1.)
- Usas, the Dawn and the terrestrial manifestation of Agni, created *jyotir* to clear away the darkness. (RV 7.77.1.)
- At the same time, Indra acted in conjunction with Usas to install within the Sun the light of *jyotir* which would guide all sentient beings. (RV 6.44.23.)
- Later, the Ptrs decorated the heavens with the asterisms so that their light of *jyotir* can be showered on the worshiper. (RV 10.86.11.)

In many instances in this book a single English word will not convey the full meaning of a foreign word or phrase. In these instances, the better approach is to resort to the foreign word along with a full explanation. The non-English word will thus be a shorthand way of conveying a panoply of different meanings. This is the situation with *jyotir*. There are many elements to Jyotis, and *jyotir* is only one. While there are two distinct meanings for *jyotir*, they are not mutually exclusive. One is Intelligence, or Mind, which is frequently represented in terms of light or brightness. *Jyotir* is a special case because of its association with Moonlight, the second element. The Lunar house of Soma is also associated with the moon, and its primary function in the Vedic dharma — the source of religious ecstacy and liberation — is especially appropriate for the Vedic dharma. Not only is moonlight related to intelligence on the basis of the light reflected from the Sun, but Soma's religiosity forms the basis for the divine principle of life and Intelligence (Mind.) These two elements act together to produce a single meaning for *jyotir*, one that recognizes the Moon and the light transmitted therefrom as the source of the divine principle of life and intelligence (Mind). *Jyotir* then represents Moonlight (the light of Soma) which is the source of the divine principle of life and intelligence (Mind). This is the combined meaning of *jyotir*.

This is not to say that there are no other meanings for *jyotir*. *Jyotir* is closely associated with the svadha, the inherent and internal essence of the individual powers, of the Lunar houses. This svadha is communicated through light and results in a form of *jyotir*. Thus, *jyotir* becomes the version of light for many Lunar houses. *Jyotir* is thereby compared to the light of the following Lunar houses and Vedic forces:

- *Jyotir* is the light of Aditi. (RV 782.10; 7.83.10; 10.185.3.)
- *Jyotir* is the light of the fire of Indra. (RV 10.35.1.)
- *Jyotir* is the light of Soma. (RV 10.43.4.)
- *Jyotir* is the light of the Angirasas. (RV 1.57.3.)
- *Jyotir* is considered a distillation of these and other qualities of the Vedic forces. A well-known rc (mantra) relates how the worshiper drinks Soma to be like the gods. (RV 8.48.3.) The complete recitation of this rc (mantra) reveals that the "immortality" of the Vedic forces and energies is indeed the light of *jyotir*.

Jyotir is also the light emitting from distinct parts of the heavenly bodies. Thus, *jyotir* becomes:

- *Jyotir* is the light of heaven. (RV 10.36.3.)
- *Jyotir* is the Daylight. (RV 7.90.4)
- *Jyotir* is the Sunlight. (RV 8.12.30.)
- *Jyotir* is the morning light at the beginning of the day. (RV 7.78.3.)
- *Jyotir* is the Moonlight. (RV 1.123.1.)

Jyotir is also a combination of the two elements of Vedic force and heavenly body. The Vedic forces both presided over and personified the heavenly bodies. This should not be surprising since it is from the Vedic forces that the heavenly bodies obtain their spiritual strength. Nevertheless, *jyotir* derives in part from the synergy of the Vedic forces and the heavenly bodies with which they represent:

- The lunar house of Agni, as the presiding deity of the Krittika asterism and in conjunction with the zodiacal houses of Mesa (Aries) and Vrsabha (Taurus), is the light of the Sun (*jyotir*). (RV 6.3.1.)
- The Lunar house of Agni is contained in the light of *jyotir*. (RV 6.9.4.)
- *Jyotir* is the light of Surya. (RV 8.25.19.) Surya is primarily the astronomical body, the Sun, but Surya's energy has the qualities of measuring the days, prolonging the days of life, driving away sickness, disease and other evils, and the Creator of all. Ancient commentators clarified the relationship of Surya and Savitr. Yaksa notes that Savitr appears when the darkness disappears. (Nir. 12.12.) Yet, commenting on RV 5.81.4, Sayana states before its rising the Sun is called Savitr and from the rising of dawn to its setting the Sun is Surya. These two conflicting commentaries are reconciled by the Vedas in the dynamic force inherent in Savitr. Savitr "approaches" or "brings" Surya. (RV 1.35.8.) "Bringing" Surya" implies a similarity but also increase. In the hierarchy of Vedic dynamic forces, Surya is accorded a greater importance.

- The Vedic energy of Surya is the highest light (*jyotir* uttaram). (RV 1.50.10.)
- The lunar house of Savitr is bright with the light of *jyotir*. (RV 10.139.1.) Savitr is the Principle of Immortality. He bestows the benefit of immortality to other dynamic Vedic forces and to us, mere mortals. He also bestowed immortality to the Rhbus, who were previously mortal and acquired life immortal by virtue of their fine character. (RV 1.110.1, 2.) He bestows immortality to the gods and duration to humans. (RV 4.54.2.) After bestowing duration to the life of humans, Savitr conducts the remains of the mortal coil, the smoke of the cremated body, upwards to the heavenly world (RV 10.17.4), under the guidance and protection of Pusan (AGS 4.4.7), another Sun deity and member of the Adityas (astrological houses). Savitr is also the Principle of Creation. This principle makes Savitr the ultimate giver of life. (RV 1.22.7.) This principle is responsible for all physical manifestation. (RV 6.71.2.)
- The lunar house of Savitr, the Sun, is lodged in the ray of intuition which creates *jyotir*, the divine light for us all. (RV 4.14.2.)
- The lunar house of the Asvins created the strength which is present in light of *jyotir*. (RV 1.92.17.)

The Vedic forces act together to endow the spiritual teachings of *jyotir* to the worshiper. In the Lunar house of Agni the fire of *Jyotir* is especially pronounced.

- Usas, a terrestrial manifestation of Agni, the presiding deity of the Krittika asterism and in conjunction with the zodiacal houses of Mesa (Aries) and Vrsabha (Taurus), created *jyotir* for the benefit of the worshiper. (RV 1.92.4.)
- Manu, the First Man (Adam), established the light of *jyotir* for the Lunar house of Agni, and this light is based on the inner essence of the Vedic dharma (*Rta*/jaata). (RV 1.36.19.)
- Agni, the presiding deity of the Krittika asterism and in conjunction with the zodiacal houses of Mesa (Aries) and Vrsabha (Taurus), is the very personification of *jyotir*, and in that capacity travels up

and down the Vedic dharma as the Lord of Heaven, guiding the worshiper through the spiritual journey. (RV 1.59.2.)

- The lunar house of Agni, the presiding deity of the Krittika asterism and in conjunction with the zodiacal houses of Mesa (Aries) and Vrsabha (Taurus), is possessed of a triple ray (*tridaa/ tuu*) of light (*jyotir*).
- The light of *jyotir* emits from Agni's eye, and the light of immortality resounds from his mouth. (RV 3.26.7.)
- The lunar house of Agni, as the presiding deity of the Krittika asterism and in conjunction with the zodiacal houses of Mesa (Aries) and Vrsabha (Taurus), purifies the Sun (*jyotir*) with three filters. (RV 3.26.8.) The light of the Sun is available for all to see and enjoy. In this sunlight is *Jyotir*, the principal means for Agni to convey his powers of purification to the worshiper.

The worshiper's attainment of *jyotir* is a classic example of the give-and-take process of the yajna. There is first the desire to obtain the spiritual endowments of *jyotir*.

- The worshiper seeks the spiritual endowments of *jyotir* from Agni. (RV 7.35.4.)
- The worshiper seeks the spiritual endowments of *jyotir* from Indra. (RV 6.47.8; 7.32.26.)

Agni is the messenger. Agni is also the presiding deity of the Sun and derives his power of spiritual endowment through the Krittika asterism, and in conjunction with the zodiacal houses of Mesa (Aries) and Vrsabha (Taurus) and has a singular purpose in conveying the spiritual endowments of *jyotir* to the worshiper. The Lunar house of Agni has primary task of presenting the light of *jyotir* to the worshiper:

- The lunar house of Agni, the Sun, through the Krittika asterism and in conjunction with the zodiacal houses of Mesa (Aries) and Vrsabha (Taurus) is himself the embodiment of the divine principle of life and intelligence found in *jyotir*. (RV 6.9.4.)

- The lunar house of Agni, the Sun, through the Krittika asterism and in conjunction with the zodiacal houses of Mesa (Aries) and Vrsabha (Taurus) presents this light of life and intelligence to the worshiper at the Sacrifice. (RV 6.9.5.)
- When incorporated in the worshiper's spiritual journey, the worshiper is enlightened in mind, body and spirit. (RV 6.9.6.)

The Lunar house of Agni, the Sun, in his capacity as the presiding deity of the Krittika asterism and in conjunction with the zodiacal houses of Mesa (Aries) and Vrsabha (Taurus), presents the light of *jyotir* in unison with the other Lunar houses to bring this light to the worshiper. Agni, in his capacity as the presiding deity of the Krittika asterism and in conjunction with the zodiacal houses of Mesa (Aries) and Vrsabha (Taurus), essentially coordinates the actions of the other Vedic forces and energies and places those forces in alignment. For example:

- Agni, the Sun, through the Krittika asterism and in conjunction with the zodiacal house of Mesa (Aries) and Vrsabha (Taurus) brings the spiritual light of *jyotir* for the spiritual benefit of the worshiper. (RV 7.5.6.)
- Usas, the Dawn and a terrestrial manifestation of Agni, the Sun, through the Krittika asterism and in conjunction with the zodiacal houses of Mesa (Aries) and Vrsabha (Taurus), brings *jyotir*, the divine principle of life and intelligence to the worshiper. (RV 1.113.1, 16.)
- Usas brings *jyotir* as reflected Moonlight of the Sun to the worshiper. (RV 1.123.1; 1.124.3.)
- Usas brings the light of *jyotir* directly from the Sun. (RV 10.35.5.)
- Usas spreads the Daylight (*jyotir*) upon every new day. (RV 5.80.2.)
- The Asvins through the power of the asterism of Asvini and zodiacal house of Mesa (Aries) brings *jyotir* to the worshiper. (RV 1.117.7; 1.182.3.)
- The lunar house of Indra, the presiding deity over Jupiter, with the power vested through Jyestra, and in conjunction with the zodiacal house of Vrscika (Scorpio), takes *jyotir*, made it his own, and conveyed it to the worshiper. (RV 3.39.7.)

- The lunar house of Indra, the presiding deity over Jupiter, with the power vested through Jyestra, and in conjunction with the zodiacal house of Dhanus (Saggitarius), brings *jyotir* to the Sacrifice to enable the worshiper to overcome evil. (RV 3.39.8.)
- The lunar house of Aditi, the head of the Adityas (zodiacal houses), through the power of Punavasu and the zodiacal houses of Mithuna (Gemini) and Karkata (Cancer), brings the light of *jyotir* to the worshiper. (RV 2.27.11.)
- The Adityas themselves, the zodiacal houses, bring the light of *jyotir* to the worshiper. (RV 2.17.14.)

Of course, Agni also acts on his own behalf to bring the spiritual endowments of *jyotir* to the worshiper. (RV 6.9.6.) The Lunar house of Agni also takes part in the grandest of all cosmic struggles

Jyotir and the Clash of the Titans

RV 1.36.8 poses an interesting twist on the struggle with the serpent Vrtra. This rc (mantra) reveals how Agni as the Bull smote and killed Vrtra, making the Vedic dharma wide and broad. Aside from the fact that it clearly shows Indra to be the incarnation of Agni in matters dealing with Vrtr, it is interesting first because the force of Agni is the presiding deity on the Sukta in which the rc (mantra) is found. The force of Agni thereby applies to the revelations obtained therein. In this rc (mantra) the Rishiis reveal that when the force of Agni unveiled the shroud of Vrtra the subtle foundation for the inner essence of the Vedic dharma was created. In its compact language pregnant with meaning, RV 1.36.8 reveals these basic elements:

- The lunar house of Agni, in his capacity as the presiding deity of the Krittika asterism and in conjunction with the zodiacal houses of Mesa (Aries) and Vrsabha (Taurus), creates the wide basis of Heaven (rodasi) and Earth. These two worlds are stated in the collective and separately. In other words, the force of Agni not only created both Heaven and Earth, but he forged the union of these polar opposites. Indeed, in so uniting Heaven and Earth, Agni shows that these worlds are not so different after all. The very act of unification indicates how similar and unitary they really are.

- The lunar house of Agni, in his capacity as the presiding deity of the Krittika asterism and in conjunction with the zodiacal house of Mesa (Aries) and Vrsabha (Taurus), releases the Water. Water is the ultimate basis of the Vedic dharma.
- The lunar house of Agni, in his capacity as the presiding deity of the Krittika asterism and in conjunction with the zodiacal house of Mesa (Aries) and Vrsabha (Taurus), makes a sound (ahuta) uttering the Word.
- The lunar house of Agni, in his capacity as the presiding deity of the Krittika asterism and in conjunction with the zodiacal house of Mesa (Aries) and Vrsabha (Taurus), releases the "herds of light," interpreted as the release of the light of knowledge.

RV 1.36.8 is an amazing rc (mantra) for another reason. It encapsulates the basic inner essence of the force of Agni described by Pandit David Frawley — speech (vak), prana and intelligence. It is the element of Speech which is the most remarkable. When Agni makes the sound uttering the Word, the Rishiis presage that which will be said millennia later. Later, it would be said that the sound of AUM is the primaeval sound which resonates after the emergence of a new cycle of creation which creates all sentient beings, things and objects in the Vedic dharma. (JUB 1.7.1, 1.9.1, 1.10.1.) The inner Vedic force of Agni is the energy lies behind and is impels that resonance. This rc (mantra) further elaborates on the first steps in the evolution of the sentient beings, things and objects in the Vedic dharma. Those initial steps are very elemental and basic but provide the basis of the inner foundation of all sentient beings, things and objects in the Vedic dharma. These are the elements:

- Agni wins the rays or "herds of starlight."
- Agni conquers and presides over the life energy (ashvo) of the Vedic dharma.

These two elements might as well be considered the constituent parts of *jyotir*. It is remarkable in that Agni, and not Indra, is the named Lunar house winning these benefits, but that the struggle with Vrtra has been posed in an astronomical context. Viewed in this light, Vrtra is seen to be more than simply a malevolent serpent. The basic nature of Vrtra, remember, is that of an enveloper, that which covers. Vrtra obscures and conceals. This is why, the Brahmanas remind us, he is called "Vrtra." (SPB 1.1.3.4.) Vrtra covers and obscures the inner truth and essence of the Vedic dharma, which is *Rta*, the second part of Vrtra's name. The act of concealment can be — and is — applied in many contexts, and these contexts have been used, certainly, in the Rg Veda. Aside from concealing the waters, Vrtra's the powers of concealment has been applied in other contexts:

In a religious context, Vrtra has been associated with Evil. When Vrtra is felled by Indra's weapon, Vrtra's evil is driven away by the New Moon. (SPB 6.2.2.18.). Astronomically considered, the subduing of Vrtra is seen as the emergence of the New Moon. "The full-moon oblation, assuredly, belongs to the Vritra-slayer, for by means of it Indra slew Vrtra; and this new-moon oblation also represents the slaying of Vrtra, since they prepared that invigorating draught for him who had slain Vrtra. An offering in honor of the Vrtra-slayer, then, is the full-moon sacrifice. Vrtra, assuredly, is no other than the moon; and when during that night (of new moon) he is not seen either in the east or in the west, then he (Indra) finishes in destroying him by means of that (new-moon sacrifice), and leaves nothing remaining of him." (SPB 1.6.4.12-13.)

In the same way Vrtra endeavors the capture and restraint of the light of *jyotir*. It is not such a huge stretch to find that the clash with Vrtra brings consequences to the creation of the light of *jyotir*. The same Vedic titans, Agni and Indra, are involved, with Soma following close behind. Surya makes a surprise appearance. The import of Vrtra to *jyotir* is deep and far-reaching:

- The light of *jyotir* was released when Indra slew Vrtra. (RV 2.11.8.)
- With the dual Lunar houses of Agni-Soma, when Vrtra was slain, the divine light of *jyotir* was created for the benefit of all sentient beings. (RV 1.93.4.)
- The Lunar house of Indra is the winner of light (*jyotir*) as a result of being victorious over Vrtra. (RV 3.34.34.)

- The light of *jyotir* resulted from the death of Vrtra at the hands of Surya. (RV 10.170.2.) According to this rc (mantra) the struggle with Vrtra was very much seen as a struggle between two forces — *rta*, the inner essence of the truth of the Vedic dharma and Vrtra, which, because he is in reality that which covers or obscures *Rta* is that which is not of the inner essence of the truth of the Vedic dharma.

All that is *jyotir* shines brilliantly. *Jyotir* explains from whence this brilliance originated. The next kind of light, *Bhanu*, describes and personifies this brilliance.

Bhanu

The Nagas are "a member of a class of mythical semidivine beings," half human and half cobra. They are a strong, handsome species who can assume either wholly human or wholly serpentine form and are potentially dangerous but often beneficial to humans.

The creator deity Brahma relegated the Nagas to the nether regions when they became too populous on earth and commanded them to bite only the truly evil or those destined to die prematurely. They are also associated with waters — rivers, lakes, seas, and wells — and are guardians of treasure." (https:// www. Britannica.com/topic/naga-Hindu-mythology.) The operative words in the description of the Nagas are that they are "associated with waters — rivers, lakes, seas, and wells — and are guardians of treasure." The Vedic astrologer believes that both of these clauses — associated with the Waters and the guardians of the treasure — refer to the same object. The treasure in this instance are the Waters, the inner essence of the Vedic dharma, and this is the treasure bestowed upon the worshiper.

Specifically, in this instance the Naga is the guardian of *Bhanu*, a specific aspect of Light. The Vedas consist of a spiritual tradition based on Light. Monier Williams, the authoritative dictionary of Sanskrit, lists upwards to five hundred different words for "light," each containing its own specific meaning and context. *Bhanu* is only one such word. It is, of course, the light originating from the asterism Ashlasha. The Light of Ashlasha, however, carries with it so many other meanings. It can mean:

- Sunlight.
- Rays of light from the sky.
- The quality of this light, including the effulgence, resplendence, brilliance, brightness, or brightness of this light.
- The Beauty of this aspect of light.

Significantly, *Bhanu* continues the work of the previous asterism, Pushya. In Pushya, Beauty incarnate was the spiritual endowment given to the worshiper. Here, in Ashlasha, the spiritual endowment given is *Bhanu*, or Beauty, with the properties of Light. This beauty is reflected in several members of the Stellar population.

- The lunar house of Agni as the presiding deity of and conveying the spiritual endowments from the asterism of Krittika, in conjunction with the zodiacal house of Mesa (Aries) and Vrsabha (Taurus).
- The Maruts as a manifestation of the Fire of Agni in the Firmament. (BD, 1.103.)
- Usas as a terrestrial manifestation of the Fire of Agni. (BD, 1.108.)
- The lunar house of the Asvins as the presiding deity of and conveying the spiritual endowments of the asterism Ashvini, in conjunction with the zodiacal house of Mesa (Aries).
- The lunar house of Naga itself acts in conveying the spiritual endowments of the asterism Ashlasha, in conjunction with the zodiacal house of Karkata (Cancer).

These are some formidable Lunar houses at work. These Lunar houses act in concert with Naga to convey the spiritual endowments of *Bhanu*. Agni as the presiding deity of and conveying the spiritual endowments from the asterism of Krittika, in conjunction with the zodiacal houses of Mesa (Aries) and Vrsabha (Taurus) represents the core spiritual qualities of the endowment itself:

- The Lunar house of Agni as the presiding deity of and conveying the spiritual endowments from the asterism of Krittika, in conjunction with the zodiacal houses of Mesa (Aries) and Vrsabha (Taurus) emits the shining brilliance of *Bhanu* with celestial splendor. (RV 10.6.2.)

- There are four elements to the shining beauty of Agni's *Bhanu* — *kavi*, the Fire of Revelation; kratu, the Fire of Divine Will; Food, the symbol of Consciousness; and *Bhanu*, the beauty of shining light. (RV 7.6.2.)
- *Bhanu* is the light of the Lunar house of Agni. (RV 1.92.5; 3.21.4.)
- The fuel powering the Lunar house of Agni is *Bhanu*. (RV 10.6.1.)
- Agni is the deification of the Beauty of *Bhanu* and shines like gold. (RV 7.3.6.)
- Agni's Beauty gleans with refulgence. (RV 7.9.4.)
- With this the Lunar house of Agni is armed with the *Bhanu* (sunlight) of the Great Impeller of the Vedic dharma. (RV 6.6.6.)

Bhanu has an ancient history:

- The lunar house of Agni as the presiding deity of and conveying the spiritual endowments from the asterism of Krittika, in conjunction with the zodiacal houses of Mesa (Aries) and Vrsabha (Taurus), was the first born of the Lunar houses, and was effulgent, the epitome of Beauty in its brilliance emanating from the light of *Bhanu*. (RV 8.7.36.)
- When the other Vedic forces created Agni, they made him resplendent in *Bhanu* (light). (RV 3.2.3.)
- Then, at this early stage of the Vedic dharma, the Lunar house of Agni gathered all traces of *Bhanu* and spread its effulgence to all corners of the dharma. (RV 6.16.2.)
- With his refulgent light of *Bhanu*, Agni, the presiding deity of and conveying the spiritual endowments from the asterism of Krittika, in conjunction with the zodiacal houses of Mesa (Aries) and Vrsabha (Taurus), overcame the Blackness which had permeated the indiscriminate, undifferentiated mass of inert matter which had enveloped the cosmos and with his Beauty and radiance bathed the Vedic dharma with light. (RV 10.3.2.)

- The radiance of Agni's *Bhanu* shines in waves, like sound waves, and in this manner reaches the highest reaches of heaven. (RV 10.3.5.) This is a clear reference to the waves of Saman discussed in the Introduction.
- Agni's light of *Bhanu* is also compared to the weaving which takes place in the subtle foundation of the Vedic dharma. As with the disha discussed in the introduction, Agni's shining light of *Bhanu* weaves like threads throughout the underbelly of the Vedic dharma. (RV 10.53.6.)

Bhanu is rightfully compared to sunlight. As sunlight, it is the only reason sentient exist on earth. Without *Bhanu* (sunlight) the material world would be a very different place. Sunlight is the basis of all life on earth, it is the basis for the Vedic astrologer's existence and the reason for the worshiper's spiritual journey. *Bhanu*, sunlight, allows the stage for the worshiper's spiritual journey:

- The Lunar house of Agni shines in the light of *Bhanu* comparable to the sunlight of Savitr, and the power of this light lifts Agni high above to the heavens. (RV 4.13.2.)
- The Lunar house of Agni shines with the power of *Bhanu*, and, like the Sun, emits a fiery flame. RV 2.8.4.)
- And why is there a general equivalence between the simple sunlight of Savitr and the light of *Bhanu* from Agni? Savitr, like Agni, is the Child of the Waters. (RV 10.140.2.) The Vedas have been handed down in highly symbolic language. As discussed in the Introduction, the "Child of the Waters" is coded language signifying from whence the Vedic forces of Agni and Savitr arose. The Waters is symbolic language signifying the essential nature of the Vedic dharma — the complete Vedic dharma. If Agni and Savitr are the "Child of the Waters," they arose from the same intrinsic forces which power the Vedic dharma. For this reason, the Veda states that an aspect of Agni, Vaisvanara, was born at the "highest place," parama vyoman, an existential plane higher than the Seven-Dimensional Universe. (RV 7.5.7.) The "Child of the Waters" signifies "the germ (seed) of waters, germ (seed) of

woods, germ (seed) of all things that move not and that move"
(RV 1.70.3.) In that capacity Agni and Savitr become the Seed
of everything in the Vedic dharma. The Lunar houses of Agni
and Savitr thereby represent the latent potentiality of all things,
alive or inert. That latent potentiality germinates and grows when
nourished by the Waters.

Bhanu is a significant part of the worshiper's life and supports the
world in which the worshiper lives and conducts the spiritual journey:

- The Vedic force of Agni, as the presiding deity of and conveying
the spiritual endowments from the asterism of Krittika, and in
conjunction with the zodiacal houses of Mesa (Aries) and Vrsabha
(Taurus), fills the heart of the worshiper with the white light of
Bhanu. (RV 10.1.1.)
- The Lunar house of Agni expiates the sins of the worshiper through
the light of *Bhanu*. (RV 1.92.1, 2.)
- The Lunar house of Agni shines with the purifying light of *Bhanu*.
(RV 6.15.5.)
- The Lunar house of Agni is the highest Hotr (officiating priest) at
the sacrifice and is resplendent in *Bhanu*.

The worshiper is not the only beneficiary of the light of *Bhanu*. The
existential levels of earth, mid-earth and heaven in the Vedic dharma
receives the blessings:

- The Lunar house of Agni spreads his light of his *Bhanu* over
the three existential levels of earth, mid-earth and heaven. (RV
10.88.3.)
- *Bhanu* indeed is the force of light with which Agni binds Heaven
and Earth (RV 3.22.2.)
- *Bhanu* is radiance itself and Agni invests this light on Heaven and
Earth. (RV 4.17.)

In concert with Agni as the presiding deity of and conveying the
spiritual endowments from the asterism of Krittika, in conjunction with
the zodiacal houses of Mesa (Aries) and Vrsabha (Taurus), is the power

of Usas, a terrestrial manifestation of Agni. These two Lunar houses act together in conveying the spiritual endowments of *Bhanu* to the worshiper.

- The daybreak dawn of Usas, a terrestrial manifestation of Agni, kindles Agni, and from there Agni emits its light of *Bhanu*. (RV 2.2.8.) This kindling of Agni is a term of art. Physical fire is "ignited," but Agni as the Sacrificial Fire is "kindled." Kindling imparts all those qualities and energies from the universe and channeled those qualities and energies into the Fire. The Sacrificial Fire plays a central role in the Sacrificial ritual, it is the center of attraction. Once kindled it is beheld by the worshiper, or, as in the Soma Sacrifice, the principal means of producing the Soma juice to be consumed by the worshiper. In all sacrificial settings, the central fire is the means by which the worshiper is transformed spiritually. The Sun is the source of all life. It is the agent which destroys the old life of the worshiper, and like the phoenix rising from the ashes, a new worshiper emerges. Breath in this above passage is prana, the subtle essence of the life force permeating the universe and sustaining the life of the worshiper. In other words, in part, the Fire of Agni is powered by and empowers the elements of the Vedic dharma, the natural order (*rta*).
- Thus, the Vedic force of Usas shines the light of *Bhanu* to the worshiper at the Sacrifice. (RV 1.48.9.)
- The daybreak dawn of Usas conveys the light (*Bhanu*) of awareness to the worshiper. (RV 6.65.1; 7.7.5; 7.79.1.) "Dawn" should be read with both and literal and figurative meaning. It is both the beginning of each new day and the beginning stage of self-realization, liberation, and salvation, which is the goal of the worshiper's spiritual journey.
- With the effulgence of *Bhanu*, the worshiper opens the doors of heaven. (RV 1.48.15.)

The Lunar house of Agni is asserted in other ways. The Maruts are a manifestation of the Fire of Agni in the Firmament The Vedic forces of the Maruts are utilized to spread the light of *Bhanu* to the worshiper. The light of *Bhanu* is compared to the brilliance of the Maruts. (RV 5.52.6.) The Maruts are radiant and powerful. (RV 1.19.5.)

The Lunar house of the Asvins also play a part. The Asvins as the presiding deity of and conveying the spiritual endowments of the asterism Ashvini, in conjunction with the zodiacal house of Mesa (Aries), conveys the benefits of *Bhanu* to the worshiper.

- *Bhanu* is the light of Asvins. (RV 4.45.1.)
- The horses convey the Asvins like the light of *Bhanu*. (RV 7.72.4.)

With regards to *Bhanu*, and the other forms of light, the rcs (mantras) reveal what they reveal. The real spiritual endowment of Light is experienced and utilized by the worshiper during the spiritual journey. The light of *Bhanu* is important to open the eyes of the worshiper. Once opened the worshiper's eyes are trained to the spiritual journey. The Vedic forces and energies themselves worship the Fire of Light, which protects Heaven and Earth. The Fire of Light therefore occupies an exalted place in the Vedic dharma.

ALL ABOUT AGNI

The Manifestations Of Agni

INTRODUCTION

Agni may be an overwhelming Vedic force and energy to comprehend simply due to his own vast powers, capabilities, manifestations, aspects and epithets — all of which are an accurate reflection of his true nature but must be taken in small portions to be fully appreciated. A great deal can be learned about Agni by the most simple method. If you read the opening rcs (mantras) of the First Mandala of the Rg Veda, you would be well on your way to learning about Agni's nature and characteristics. But first let's consider the place the divine Vedic power of Agni occupies in the Vedic dharma. It's true that the Vedas speak of the world of Light, but it also is a world of Fire. Fire plays a more important role, because what is Light but a by-product of Fire? Without fire could there possibly be light? First, a recap.

Prajanya recycles the worshiper's soul as well as and in the manner of rain. This process is described in the Five Fires of the Vedas. According to the Upanishads there are five fires. Let's recap:

- *The Heavenly Fire*

  Humans are sacrificed at death by cremation, becoming food for the divine Vedic energies and principles and transformed by the heavenly fire into Soma, the purified mind. This fire transforms the human body at death and upon the funeral pyre. The smoke, ciders, and ashes carrying the soul upwards to the heaven. (BU, 6.2.14, Ch.Up., 5.4.1.)

179

- *The Fire of Parjanya.*

This fire transforms Soma and the souls in its command into rain. Parjanya is the Vedic divine force for rain. The soul is carried upwards to the heavens to be met by Parjanya. (BU, 6.2.10, Ch.Up., 5.5.1, 5.6.1.)

- *The Vegetative Fire.*

Soma, the divine food, releases the rain, its essence, to earth, where it is transformed into vegetation. Rain is the essence of Soma (Purification), as divine food, falls to the earth with the souls in transmigration. (BU, 6.2.11, Ch.Up., 5.4.2.

- *The Digestive Fire.*

When these food plants containing the human remains are eaten, they are transformed into seamen by the man-fire, the digestive fire. The rain containing the seeds of the souls in transmigration are transformed to semen and are absorbed by the plant life and fauna and eaten by man or animal. (BU, 6.2.12.,)

- *The Female Fire.*

This semen is transformed into a Purusha, a person, by the woman-fire. The semen is transformed into a Purusha. (BU, 6.6.2.13.)

Fire however is a vast concept and assumes many forms. The Veda speaks of many Agnis. The many forms of Agni are contained in the names referring to his inherent, essential powers (*svadha*). The many fires of Agni and the nature of fire were featured in our first installment of the examination of Agni. In this examination Agni consists not simply in the physical flames but many other permutations of fire. A great deal of what the Vedas have to say about fire can be read in the First Mandala of the Rg Veda. These fires are defined in the opening rcs (mantras) of the First Mandala of the Rg Veda. Let's look at these opening rcs (mantras) of the Rg Veda and what they have to say about Agni:

- Agni is *Agni/m*, the Sacrificial Fire, found in RV 1.1.1.
- Agni is *Agni/h*, the Mystic Fire, found in RV 1.1.2.
- Agni is *Agnina*, the Celestial Fire, the Fire of the Inner Vedic dharma, found in RV 1.1.3.
- Agne is *Agne*, the Physical Fire, the Digestive Fire, found in RV 1.1.4.
- Agni is *Agnir*, the Fire of Divine Will, found in RV 1.1.5.
- Agni is *Agna*, the Spiritual Fire, found in RV 1.14.2.
- Agni is *Agnau*, the Fire of Self-Surrender, found in RV 1.169.19.

In RV 1.164.46 it is revealed that "[t]hey speak of Indra, Mitra, Varuna (Lord Protector of the Dynamic Cosmic Order), and fire (Agni). The learned speak of many names, but there is only one. The one is a winged bird." This rc (mantra) says, in effect, that the Wise know the One ("Ekam") by many names, and they call the One Agni, Indra, etc. RV 1.164.46 represents a fundamental truth, a philosophy that pervades in every Veda, every Brahmana, every Upanishad. The many deities mentioned in the same breath as the One are simply the many manifestations of the One, Ekam. The fundamental truth is that there is but One God, and the deities associated from the One are its manifestations. These manifestations are what the word means — they manifest in the material world. In the same way, there are many manifestations of fire. Fundamentally, however, all are called Agni in the Veda and all the permutations of fire share a common core. In each of these forms of Fire, the divine Vedic force of Agni serves as a catalyst for the variations of experience encountered by the worshiper during the spiritual journey. During that journey Agni in the capacity of the Sacrificial Fire protects the worshiper (RV 3.27.6) and provides the flame to guide the worshiper along the spiritual path. (RV 3.27.12.) Yet these are only names, categories of the fire of spiritual experience. These categories tell us nothing of the contours of each fire and how the fire changes the worshiper to achieve the goal of spiritual liberation and salvation. These fires contribute to the incredible omnipresence of Agni. This omnipresence in Agni runs across every level:

- On a material, microcosmic level Change represents the digestive fire which supports the individual and operates the material world.

- In a mental level Change represents the light of knowledge.
- On a spiritual level, Change represents the fire which burns away impurities, sins, of the worshiper, providing the forgiveness of sins.
- On cosmic level Change represents the Cosmic Fire.

Thus, we saw in the first installment that the fires of Agni took many forms and permutations. This is called the "Aspects" of Agni, the *svadha*, essential, inherent, nature of Agni:

- Agni as the Sacrificial Fire, *Agnim*.
- Agni as the Mystic Fire in all its permutations which is inherent in the universe, signified in the Rg Veda as *agnih*.
- Agni as the Fire of Divine Will, called *Agnir*.
- Agni as the Celestial Fire, or Fire from Heaven, called *Agnina*.
- Agni as the Fire of the Mid-World, *Agner*.
- Agni as the Terrestrial Fire, *Agne*.
- Agni as *Agnaye*, the Fire of Transcendence.
- Agni as the Fire of Self-Surrender, *Agnau*.
- Agni as the source of the light of consciousness, or awareness, signified in the Rg Veda as *agnii/na, agnii/*, and *agna*.

There are also manifestations of Agni. The manifestations are those which are translated into the material world. The principal manifestation of Agni is in physical fire. Agne, physical fire, consists of four components:

- Agni as the Digestive Fire.
- Agni as the Vegetative Fire.
- Agni as the Fire Altar.
- Agni as physical fire.

There are other Manifestations. These forms of Agni are called "Manifestations" because these refer to the manner in which Agni appear in the Vedic dharma. They include fires located in the three worlds of existence, namely Earth, the Mid-World or the Firmament, and Heaven. This book part of Agni is concerned with his Manifestations. To fully appreciate the extent to which Agni pervades as a Manifestation in the material world, a refresher course in the cosmology of the Vedic dharma must first be explained.

The Cosmology of the Vedic dharma

In the Vedas, Dharma is the totality of the natural order. (VaS, 1.1.1.) What does this actually mean? What does it consist of?

At first there was a great mass of indiscriminate, undifferentiated, matter. Then, when Indra felled Vrtra with Vayra, he divided the world into two parts: one part, *rtasat* ("What is") and the other *asatanrta* ("What is not"). (RV 6.24.5.) The forces of Indra and Soma cast *Asatanrta* below the triple structure of the world. (RV 7.104.11.) From there, in the beginning stages of all creation, described in RV 10.190, *Satyam* and *Rta* are found at the highest level of Being. (RV 10.190.1.) Of the two, *Rta* prevailed over and pervades over *Satyam*. As Hickman notes in his "Toward a Comprehensive Understanding of *Rta* in the Rg Veda," *Satya* is "being" manifested by the establishment of the universe, but *Rta* is the mode of that being which promotes and supports the freedom and mobility of *Satyam*. The former, *Rta,* furnishes the framework for the latter, sat, and allows it, as well as all other subjects in the cosmic order, to function. *Rta* is the internal mechanism of the proverbial watch which regulates the ticking of the universe.

And so it is for the Vedic dharma. The Seven-Dimensional is a combination of the three upper and three lower levels of existence, conjoined together by the Svar. *Satyam* and *Rta* together create the second highest level of being, *Tapas*. (RV 10.190.1.) After *Tapas*, Madhuunaam, or Bliss, is on the bottom tier of the higher world. In the Arthavada, those highest stations are *Rta, Satyam* and Brhat (Infinity). (AV 12.1.1.) On the bottom level exists the three levels of sensible appearance: the earth, mid-world, and heaven. (RV 1.34.7; 1.154.4.) This schema is referred to differently. In some passages, these lower three regions have been referred to as "tridhaatu prthhvim," (RV 1.34.7; 1.154.4) which can be roughly rendered as the "three levels of the material plane." Sometimes these two general existential planes are referred in terms of the Ocean, one Higher and one lower. Other times, these two existential planes, one higher and one lower, are what are more commonly set forth as simply Heaven and Earth.

Whatever their denomination, each level contains three subdivisions. There are three levels of the Higher Ocean, Heaven, *dyaus*. (RV 1.35.6; AV 8.9.16.) The three divisions of this existential level are:

- *Uttama(m)* (RV 1.24.15; 1.25.21; 1.50.10; 1.91.8; 1.108.9; 1.156.4; 1.163.7; 2.1.2; 2.23.10; 3.5.6, 8; 4.315; 436.8; 4.54.2; 5.25.5; 5.28.3; 5.59.3; 9..22.6; 9.51.2; 9.63.29; 9.67.3, 28; 9.85.3; 9.107.1; 9.108.16; 10.75.1; 10.97.18; 10.159.3; 10.166.5; 10.78.3) or *uttame* (RV 1.31.7; 2.41.5; 5.60.4; 6.60.3, 8; 8.51.4; 9.61.29.)
- *Madhyama* (RV 1.24.15; 1.25.21; 1.108.9, 10; 2.29.4; 4.25.8; 6.21.5; 6.62.11; 7.32.16; 8.61.15;9.70.4; 9.108.9; 10.15.1; 10.81.5; 10.97.12) or *madhyame* (RV 1.27.5; 2.23.13; 5.60.6; 6.25.1); and
- *Avama* or *avame*. (RV 1.105.4; 1.108.9, 10; 1.163.5; 2.35.2; 3.54.5; 6.251; 6.62.11; 7.71.3; 1.185.11.)

Even here there are other expressions of Heaven. In the Atharvaveda there are also three levels of heaven. The highest level is that level where the *ptrs* (fathers) and angirasas reside. (AV 18.1.6; 8.2.48.) The second level is the "starry" heaven (AV 18.2.12, 48), and the third, lowest, level is the "watery" heaven. (AV 18.2.12, 48.) Sri Aurobindo, the noted philosopher and Vedic scholar called this the Upper Ocean.

In the Rg Veda and Atharvaveda there are three levels to the lowest level of the material world. (RV 1.34.8; AV 8.9.16.) The Fire of Change, in its three aspects of Agne, Jatavedas, and Vasivanara, is the embodiment of the lower three regions. (BD, 1.6.6.) Agne is the embodiment of the earth; Jatadevas is the embodiment of the mid-earth (RV 1.77.5; 2.4.1; 3.1.20; 4.1.20; 4.58.8; 6.4.2; 6.10.1; 6.12.4; 6.15.13; 7.9.4; 7.12.2; 10.45.1; 10.61.14; 10.83.2; 10.88.4); Vasivanara is the embodiment of heaven. (RV 1.59.3, 4, 6, 7; 1.98.1, 2; 3.2.1, 11, 12; 3.3.1, 5, 11; 3.26.1, 2, 3; 4.5.1, 2; 5.15.13; 6.7.1, 2, 6, 7; 6.8.1, 2, 3, 4; 6.9.1, 7; 7.5.1, 2, 5; 7.6.6, 7; 7.13.1; 7.49.4; 8.30.4; 9.61.16; 10.45.12; 10.88.12, 13, 14.) Indra, in his representation of strength and vitality, embodies the mid-world. The Purified Mind (Soma), the inherence of the Eternal Law of God-Realization and Purification, embodies heaven.

There are then these two broad levels of existence — the earth and heaven — are sometimes referred to as the Lower Ocean and Upper

Ocean. This Earth/Heaven distinction will prove important to a Vedic force like Agni, since his power is the unifying agent for these two levels.

There is an intermediary level binding the Upper Ocean and Lower Ocean. Materially, the binding level is represented by the Mid-World, the Firmament. The firmament is the upper atmosphere, the canopy which lies between the surface of the earth and the Stas. Both in the Rg Veda and Atharvaveda there are three levels to the atmosphere, the mid-world, firmament. (RV 1.34.8; AV 8.9.16.) The mid-world binds the two levels, the Upper Ocean and Lower Ocean. Subtly, these two levels of existence, the Upper Ocean and the Lower Ocean, are bound by the Svar.

The Svar is the transitory world of heaven and light. The Svar can be viewed as the subtle counterpart for the Firmament. This middle region, the svar, is an intermediate world of heaven and light. (RV 1.35.6.) Here again, as is the Vedic force of Agni, the Svar is characterized by triads. There are three subdivisions to each region and has three subdivisions. (RV 3.56.8.) There are three regions of light in the svar. Those regions are *rocanna*, svar, and *raajati* (*raajati*). (RV 1.102.7; 2.27.9; 1.149.4; 4.33.5; 5.29.1; 5.69.1; 9.17.5.) These regions of light are sometimes indicated as general regions of light. (RV 1.102.7; 1.149.4; 3.56.8; 4.53.5; 5.69.1; 5.29.1; 9.17.5.) Those three regions of light are:

- *Rocanna*. (RV 1.49.1; 1.49.4; 1.50.4; 1.81.5; 1.93.5; 1.102.8; 1.146.1; 1.149.4; 2.27.9; 3.2.14; 3.5.10; 3.12.9; 3.44.4; 3.56.8; 3.61.5; 4.53.5; 3.61.5; 5.29.1; 5.56.1; 5.61.1; 5.69.4; 6.6.2; 6.7.7; 8.1.18; 8.5.8; 8.8.7; 8.14.7; 8.14.9; 8.93.26; 8.94.8; 8.98.3; 9.17.5; 9.37.3; 9.42.1; 9.85.9; 10.32.9; 10.46.3; 10.49.6; 10.65.4; 10.89.1; 10.170.4; 10.189.2.) *Rocanna* is the highest sphere of light. (RV 1.6.1, 9; 1.19.6; 1.81.5; 1.86.1; 1.92.17; 1.113.7; 1.121.9; 1.124.3; 1.146.1; 3.2.14; 5.41.3; 6.7.7; 6.44.23; 8..1.8; 8.14.9; 8.25.19; 8.52.8; 9.42.1; 9.85.9; 9.61.10; 10.32.2; 10.70.5; 10.143.3.) The highest region of light is sometimes indicated as upa nam ketu. (RV 5.34.9);
- The Svar.
- *Revati* (RV 1.164.12; 6.2.2; 6.66.7; 9.84.4; 9.108.2), also known as *rajas*. (RV 1.125.20; 1.36.12; 1.188.1; 5.8.5; 5.28.2; 5.81.5; 7.32.16; 8.13.4; 8.15.3; 8.15.5; 8.19.31; 8.37.3; 8.60.15; 9.66.2; 9.86.5, 28; 10.140.4; 10.167.1.)

It is a grand, sometimes confusing, structure, and on top is *parame vyoman*, "the highest heaven." The *parame vyoman* is or than the highest heaven. it is where Divine Grace (Indra) and Transformation (Agni) were born RV 3.32.10); it is where the very source of Deification and Divination (Soma) dwells with the power of Divine Grace (Indra). (RV 9.86.15.) It is the place of origin where all the principles inherent in the divinities reside (RV 1.164.39.) It is a place beyond space and time. It is a region of Pure Being.

Parame Vyoma is also a psychological state. It is made up of a psychological state through the agency of select divine attributes. The Fire of Transformation (Agni), as soon as it appeared in the realm of Pure Being (*parame vyoma*), placed the spark of consciousness in the firmament. (RV 4.50.4.) Brihaspati, as soon as it appeared in this region, created the seven layers of consciousness and the entire multitude of physical forms. (RV 5.15.2.) These divine qualities and others are crystallized in the place of the sacrificial altar (RV 5.15.2), where, once reborn, the worshiper is united with this highest place of Pure Being. (RV 1.143.2.) The Vedic force representing this highest state of Pure Being is Brihaspati. Brihaspati is the Supreme manifestation of consciousness. The appellation literally means "Lord of Infinity (the psychological state of Pure Being)."

Pure Being is infused in the Vedic dharma. The transition into the material world corrupts the pure state of Being and transforms it to a material state of Becoming. It is in this transition that this pristine state is transformed into the existential planes that we know today.

Schematically, this edifice looks like this:

Parame Vyoma "the Highest Heaven"

UPPER HEAVEN (Upper Ocean):

ELEMENT	ATHARVAVEDA	RIG VEDA
Fire	Ptrs (Angirasas)	Uttama (Uttame)
Akasha Ether)	"Starry" Heaven	Madhyama (Madhyame)
Water	"Watery" Heaven	Avama (Avame)

THE SVAR

THE SVAR (REGION OF LIGHT)
Rocanna
Svar
Recast (Rajasic)

THE INTERMEDIARY REGION BETWEEN HEAVEN AND EARTH:

THE SENSIBLE WORLD (Lower Ocean):

Lower Heaven

Mid-World
Earth

This cosmological schema will prove important to our discussion here. The importance lies in the many faces of Agni:

- The Aspects of Agni — the inherent, essential characteristics of Agni explored in a companion volume — relate to the subtle aspects of the Vedic dharma contained in the Upper Ocean.
- The Manifestations of Agni — the subject matter of this portion —implicate the various elements of the material world found in the Lower Ocean of the Vedic dharma.

Specifically, we are only concerned for the moment with this last, lower level of the Vedic dharma. It is here that the manifestations of Agni live. An understanding of the running parts of the Vedic dharma gives us a true appreciation of the pervasion of Agni. The Vedic force of Agni encompasses the Vedic dharma at every level. It is a characteristic few other, if any, Vedic forces can aspire. The Aspects of Agni pertain to the Upper Ocean, the three higher levels of existence. The general manifestations of Agni, however, correspond to these three lower existential levels in the Lower Ocean. (B.D., 1.66.) Agni is known by a different name for each existential level. The Manifestations of Agni are found in three general groups. Those groups coincide with the three major levels of existence — the material world, Mid-World (or firmament) and Heavenly world. Those qualities manifest themselves in various fires. Thus, Agni is transformed and includes:

- Agni Suci, the manifestation of the Celestial Fire found in the Lower Heaven.
- Agni Vanaspati, the manifestation of the Fire in the Mid-World or Firmament, and
- Agni Pavamana, the manifestation of the Terrestrial Fire.

The specific celestial fires of the Lower Heaven in Agni Suci are:

- Agni Bharati and
- Agni Vaisvanara.

The specific fires of Agni Vanaspati is the fire of the firmament. The fires found in this region belong to:

- Maruts,
- Agni Jatavedas,
- Rudra, and
- Saraswati.

Agne is the terrestrial aspect Agni manifested on Earth and is Agni Pavamana. Agni Pavamana presides over these divinities possessing the following manifestations; let's recap:

- Agnayi.
- Ajith.
- Apva.
- Aranyani.
- Barhi.
- The Bull.
- Dhumaketu.
- Dravinodas.
- The Frog.
- Idhma.
- Ila.
- *Kavi.*
- The litter and the Divine Doors.
- Narasamsa.
- Pestle and Mortar.
- Prthvi (Earth).
- The Pressing Stones.
- Ratri.
- The Rivers.
- Sraddha.

- The Steed, the Horses.
- Svadha.
- Svahakritis.
- Tanunapi.
- Tvastr, the Architect, the Demiurge.
- Usasanakta, "Dawn and Night."
- Vanaspati.
- The Waters
- The Whip

There are many sides to the manifestations of the Vedic force of Agni. These fires touch every aspect in every level of existence. They are the fires found in the material world. The manifestations of Agni touch all three existential levels in the material world:

- The Celestial Fire.
- The Fire of the Firmament.
- The Terrestrial Fire.

THE FIRE OF THE
HEAVENS

Agni's Fire of the Heavens belong to the upper level of Vedic existence. In the sensible world, these fires belong to the Lower Heaven, the lower ocean referred to occasionally in the Veda, if you will. In the Upper Heaven it belongs in the Rg Veda these fires belong to the existential plane of Uttama, and in the AtharvaVeda it belongs to the Forefathers, the ptrs. As an element itself it is Fire itself.

Saunaka, the Medieval Vedic scholar, describes a scheme of Agni distributed over the three tiers of existence and under which distributes the divinities which belong to each existential level. These divinities each inform a different aspect of Agni. There are three principal manifestations of the Fire of Change (Agni): Celestial, the "Middle" Agni, and Terrestrial Agni. (BD, 1.91, TB 1.2.1.56, 57.)

Recognizing that there is a tripartite nature to Agni, the properties and appearances of the three Agni differ. The terrestrial Agni is hairy with flames, the middle Agni is hairy with lightening, and the celestial Agni is hairy with rays. (BD, 1.94.) The terrestrial Agni is led by men, and the celestial Agni leads the worshiper from this world to heaven, namely liberation and salvation. (BD, 1.91.)

The force of Agni also is possessed of its svadha, its essential, inherent nature. The Svadha of Agni is expressed in his Aspects. The essential qualities of Agni's aspects are expressed in the principal aspect of his Celestial or Heavenly Fire, *Agnina*. The First Mandala gives a good introduction of the benefits of the Celestial Fire:

- RV 1.1.3.
  Agnina, the Celestial Fire bestows the essence of the Vedic dharma on the worshiper

- RV 1.12.6.
  Agnina, the Celestial Fire is kindled by Agnir, the Mystic Fire. We are dealing with terms of art here. "Kindled" itself signifies the ignition of mystic powers.

- RV 1.36.18.
  Agnina, the Celestial Fire summons Yadu, Turvasha and Ugradeva the "upper regions" to do its work. Kashyap in his commentary of This rc (mantra) explains that these are names of RgVedic Kings since endowed with spiritual powers. Yuda does the bidding of the Vedic force of Indra, Ugradeva means One Who Has a Terrible God, and Turveda is One with Conquering Speed.

Agni is possessed of its manifestation as the Celestial Fire. The celestial, heavenly aspects of the Fire of Change (Agni), is also known as Suci Agni. Suci Agnis is better known as possessing various manifestations:

- Bharati. (BD, 3.13.)
- Agni Vaisvanara. (BD, 1.67.)
  Here is what the Vedas reveal of Agni Bharati and Agni Vaisvanara.

AGNI BHARATI

Bharati is the Vedic force which "knows the minds of gods," who is "omniscient" and "all-knowing." The qualities of this manifestation of Agni, Bharati, then, address issues of Knowledge, Divine Mind, and Omniscience, the knowing channeling of the mind, spirit and force permeating the Vedic dharma. The qualities of this manifestation of the Celestial Fire is definitely a mixed bag. But as we will soon see, like the song says, Bharata is "part sinner, part saint," it is not one or the other but both. This is what the Veda has to say about Bharati:

- RV 1.96.3: Agni, in his incarnation as Bharata the Celestial Fire, is the Sustainer. As the Sustainer, in this incarnation Agni is the "perpetual giver" of spiritual wealth.
- RV 1.104.3: Agni, in his incarnation as Bharata the Celestial Fire, "knows the Mind of the Gods." This phrase needs a more precise explanation beyond the mere epithet. We are of course familiar with our own consciousness, if only as a whirl of meandering and fleeting thoughts, feelings, and sensations. "The Mind of the Gods" is a different animal. The worshiper may be able to "Know" things, know the world. Before an object may be "known," that object must first exist in some tangible or intangible form so that it may be capable of identification. Once that object is available for cognition, the perceiving subject will attach a name to distinguish that object from others. Human Speech is the articulation of the world, attaching a word to an object in the world. For the worshiper to assign the word "tree" to the actual object implies

195

knowledge of that object, albeit through the sense perceptions. It's all some heady stuff, but that in a nutshell is a very short description of consciousness. The essence of Vedanta is that the perceiving subject superimposes the objects of the world for mortals to perceive. As Adi Sankara opens in his Drg-Drsya-Viveka, "The forms are perceived and the eye is its perceiver. The Eye is perceived and the mind is the perceiver. The mind with its modifications is perceived and the Witness (the Self) is verily the perceiver. But it, the Witness or Self, is not perceived by any other." Error occurs when the perceiving object — namely, us — believe we are the subject responsible for the perception of the objects in the material world, when in reality it is the Atman, the Self, superimposing itself on the universe. The quality of Agni, then, in his incarnation as Bharata and as the "Knower of the Mind of the Gods," has this meaning. This aspect of the Celestial Fire is a precursor to the Universal Atman.

- RV 2.14.8: Agni, in his incarnation as Bharata the Celestial Fire, is the power behind the "Rays of Knowledge." In this rc, Bharata represents the rays of knowledge given not to the worshiper, but from Soma, the Vedic force of divine ecstasy, to Indra, the divine force of Articulation and Might.
- RV 2.26.3: Agni, in his incarnation as Bharata the Celestial Fire, is used as the generalized groups of spiritual endowments intended for the worshiper.
- RV 3.10.5: This rc (mantra) highlights yet another aspect of this incarnation of Agni. Bharata in this rc (mantra) signifies a "priest," or, in this rc, the "Priest of the Call."
- RV 2.37.1: This rc (mantra) highlights another aspect of this incarnation of Agni. In this rc (mantra) Bharata is seen as the "benefactor of men." Thus, here, the Soma is brought to the Vedic forces and energies such that they can be the "benefactor of men."

Now, as they say, for something completely different. In RV 3.33.11, Bharata is straightforwardly referred herein as the "Offspring of Bharata." In RV 3.33.12 the rcs (mantras) refers to the "Sons of Bharata." This is where the Rg Veda ceases to be a spiritual and metaphysical scripture and is transformed into a source of ancient historical record. The Bharatas are an Aryan tribe mentioned in the Rigveda, especially in those portions of the Third Mandala and Seventh Mandala attributed to the Bharata Rishii Vishvamitra. There are noble and nefarious connotations of Bharata. Bharata has the meaning of "foe," or "enemy." For example:

- In RV 4.17.9, for example, Bharata has the meaning over those which Indra is victorious in battle.
- In RV 7.8.4 the Bharatas are enemies of the Purus, another Aryan tribe.
- In RV 9.106.3, Indra wins back riches (spiritual?) which were being held by the Bharatas.
- In an odd twist in RV 10.147.4, the Bharatas were called the "associates of Indra."
- In RV 8.100.3, the Bharatas were again referred to as the enemy from whom Indra wins back the truth and which they held.
- In RV 10.40.8, the Bharatas are the enemies over which the Asvins conquer and subdue.
- In RV 10.76.4 the Bharatas were called the "demons."
- In RV 10.138.6 the Bharatas were the enemies who opposed the sacrifice.

The historical and spiritual meanings merge in RV 3.52.8, where Bharata was called the "hero among the Gods." Bharata undeniably has its spiritual meaning. The difference is in the pronunciation. Bharatá, emphasis on the last syllable, is the spiritual side of Bharata and in this incarnation is the Celestial Fire of Agni. In this context it literally means, "to be maintained," viz. the fire having to be kept alive by the care of men). Bharata is also the name of Rudra in RV 2.36.8 and RV 7.46.1.

Bharata has other meanings. In one of the "river hymns" RV 3.33, the entire Bharata tribe is described as having crossed over the river, with their chariots and wagons, at the confluence of the Vipash (Beas) and Shutudri (Satlej). One can construe this meaning in a spiritual setting, but this is one instance where the intent of the Rishiis was historical. The hymns by the Rishii Vasistha in the Seventh Mandala, RV 7.18, for example, mention the Bharatas as the protagonists in the Battle of the Ten

Kings, where they are on the winning side. In this portion of the Veda, the purpose is clearly historical, and is likely an answer to that age-old question of the Aryan Invasion, although this issue is obviously the subject of a separate treatment. The Bharata tribe, for all their historical and spiritual connections, are clearly favored by the Vedic dharma. RV 5.11.1 relates that the force and energy of Agni protects the Bharatas. What better protection can be given to any group or tribe than to be associated with the Celestial Fire of Agni? For this reason perhaps they appear to have been successful in the early power-struggles between the various Aryan and non-Aryan tribes so that they continue to dominate in post-Rigvedic texts, and later in the (Epic) tradition, the Mahabharata, where the eponymous ancestor becomes Emperor Bharata, conqueror of "all of India," and his tribe and kingdom is called Bharata. It is in this meaning that the name Bharata has continued relevance. "Bharata" today is the official name of the Republic of India.

A rc (mantra) with historical and spiritual meaning is found in RV 5.54.14. This rc (mantra) simply reads that the Maruts give the Bharata their power. Can this be interpreted to mean the historical Bharata? Is this a declaration of where the divine quality of Bharata originates? This rc (mantra) could genuinely be interpreted both ways. The force and energy of Agni is responsible in empowering the Maruts, just as Bharata is another name for Agni in its manifestation as the Celestial Fire. Moreover, as a historical matter the Bharata have also had a special status.

In RV 3.33.11, 3.33.12, and 6.16.4, Bharata, the manifestation of the Celestial Fire of Agni, is known as the "Bringer of Treasure." As in other contexts, "treasure" should be understood as the gift of spiritual endowments. Those endowments are those tools used by the worshiper in the course of the spiritual journey. Essentially, these treasures are the gifts from the Vedic dharma, the vast expanse of the universe.

Bharata is associated with "continuous speech" in RV 7.24.2. The speech intended is not ordinary speech. It is the most subtle form of speech found in the Vedic dharma. Vak, speech, is three-fold, and belongs to the Celestial, Middle and Terrestrial Fires. (BD, 3.14.) RV 1.164.45, on the other hand, teaches there are four elements and they correspond to the four, broad, dimensions of the multi-universe of the Vedic dharma. It is a gradual process, and as the worshiper progresses in the spiritual journey, the level of speech practiced and communicated becomes more and more subtle.

Level of Vak	Corresponding Dimension of the Universe
Vaikhari	Two-Dimensional Universe
Madhyama	Three-Dimensional Universe
Pasyanti	Five-Dimensional Universe
Para	Seven-Dimensional Universe

These levels of speech correspond to the ever-more subtle levels of communication experienced by the worshiper during the spiritual journey.

- The natural order begins at Vaikhari, the underlying basis of material existent present in the Two-Dimensional Universe, where the worshiper experiences the insane tug and pull of maya. This is the verbal speech we all engage in everyday life in the material world.
- Beginning to break free of the chains of maya, the worshiper begins to live and experience in the material world reflected in the Three-Dimensional Universe.
- Through meditation the worshiper discovers the subtle basis of the material world in the Five-Dimensional Universe.
- Through intense worship, ritual and meditation (*Tapas*) the worshiper, if lucky, transcends and is teleported to liberation in the Seven-Dimensional Universe. This is the completely non-verbal level of speech associated with and experience during the intense worship, ritual and meditation.

In RV 9.48.3 Bharata was called the "King of the Heavens." While associated with the Celestial Fire of Agni, here Bharata is associated with Soma, the divine force of Ecstasy. More than being merely associated, in this rc (mantra) Soma becomes Bharati, the manifestation of Agni as the Celestial Fire, once placed on earth by the falcon.

Bharata is given a different context in RV 9.97.1. Here, Bharata is used to identify the invoking priest who presses the Soma juice from the pressing stones. This is not inconsistent with the overall meaning of Bharata as the Celestial Fire. Soma, the liquid sacrament which urges direct communication with the divine, is the product of the Celestial Fire. It takes a fire of celestial origin to bring about union with the divine.

In RV 10.100.2 the Bharatas acquire the epithet of the "cherisher of all." This is a reference to the divine force of Indra, an incarnation of the Vedic force of Agni.

So Agni in its aspect as the Celestial Fire, in its manifestation of Bharata, is a mix of qualities, some spiritual, some evil, some utterly historical, some not. It is confirmation that God as the highest power and creator of the Vedic dharma created everything and encompasses everything, the good and the bad and the ugly. It is the Vedic answer for the creation of evil. Not the only answer, however, there is another story of the origin of evil in Vrtra. This, however, deserves its own treatment. If God is the Creator, surely He must have created everything, and the fact that He is the highest power does not necessarily mean that He was only responsible for the good things in life. This is a tradition which was carried on to Christian theology. Before becoming the Prince of Darkness, Satan was one of God's most trusted Angels. This is Christian recognition that God the Creator was responsible for all in His creation. That Bharata could be considered a "foe" and "enemy" and at the same time be the manifestation of the Celestial Fire is confirmation that of the wide scope of the Vedic dharma.

AGNI VAISVANARA

We saw Agni Vaisvanara earlier in this book. Earlier Agni Vaisvanara was described as the Sacrificial Fire. There are in fact three aspects to Agni Vaisvanara: (1) the Fire of Knowledge, (2) the force of Vital energy, and (3) the sacrificial fire. The characteristics and qualities of Agni Vaisvanara could easily fill an entire book. It is a major Vedic force and energy.

Agni Vaisvanara is one of the brothers of Agni. (BD 7.61.) Vaisvanara is a principal manifestation of Agni Suci, the Celestial Agni. (BD, 1.67, 7.142.) A defining characteristic of this aspect of Agni Suci is its power to bestow spiritual bliss and happiness, either to the worshiper, to the Vedic dharma, to other Vedic forces and energies, or consumed with draughts of Soma as do the other Vedic forces and energies. Agni Vaisvanara is that aspect of Fire of Change through which the worshiper is purified. (TB 1.4.8.7.) Agni Vaisvanara is that power in Change which bestows bliss, happiness, and expiation of sins, such that these qualities pervade the universe. (TB 1.2.1.1-6.) Agni Vaisvanara is a part of the celestial fire because it is possessed of many subtle and divine characteristics. There are numerous references to Agni Vaisvanara in the Veda.

- All spiritual endowments and riches are vested in Agni Vaisvanara, and those endowments are spread throughout the pervasion of the Vedic dharma. (RV 1.59.3.)
- Agni Vaisvanara unites the respective powers of Heaven and Earth and establishes the existential levels in the Vedic dharma. (RV 1.59.4.)

- Agni Vaisvanara is the "knower of all births" (*jatavedo*), a quality shared with the other aspect of Agni, Agni Jetavedas. (RV 1.59.5.) Just as there are many fires of Agni, there are many areas in which the Knower of Things touch. As the Knower of all Things, Agni in its manifestation in Jatavedas gives strength to the worshiper during the spiritual journey; is strengthened itself as a result of the Sacrifice for the benefit of the other Vedic forces and energies and the worshiper; is the Godhead, the accumulation of all Vedic forces and energies in One; knowing the eternal births of the Vedic force of Agni and knowing the birth of the worshiper who attends the sacrifice; is constantly in the worshiper's thoughts; has perfect vision; overcomes all evils; and other powers. Indeed, the "knowing" power of Agni Vaisvanara and Agni Jatadevas has more to do with providing the subtle essence of the material universe in which the worshiper and we all live.
- Indra is the incarnation of Agni Vasivanara when battling the "enemies." (RV 1.59.6.) The enemies the Rishiis mentioned in This rc (mantra) are Vrtra and Shambara, although it is conceivable that any evil force obstructing the Waters can be considered an "enemy" which transforms Indra into an incarnation of Agni Vaisvanara.
- Agni Vaisvanara is the Universal Godhead, the Universal Self. (RV 1.59.7.)
- Agni Vaisvanara is the Lord of the Vedic dharma, he unites with the Sun, and the powers inherent therein are channeled to the worshiper through his grace (syama). (RV 1.98.1.)
- Agni Vaisvanara is present in all things and pervades all. Agni Vaisvanara protects the worshiper "day and night." (RV 1.98.2.) "Day and Night" is coded language signifying the fire urging from the progression between the two equinoctial asterisms, the Vernal to the Autumnal Equinox.
- From this fire, the fire emitted from the progression between the Vernal and Autumnal Equinox, the worshiper develops a true understanding of pure light (*ghrta*) and increases the understanding of *Rta*, the inner essence of the Vedic dharma. (RV 3.2.1.)

- Agni Vaisvanara bestows the vast array of spiritual endowments. (RV 3.2.11.)
- As he bestows these spiritual endowments to the worshiper, Agni Vaisvanara ascends to the mid-world, then to Heaven, while he creates other spiritual endowments. (RV 3.2.12.)
- The effulgence of Agni Vaisvanara shines upon the paths of spiritual journey of the worshiper. (RV 3.3.1.)
- Agni Vaisvanara, sitting in the Waters, discovers the Heaven, the svar, and in this brilliant light, enlighten the world. (RV 3.3.5.)
- In finding the Sun world, the svar, Agni Vaisvanara follows the truth. (RV 3.26.1.)
- Agni Vaisvanara is the Lord of Heaven and the Traveler of the Earth. The Collective Vedic gods gave birth to Agni Vasivanara from the inner essence of the Vedic dharma *(rta)*. (RV 6.7.1.)
- When Agni Vaisvanara was created, all the forces and energies of the Collective Vedic gods were funneled into him. He leads the way of the paths, including the worshiper's spiritual journey. (RV 6.7.2.)
- The heights of Heaven take form in Agni Vaisvanara's eye. All worlds stand on his head. The Seven Rivers flow from him like a spring. (RV 6.7.6.)
- The Will of Agni Vaisvanara formed the Mid-World; he shaped the effulgent planes of Heaven. He is the guardian of eternity. (RV 6.7.7.)
- Pure Thought streams from Agni Vaisvanara. (RV 6.8.1.)
- Agni Vaisvanara oversees and monitors the laws of religious austerities, ceremonies, and practices. He perpetuates the laws of motion and action in the material space. He shapes that space of Pure Being, parame/ vyo\mani, and the material world. (RV 6.8.2.)
- Agni Vaisvanara supports Heaven and Earth. (RV 6.8.3.)
- Night and Day revolve according to their own laws. Agni Vaisvanara governs the progression of Night into Day. (RV 6.9.1.)
- The Word (logos) powers the Fire of Agni Vaisvanara. (RV 7.5.1.)

- The Fire of Agni Vaisvanara establishes the Heavens and the Earth. He is the Lord of the Rivers (Consciousness) and the Bull. (RV 7.5.2.)
- The Word (*logos*) are the horses of Agni Vaisvanara. (RV 7.7.5.)
- Agni Vaisvanara took the riches from the upper and lower oceans to give them to sentient beings on earth. (RV 7.6.7.)
- Agni Vaisvanara is adamantine, the creator of Thought, and the slayer of demons. (RV 7.13.1.)
- The Collective gods created Agni Vaisvanara as Pure Intuition (ketu) for the sake and enjoyment of all sentient beings in the material world. (RV 10.88.12.)
- Agni Vaisvanara gives power to the constellations (Nakshastras) to move in their paths. (RV 10.88.13.)

Agni Vasivanara is also the Presiding Deity in several Suktas. These Suktas tell us much about Agni Vaisvanara. Reading these Suktas is the best way to learn about the properties and powers of Agni Vasivanara. One such Sukta is found in the Third Mandala. This is what Sukta 3.3 of the Third Mandala says of Agni Vaisvanara:

- RV 3.3.1: Agni Vaisvanara, through the sponsorship of the Sacrificial Fire of Agni, establishes the paths of all material and subtle objects in the Vedic dharma through its luminous powers.
- RV 3.3.2: Agni Vaisvanara, though the Fire of Divine Will of Agni Messenger, travels up and down heaven and earth, aiding the Fire of Divine Will of Agni with the thoughts of the worshiper. A word of explanation is required as to Agni Vaisvanara's capacity of "traveling" up and down Heaven and Earth. As with Agni the Messenger, whose ability is to summon, unify, the other Vedic forces and energies to the sacrifice, Agni Vaisvanara travels up and down Heaven and Earth in an effort in unifying both opposing existential planes. In other contexts Agni Vaisvanara travels up and down to deliver lessons or messages from each to the other level. Principally, the traveling of Agni Vaisvanara performs a service to the worshiper by delivering the worshiper's thoughts and concerns to the greater Vedic dharma. From time to time among

the rcs (mantras) concerning Agni Vaisvanara these meanings will alternate and change to the context intended.

- RV 3.3.3: Agni Vaisvanara, again working in concert with the Sacrificial Fire of Agni, bestows on the worshiper the knowledge and harmony required for the spiritual journey. RV 3.3.4: Agni Vaisvanara, as well as the Fire of Divine Will of Agni, are manifestations of Knowledge to the worshiper.

- RV 3.3.5: Agni Vaisvanara and the Sacrificial Fire of Agni were "born in the Waters." This is code for the inner essence of Agni. "Born in the Waters" means Agni, Agni Vaisvanara and the Sacrificial Fire of Agni share and consist of the inner essence of the Vedic dharma which is Water.

- RV 3.3.6: The sacrificial fire is constructed through the thoughts of the worshiper so that Agni Vasivanara and the Fire of Divine Will of Agni may move up and down Heaven and Earth.

- RV 3.3.7: Agni Vaisvanara through the sacrificial altar nourish the impulsions triggering the thought waves of the worshiper. The terminology and application of "Impulsion" is a term of art as used in the Veda. Impulsion it supplies the very impetus for consciousness, Mind, thoughts, indeed, all forms of mental activity.

- According to the Vedas, the subtle energies which kick-start the living force of the worshiper is called, isas, translated as "impulse" or "impulsion." Not to be confused with a related topic, "life Force," more commonly known as "breath" or "prana," with isas as the ignition starts a motor vehicle, so the impulse provides those energies required to run the many other physiological functions of the worshiper. So without the impulse, prana, breath and the other bodily functions of the worshiper would be impossible, or, so to speak, stuck in neutral. The bodily function focused in the Vedas concern Consciousness and mental activity. This is an important function of Agni Vaisvanara.

- RV 3.3.8: Agni Vaisvanara is the driver of the Worshiper's thoughts. We knew this already, however, because this was essentially stated in the previous rc. This rc (mantra) also says that Agni Vaisvanara

is the agent which awakens the consciousness of the worshiper
during the spiritual journey.

- RV 3.3.9: Agni Vaisvanara, with the Fire of Divine Will of Agni,
  completely purifies the worshiper.
- RV 3.3.10: Agni Vaisvanara, in the form of the Fire Altar, is the
  Knower of the Sunworld (Svar) and with that knowledge fills the
  Heaven and Earth.
- RV 3.3.11: The Fire of Divine Will of Agni detached itself from
  Agni Vaisvanara to accomplish its functions, leaving Agni
  Vaisvanara to be the seed of Heaven and Earth.

There are other Suktas in which Agni Vaisvanara is the Presiding
Deity. Another such Sukta is located in RV 4.5.1 – 15. This Sukta is
presented as a dialogue between the worshiper and Agni Vaisvanara and
unlocks the secrets the worshiper will use during the spiritual journey.

- RV 4.5.1: This rc (mantra) begins by asking, rhetorically, how the
  worshiper should serve Agni Vaisvanara.
- RV 4.5.2: This rc (mantra) cautions the worshiper from "blaming"
  Agni Vaisvanara. This rc (mantra) is the Vedic answer to the age-
  old question: How can a good God permit a world where Evil
  exists? This rc (mantra) replies that Agni Vaisvanara is divine,
  immortal, and has given the gift of life to the worshiper. Now,
  that life may include the good with the bad, it includes the bad
  simply because God created Everything, which includes the bad,
  Evil. This capability is part of the inherent power (svadha) of Agni
  Vaisvanara.
- RV 4.5.3: Agni Vaisvanara, in conjunction with the larger
  Mystic Fire of Agni, has a "two-fold" force, implicating the Two-
  Dimensional Universe. This is the world of the material universe
  in which the worshiper lives. It is augmented, this rc (mantra) says,
  by the Bull, the Regenerative Principle, who spreads its seed to
  rejuvenate the world. In this way, the material world continues to
  exist and renew itself. It is in this world that this rc (mantra) says
  the worshiper strives to discover the "ray-cows," another exercise
  in symbolic speech, representative of Knowledge. The worshiper

thereby is in a quest for knowledge in the spiritual search that necessarily must play out in this material universe. Agni Vaisvanara makes the successful completion of this search possible.

- RV 4.5.4: Agni Vaisvanara revels in this service to the worshiper. Again in conjunction with the Mystic Fire of Agni, Agni Vaisvanara destroys, through the effulgence of his brilliant illumination, the enemies of the Vedic dharma and fellowship.

- RV 4.5.6: We just saw that fire can be used as an agent of destruction. In this rc (mantra) it is used as a means of purification. The Fire of Agni Vaisvanara when it appears in the Fire Altar is a purifying fire by placing the worshiper within its seven layers. Is this an implication of the Seven Dimension Universe? It is a reference to the Fire Altar which consists of seven layers (SPB 8.5.3.5, 6), itself representative of the Seven-Dimension Universe.

- RV 4.5.7: Through the Fire Altar and Agni Vaisvanara the thoughts and aspirations of the worshiper are raised upward to the Vedic forces and energies.

- RV 4.5.8: In this rc (mantra) the worshiper wonders what hidden Word is in the cave and asks Agni Vaisvanara to protect the worshiper's soul.

- RV 4.5.9: Agni Vaisvanara by virtue of its flaming light discovered the hidden truth which was located in the cave. It is likely belaboring the symbolism to interpret this "cave" as the unconscious as some have done. A more likely explanation comes from Plato and the Allegory of the Cave. According to this Allegory, Plato has Socrates describe a group of people who have lived chained to the wall of a cave all of their lives, facing a blank wall. The people watch shadows projected on the wall from objects passing in front of a fire behind them and give names to these shadows. The shadows are the prisoners' reality. Socrates explains how the philosopher is like a prisoner who is freed from the cave and comes to understand that the shadows on the wall are not reality at all, for he can perceive the true form of reality rather than the manufactured reality that is the shadows seen by the prisoners. The inmates of this place do not even desire to leave their prison, for they know no better life. The prisoners manage to break their bonds one day and discover that their reality was not what they thought it was. They discovered the sun, which Plato used as an analogy for the fire that man cannot see behind. Like the fire that cast light on the walls of the cave, the human condition is forever bound to the impressions that are received through the senses. As applied to this rc (mantra), the Rishiis are attempting to say that Agni Vaisvanara discovers for the worshiper the secret hidden in the cave, the true nature of the Vedic dharma.

- RV 4.5.10: In this rc (mantra) Agni Vaisvanara discovers another truth for the worshiper for use in the spiritual journey: The true nature of Knowledge (symbolized as the Cows) and the nature of the transmigration (or regeneration) of the Soul (symbolized by the Bull.)

- RV 4.5.11: Armed with these spiritual endowments, thanks to Agni Vaisvanara, the worshiper can now know and articulate the truth.

- RV 4.5.12: The worshiper, says this rc, does not know the nature of the Truth, but this nature is known and revealed by Agni Vaisvanara.

- RV 4.5.13: The worshiper, says this rc (mantra), wonders what the boundaries of the true knowledge are. The worshiper wonders what it feels like to feel the bliss in bathing in this true knowledge.

- RV 4.5.14: The worshiper, says this rc (mantra), wonders what will become of those unenlightened by this true knowledge or, in what is the functional equivalent, the experience of the Fire Altar. The worshiper ultimately dismisses those who do not know the true knowledge.

- RV 4.5.25: The Sukta concludes with the worshiper in amazement of the Principle of Regeneration and Transmigration, the Bull.

Three are located in the Sixth Mandala. One such Sukta is 6.7.1-7:

- RV 6.7.1.: Agni Vaisvanara is Lord of Heaven and travels up and down Heaven and Earth to bring to the worshiper the inner essence of the Vedic dharma.

- RV 6.7.2: The sum total of all the Vedic forces and energies congregate in Agni Vaisvanara. Agni Vaisvanara is the central link to the conduct of the sacrifice.
- RV 6.7.3: The Fire Altar gives birth to the Rishiis and Horses. "Horse" is another code word. There is an esoteric meaning to horses in the Veda. Horses in the Veda has the metaphorical meaning of the "senses," sight, touch, hear, smell, and feel. Horses represent the senses, the mind's perception of the senses, in all their unbridled glory. Unyoked, the Horses represent the Monkey Mind, distracted, unfocused, confused, going from one thought to another. There is yet another level to this esoteric meaning. When the worshiper perceives the surrounding world, that sense data creates a mental impression on the worshiper's mind. This mental impression is the vrttis about which Patanjali in his Yoga Sutras makes the goal in yoga. Just as once a thumb is lifted from a clump of dough, these mental impressions remain long after the worshiper undergoes any kind of mental activity — perceiving the sensible world, feeling happy, sad, joyous, depressed, the memories, hearing a tune in your head that you heard earlier in the day and which you liked. All these mental events are impressions lodged in the consciousness. When you stop to think of the dynamics involved here, it all makes perfect sense. The object of yoga is not to eliminate the vrttis, the worshiper would be brain-dead if the mental impressions were eliminated. The goal is to manage the vrttis, control them in such way that they are not an impediment to the spiritual or mental growth of the worshiper. The passage from the Katha Upanishads emphasizes the consequences of and need to yoke — i.e., restrain, control — the senses and vrttis, metaphorically represented by horses, to achieve liberation and salvation. "Yoked horses" thus becomes a metaphor for the yogic practice of pratyahara, the restraint and withdrawal of senses and the organs of sense perception which create the mental impressions in the worshiper's mind.
- RV 6.7.4: The sum total of all the Vedic forces and energies congregated in him at the birth of Agni Vaisvanara.

- RV 6.7.5: At its birth Agni Vaisvanara, with the Fire Altar, discovered the regulation of days.
- RV 6.7.6: The vast expanse of the Heavens emits from the eye of Agni Vaisvanara. The remainder of this rc (mantra) describes the vastness of Agni Vaisvanara. All the plains of Existence stand on the head of Agni Vaisvanara, and the seven rivers branch outward. These words refer to the structure of the Vedic dharma. The cardinal numbers in the Vedic universe are two, three, five and seven. The cardinal numbers pertain to ever-greater levels of subtly: As the numbers progress to higher levels, so does physical matter become ever subtle and so intensify the worshiper's journey to liberation. These numbers are coordinates which are incorporated into the structure of the universe. The Seven-Dimensional Universe, the reference in this rc, is that existential level which transcends the material world.
- RV 6.7.7: This rc (mantra) describes further the influence of Agni Vaisvanara on Existence. Agni Vaisvanara establishes form in the Mid-World. Agni Vaisvanara shapes the luminous plane of Heaven. He is the guardian of immortality.

Another is the next Sukta, at RV 6.8.1-7.

- RV 6.8.1: Agni Vaisvanara, with Agni the Transcendental Fire, fills the world with its brilliance and might. Agni Vaisvanara is the Knower of all things and represents Knowledge itself.
- RV 6.8.2: Agni Vaisvanara is the guardian of religious austerities and practices. Agni Vaisvanara sees that the mechanical laws of motion are not disturbed. Agni Vaisvanara gives shape to the mid-world and informs the workings of Heaven.
- RV 6.8.3: Agni Vaisvanara supports the Earth. Agni Vaisvanara casts away the darkness with its luminous light.
- RV 6.8.4: Agni Vaisvanara sprang from the lap of the waters. Agni Vaisvanara arrived from the existential plain beyond the material universe. Agni Vaisvanara is the Messenger from Heaven. In these actions Agni Vaisvanara acts as the Sacrificial Fire of Agni.

- RV 6.8.5: Agni Vaisvanara makes available to the worshiper the spiritual endowment of the Word, the principle of Articulation.
- RV 6.8.6: Agni Vaisvanara as the Fire Altar guards in order to be available for the worshiper the other spiritual endowments.
- RV 6.8.7: Agni Vaisvanara is the guardian and impeller of the "triple session." The meaning in this rc (mantra) is the three sacrifices, morning, afternoon and evening.

The next Sukta, RV 6.9.1-7, moves to a more esoteric stage with astronomical and mystical connotations.

- RV 6.9.1: The rc (mantra) states that one half of the day is dark and one half is brilliantly bright and concludes conventionally that Agni Vasivanara drives out the darkness. The meaning may be as straightforward as meaning that Agni Vaisvanara ushers the daylight by bringing in the dawn. Or that a more complex phenomenon is intended. The rcs (mantras) may refer to something more catastrophic, such as an eclipse or dust storm or similar event which covers the daylight. Thus, the rcs (mantras) could be a reference to the cataclysmic atmospheric phenomenon which engendered the birth of Vrtra, the "enveloper," that Vedic force which covers and obscures and obfuscates. Given the Veda's love of veiled, layered meaning, either one or all possibilities are likely.
- RV 6.9.2: Similar to the wonder expressed in RV 10.129, This rc (mantra) expresses the Rishii's befuddlement and nonfamiliarity with the "web" that is woven "in the field of motion." This rc (mantra) deals with the Vedic Field. The Vedic Field is what the Vedic scripture frequently speak of as the "directions," but more precisely known as disha. In the Vedic dharma disha has a specialized meaning and does not simply mean terrestrial direction but the substance which weaves the fabric of the material universe. As recently explained by Sindhu S. Dange, *Vedic Beliefs and Practices* (2005), pp 85, et seq.), the *disha* are not simply the spatial and directional distribution of matter but possess a mystical meaning and significance. The *disha* are of divine origin. (SPB 6.1.2.4.) The East is the direction of the Gods (SB 3.1.26.) and

is associated with Vedic forces of Agni (KB, 7.6, SPB 1.4.1.10-14, 6.3.3.2, 6.8.1.8, 1.7.12, 8.3.18, 9.3.1.3, 1.2.5.17, 3.6.4.12), the South is the direction of the fathers (SB 3.1.27, SPB 3.6.4.12, 2.6.1.8, 9, AB 1.7-2.1), and the West is associated with Evil (KB 2.2, TS 5.2.5.3, SPB 3.1.1.7, but See SB 3.1.28, where the Westerly direction is associated with Mankind) and the North is associated with the asterisms (SB 3.1.29) or mankind. (SPB 1.8.3.18, 1.7.1.12, 1.2.5.17, 3.6.1.23.) The disha are the essence of Ethereal Space, the aether — the element of akasha — and spread in all directions from the radiating soul in lines of living energy like subtle strands of woven cloth. Once radiated from the worshiper's soul they recoil to return to the radiating soul. (The Wisdom of the Vedas (1992), pp. 62-65, 131.)

Disha, the web of interconnected beams of energy in the Vedic dharma, is the web the glue of subtle matter which bonds the material universe. The Vedic force of Soma is lord and master of the disha. In the Ninth Mandela Soma is Lord of the Quarters, *dishaam pata.* (RV 9.113.2.) Soma is the King of the North. (AB 1.18-22, BSS 5.5.6.12.)

Direction	Presiding Deity
East	Gods, Agni
South	Ptrs (fathers)
West	Evil (Humans)
North	Asterisms (Humans)

- RV 6.9.3: While Soma is the Lord of disha, Agni Vaisvanara "knows" this network, the Vedic Field, which is web of subtle matter binding the material universe. This word "know" needs to be defined. Through its exercise of intense contemplation and meditation, between the lines this rc (mantra) establishes that Agni Vaisvanara created and installed this systems of subtle webbing that is the Vedic Field.
- RV 6.9.4: Agni Vaisvanara is the divine spark which exists in the worshiper and all sentient beings.

- RV 6.9.5: Agni Vaisvanara is the inner light of responsible for spark of consciousness in the worshiper and all sentient beings.
- RV 6.9.6: While the eyes see, the ears hear, and so forth, Agni Vaisvanara is located at the heart which is the center of consciousness. In the Vedic dharma, the Heart is something more than the physical organ. This is shown in expressions such as taking something "to heart," which signifies serious considerations of an issue, or knowing something "by heart," which signifies knowing something so well that it is engrained into the mind of the sentient being. The Heart, then, is the repository which warehouses the thoughts, desires, emotions and all other mental activity of the worshiper. Agni Vaisvanara is the source of the heat and energy required to have the heart function. The worshiper achieves final liberation when that bucket of impulses is discarded. When Heart discards and destroys those material desires the worshiper achieves immortality (BU, 4.4.7), literally liberated from the burden of carrying this bucket of sensations. This rc (mantra) clarifies, however, that what remains when all that is said done is the presence of Agni Vaisvanara, wherein the Heart resides.
- RV 6.9.7: So awesome and far-reaching are the powers of Agni Vaisvanara that even the Vedic forces and energies are subordinate before it at the Fire Altar.

There is Sukta 7.5.1 – 9. This Sukta gives a broad overview of the characteristics of Agni Vaisvanara.

- RV 7.5.1: Agni Vasivanara represents the collective Vedic forces and energies in the Vedic dharma. That power is Increased in the worshiper when the worshiper awakens, becomes enlightened, at least in its beginning stages. There are stages to the worshiper's liberation and salvation. The Awakening is the first step in the elevation of consciousness during the worshiper's journey towards salvation and liberation. From the Awakening, or Enlightenment, the worshiper acquires Knowledge. From Knowledge, he worshiper gains Consciousness. From Consciousness, the worshiper has the capacity to be engaged in Contemplation or Deliberation. From the act of Contemplation or Deliberation the worshiper gains Insightful Knowledge. From Insightful Knowledge, the worshiper obtains Discernment. From Discernment, the worshiper obtains Divine Vision. From there, Rapture, the worshiper gets a taste of Liberation. Agni Vasivanara is the guiding force in the Increase experienced by the worshiper in this spiritual journey.

- RV 7.5.2: This rc (mantra) describes the interaction of Agni Vaisvanara and the Fire Altar. He is described as the Lord of the Rivers and the Lord of the Bulls. This is, of course, symbolic speech for broader concepts. To be Lord of the Rivers is to be Lord of the stream of consciousness. This does not refer to the literary art form, but symbolic for the flow of consciousness in the mind of the worshiper. The Bull is symbolic to the Principle of Regeneration, that process that guarantees the continuation of life. That is Agni Vaisvanara.

- RV 7.5.3: This rc (mantra) emphasizes how Agni Vaisvanara drove out the "Black Tribe," and cast light upon the worshiper. This is another example of the quasi-historical connotations applied to a metaphysical context.

- RV 7.5.4: The three existential levels of heaven, mid-world, and earth depend on the support of Agni Vaisvanara. That support comes from the light of Agni Vaisvanara which spread over heaven and earth.

- RV 7.5.5: This rc (mantra) mentions a string of epithets for Agni Vaisvanara. Agni Vaisvanara is the Word. When the worshiper attaches a word to an object in the world, the worshiper's speech relates to the object's inner meaning in its articulation. There is thus a three-step process from Speech, to the Word spoken, to the objects inner meaning. Since it is a manifestation of the mid-world, it is appropriate that Agni Vaisvanara represent the second step in this process. Also, with Agni Vaisvanara's shining horses it is the "charioteer of the treasures." We know treasures as the spiritual endowments from the Vedic dharma. Horses and charioteers both refer, respectively, to the sense perceptions and the Universal Self. (Kat. Up., 3.3 – 10.) As in the previous rc, the Fire Altar is working in conjunction with Agni Vaisvanara in this context. The message herein then is that with the agency of Agni Vaisvanara, the worshiper receives the blessings of a right discrimination on contemplation of the Fire Altar.

- RV 7.5.6: Another quasi-historical rc. The rcs (mantras) says that Agni Vaisvanara threw the destroyers out of the house so that the light could shine on the Aryans. A metaphysical meaning does not appear to be implicated in this rc. What appears to be implicated is an ancient battle in which the Aryans were victorious over the "destroyers," whoever they were.

- RV 7.5.7: This rc (mantra) has cosmogonic connotations. Here, Agni Vaisvanara was born at the "highest place." The Sanskrit is *parame vyoman*. *Parame vyoman* is a that existential place beyond even Heaven, it is above heaven, above all existential planes. There, Agni Vaisvanara was born as Vayu, the Vedic force of the Vital Force of Life, prana. Agni Vaisvanara thereupon uttered a cry and gave birth to all the worlds. This, says the rc, was Agni Vaisvanara's gift to the Sun. In these few words, the Rishiis restate the creation myth. *Parame vyoman* is a restatement of the indeterminate mass that existed before the beginning of the present Yuga. (RV 10.129.1.) Agni Vaisvanara born as Vayu is a restatement of the One appearing by breathing by its intrinsic power. (RV 10.129.2.) Agni Vaisvanara creating all the worlds is a restatement of the Vedic dharma *(rta)* and existence (Satya) being born of a flaming *Tapas.* (RV 10.190.1)

- RV 7.5.8: Here the worshiper invokes Agni Vaisvanara to receive impulsions. Impulsion supplies the very impetus for consciousness, Mind, thoughts, indeed, all forms of mental activity. According to the Vedas, the subtle energies which kick-start the living force of the worshiper is called, isas, translated as "impulse" or "impulsion." As was explained earlier, isas is not to be confused with a related topic, "life Force," more commonly known as "breath" or "prana," with isas as the ignition starts a motor vehicle, so the impulse provides those energies required to run the many other physiological functions of the worshiper. So without the impulse, prana, breath and the other bodily functions of the worshiper would be impossible, or, so to speak, stuck in neutral. Agni Vaisvanara supplies impulsions to the worshiper.

- RV 7.5.9: With these impulsions Agni Vaisvanara guides the worshiper to inspired knowledge, a later stage towards liberation and salvation.

Agni Vaisvanara is the Presiding Deity governing the Sukta at RV 7.6.1 – 7. Some rcs (mantras) and Suktas are grounded by quasi-historical events, and those events take on metaphysical, philosophical, or religious overtones. Recent historical events have demonstrated that opponents in internal and geo-political rivalries and conflicts are labeled as "unholy" or "evil" or "demonic." We do not have to search far to find examples. We are all too close to recent events to correctly interpret the political merits of "the Enemy" or "the Other," and the historical basis of "the Enemy" or "the Other" in the Rg Veda is lost to ancient history. All that remains are the metaphysical ruminations that had their origin from these conflict with these groups, and for good or ill they remain as personifications of the powers of darkness found in the verses of the Veda. Accordingly, these rcs (mantras) emphasize Agni Vaisvanara as a Destroyer, one of the essential powers of Fire.

- RV 7.6.1: This rc (mantra) proclaims Agni Vaisvanara's admiration for the Vedic force of Indra, whom is called the Almighty, the Ruler of All, and the Destroyer. The rcs (mantras) goes on to place Agni Vaisvanara at the same place and stead as Indra. Agni Vasivanara is an expression of the Vedic forces and energies in the Vedic dharma, who have collectively given him birth.
- RV 7.6.2: This rc (mantra) says that Heaven and Earth sends Agni Vaisvanara as its Messenger. This phraseology signifies that Agni Vaisvanara is the foundation of Heaven and Earth, for which Agni Vaisvanara is a unifying agent. This rc (mantra) makes another interesting statement. Agni Vaisvanara is known as the Destroyer of Cities.
- RV 7.6.3: Agni Vaisvanara drives away and destroys the Panis. Panis were a specific enemy found in the Veda. Quite possibly grounded from historical fact but immortalized in the verses of

the Rg Veda, the Panis were singled out for special condemnation. Historically, the Panis were a tribal group located in Afghanistan, and were thought to be the ancient Parthians. The historical basis for the Panis are indicated by their description. The Panis were described as wealthy traders, (RV 4.25.7), "taking advantage of people" (RV 1.33.3), a "wolf" (RV 6.51.14), only thinking of himself. (RV 6.61.1.) The actual historical origins of the Panis are also indicated when it is said that they were "defeated" and "slaughtered." (RV 1.83.4, 1.184.2, 3.58.2, 5.34.7, 5.61.8, 6.13.3, 6.20.4, 6.33.2, 8.64.11.) As what usually happens when the Victor writes the history of past battles and consistent with what has happened time and time again in human history, the enemy, the Panis, were singularly demonized. This demonization took metaphysical dimensions, so that not only historically were the Panis adversaries in the tribal conflicts with the Aryans, but that they were considered the epitome of what is not considered Aryan. Thus, the Panis bring calamities (RV 6.51.13), a hostile force which covers the truth (RV 6.51.14), the divider, the unblessed, the unholy (RV 6.44.22), and a hostile power. (RV 6.61.3.) In addition to destroying Cities Agni Vaisvanara destroys the Panis.

- RV 7.6.4: Agni Vaisvanara is known as the Lord of Treasure. In this context, treasure takes on a new dimension. Those treasures come about when Agni Vaisvanara destroys the "enemies."

- RV 7.6.5: Agni Vaisvanara destroys the limiting walls. It is tempting to give an expansive reading to the phrase the "limiting walls." It is very possible that "limiting walls" signify the barriers that we all place between ourselves and other people or the divine. And it is very possible that there is a further metaphorical meaning to this phrase. However the context in which this rc (mantra) is recited should be remembered. There is a quasi-historical character to this Sukta, and the same holds true about the meaning of these "limiting walls." This Sukta elaborates on Agni Vaisvanara the Destroyer, and, as we will see in the next rc, as the Victor against historical, ancient tribal groups such as the Panis and others. Thus, when the rcs (mantras) speaks of the "limiting walls," the meaning is more likely the actual, physical walls erected by the Panis in some ancient battle. At the same time, like so many rcs (mantras) in the Vedas, the original meaning, or the meaning giving the metaphorical birth to the words of the rc, may forever lost in the fog of ancient history, leaving only the words of this rc.

- RV 7.6.6: With all the conflict presented by the Panis and other enemies, the worshiper comes to Agni Vaisvanara to find a peaceful place. That place, This rc (mantra) says, is beyond Heaven and Earth, in other words, the Seven-Dimensional Universe beyond all existential levels.

- RV 7.6.7: Agni Vaisvanara is the repository of the spiritual riches of the Vedic dharma. These riches included the spiritual endowments from the upper and lower ocean. Ocean here is symbolic speech for the existential basis of the Vedic dharma. The subtle raw material of these existential levels is communicated to the worshiper as a road map for the spiritual journey.

Another Sukta dealing with Agni Vaisvanara is RV 10.88.1 – 19. Agni Vaisvanara shares this Sukta with Surya. Surya is the Vedic force which represents the energy emanating from the Sun. Surya is called the "invoker." The invoker is called the highest deity according to the Medieval commentator Sayana. Surya is also known as Aditya, *Bhanu* or Ravi Vaisvanara, is the chief solar deity in Hinduism, and generally refers to the Sun. The Rishiis recognized the Sun is the source of life on earth. It's one thing to call Surya the "invoker," but what does that term actually mean? In keeping with its capacity as an astronomical body, Surya (Energy) has the following qualities as the "invoker": Surya measures the days. (RV 1.50.7.) Surya prolongs the days of life (RV 8.48.7), drives away sickness, disease and other evils, (RV 10.37.4), is the Visvakarmen, the Creator of all, (RV 10.170.4), the source of all actions (RV 10.170.4), and establishes movement in all things. (RV 1.50.10, 1.115.1, 10.37.10.) Surya is described as the "soul of all that moves," which is to say that it provides the inner catalyst that creates all movement, from the tiniest atom to the largest astrological body. (RV 1.115.1.) Thus, Surya "invokes" — is a principal mover — of the material universe.

There is an intimate relationship between the Invoker (Surya) and the first brother (Agni): Surya is the light of the Sun which is converted into the heat of Agni. (RV 10.114.1.) Further, the light of the Sun is Agni. (SPB 2.3.1.30.) So while Surya provides the mechanism of the material universe, the internal Fire of Agni translates that mechanism to a force of energy illuminating that universe. These are necessarily two different processes. Surya provides the raw material, Agni converts that raw material into raw energy. It is a symbiotic relationship, one that contributes to the continued existence of the material level of the Vedic dharma. With astronomical and metaphysical connotations, that relationship between these two is explored in this Sukta.

- RV 10.88.1: Agni Vaisvanara represents the existential regions of heaven and earth and the Svar, the region of the transitory vortex. Agni Vaisvanara drinks Soma and in the process knows the Svar and touches Heaven. By consuming Soma the heavens are unified and solidified. The Svar is an intricate, confusing, sometimes contradictory, area of the Vedic dharma cosmology. What follows is a description of this cosmology, aided by charts on the following page. The Seven-Dimensional Universe is a combination of the three upper and three lower levels of existence, conjoined together by the Svar. There are three levels of sensible appearance, the earth, mid-world, and heaven. (RV 1.34.7, 1.154.4.) There are also two levels of existence, the upper and the lower, Heaven and Earth. There are three levels of heaven, *dyaus*. (RV 1.35.6, AV 8.9.16.) The three divisions of heaven are: *uttama(m)* (RV 1.24.15, 1.25.21, 1.50.10, 1.91.8, 1.108.9, 1.156.4, 1.163.7, 2.1.2) or *uttame* (RV 1.31.7, 2.41.5, 5.60.4, 6.60.3, 8, 8.51.4, 9.61.29), *madhyama* (RV 1.24.15,1.25.21,1.108.9,10, 2.29.4, 4.25.8, 6.21.5, 6.62.11, 7.32.16, 8.61.15,9.70.4, 9.108.9, 10.15.1, 10.81.5, 10.97.12) or *madhyame* (RV 1.27.5, 2.23.13, 5.60.6, 6.25.1), and *avama* or *avame*. (RV1.105.4, 1.108.9, 10, 1.163.5, 2.35.2, 3.54.5, 6.251, 6.62.11, 7.71.3, 1.185.11 (avame).) In the middle, the svar, is an intermediate, transitory, world of heaven and light. (RV 1.35.6.) The two levels of existence, the upper and the lower, heaven and earth, are bound together by the Svar. The edifice consists of triads: The Upper Heaven, the Lower Heaven, and the Svar that lies in between. The Svar serves as a vortex between these two worlds, and Agni Vaisvanara is their unifying agent. In this way, Agni Vaisvanara represents the existential regions of heaven and earth and the Svar, the region of the transitory vortex. Agni Vaisvanara accomplishes this as a manifestation of the Fire of Self-Surrender.

- RV 10.88.2: Also as a manifestation of the Fire of Self-Surrender Agni Vaisvanara cast away the darkness which engulfed the entire world. It is very likely This rc (mantra) may be read that Agni Vaisvanara casts away the astronomical phenomenon of eclipses. It is not uncommon for the Vedic forces and energies to have the power to allow the Sun to appear in the course of eclipses. The Vedic force of Indra also has the power to cast away eclipses. (RV 5.90.1, 3.) Here, Agni Vaisvanara casts away eclipses, metaphorically and metaphysically simply "darkness," with the light of the Svar, the very epitome of the region of Light. As a result of this casting away, Vedic forces and energies, the worshiper, the entire Vedic dharma, benefits.

- RV 10.88.3: In this rc (mantra) Agni Vaisvanara is an expression of the Sacrificial Fire. Here, Agni Vaisvanara is called "ageless," in other words, eternal, created in the primeval beginning of the present cycle. The unifying influence of Agni Vaisvanara spreads to the two worlds, Heaven and Earth.

- RV 10.88.4: As an expression of the Fire of Divine Will, Agni Vaisvanara created the world in a blink of an eye. Could this be another astronomical or cosmogonic reference? Modern Cosmology indicates that the Big Bang which created the universe happened in an instant. Similarly, this rc (mantra) appears to say the same.

- RV 10.88.5: This rc (mantra) speaks of Agni Jatavedas. Is this a misplaced mention? Hardly. Both Agni Jatadevas (RV 3.3.8) and Agni Vaisvanara are the "Knowers of All Things."

- RV 10.88.6: Returning to Cosmogony, this rc (mantra) says that Agni Vaisvanara as an expression of the Fire of Creation is the first principle that created Surya (the Sun) and caused its movement in the sky (mid-world). We have known for centuries, of course, that the Sun does not "move," at least not in our Solar System. The Sun, however, does move, relative to its position in our galaxy and as against the greater universe beyond our own galaxy. The Rishiis reveal that the scope of Agni Vaisvanara is not limited to our own, rather insignificant and ordinary, Solar System, but to the greater cosmos beyond, which is all part of the Vedic dharma. This is the import of this rc. This is, as the rcs (mantras) states, "the wisdom of the gods."

• RV 10.88.7: This is a series of epithets of Agni Vaisvanara. He represents the collective dynamism of the Vedic forces. In This rc (mantra) Agni Vaisvanara is an expression of the Fire of Self-Surrender. When Agni Vaisvanara is kindled, he shines in the very center of heaven. When Agni Vaisvanara shines he becomes visible to all the world. "Kindled" carries a special meaning. Physical fire is "ignited," but the Sacrificial Fire is "kindled." Kindling imparts all those qualities and energies from the universe and channeled those qualities and energies into the Fire and later to the worshiper. Those Vedic forces thereupon create and protect the chants and offerings at the sacrificial ritual.

• RV 10.88.8: A continuation from the previous rc (mantra). The Vedic forces initially created the sacrificial ritualistic chants, and then they created Agni Vaisvanara, and then they created the offerings presented at the sacrifice. In this rc (mantra) Agni Vaisvanara is an expression of the Sacrificial Fire. There is an odd dynamic happening in these rcs: Agni Vaisvanara is the collective Vedic forces themselves, those forces create the sacrificial chants, then the collective forces created Agni Vaisvanara, and afterwards the offerings of the sacrifice, Agni Vaisvanara then becomes the sacrifice. In a good example of the Veda's love of paradox. The Rishiis purport to say that there is a self-referential identification between the Vedic forces and energies, Sacrifice, and Agni Vaisvanara. An identification primarily between the collective Vedic forces and energies and Agni Vaisvanara. Those forces and energies are funneled into Agni Vaisvanara, who in its powers and functions relate back to the collective Vedic forces and energies. Sacrifice, the yajna, is a by-product of this self-referential union.

• RV 10.88.9: Another continuation from the previous rc (mantra). In this rc (mantra) Agni Vaisvanara is an expression of the

Sacrificial Fire. That rc (mantra) reveals Agni Vaisvanara, the Protector, becomes the Sacrificial subject itself. The Rishiis restate what had been revealed previously. In this rc, they reveal that when the collective Vedic forces created the world, they offered Agni Vaisvanara as the ultimate sacrifice to the world. In effect, the Rishiis purport to demonstrate another example of the give-and-take process displayed at the sacrifice. Here, it is Agni Vaisvanara which is the offering, which is given to the Sacrifice.

- RV 10.88.10: In this rc (mantra) Agni Vaisvanara is an expression of the Sacrificial Fire. The Rishiis restate that the collective Vedic forces and energies created Agni Vaisvanara through their stoma hymns. Stoma is a hymn of praise. Coincidentally, "stoma," στομα, is the Ancient and Modern Greek word for "mouth," out of which these chants are sung and all other verbal communication effected. Having created Agni Vaisvanara, this manifestation of Agni fills the Vedic dharma with its presence. The collective Vedic forces and energies fashion Agni Vaisvanara to have a three-fold nature. This implicates the existential level of the Three-Dimensional Universe and is a reference to the larger Vedic dharma of Heaven, Mid-World and Earth.

- RV 10.88.11: In creating Agni Vaisvanara, the collective Vedic forces and energies placed Agni Vaisvanara in heaven, the highest existential level, along with Surya. Surya is identified as a member of the Adityas. There are twelve Adityas. Academically, the Adityas are known as the "atmospheric gods." In the Vedic dharma, they are the twelve houses of the zodiac. This latter definition is consistent with what the Rishis reveal. Having placed Agni Vaisvanara and Surya in heaven with the other Adityas, the world is under their influence. More on this when the Vedic astrologer is discussed in a future installment of this series, The Secret History of the Vedas.

- RV 10.88.12: In this rc (mantra) Agni Vaisvanara is an expression of the Sacrificial Fire. The collective Vedic forces and energies created Agni Vasivanara as the light of consciousness and intuition that he may thereby illumine the world. With this light Agni Vaisvanara scatters the darkness and ushers the dawn. "Dawn" can be taken to mean both daybreak and the beginnings of enlightenment.

- RV 10.88.13: A rc (mantra) with astronomical connotations. As the masters of the Sacrifice, the collective Vedic forces and energies created Agni Vaisvanara to rule over the Nakshastras, the Constellations, so that the Constellations may supervise the collective Vedic forces.

- RV 10.88.14: In this rc (mantra) Agni Vaisvanara is an expression of the Sacrificial Fire. Agni Vaisvanara pervades over the Vedic dharma by his light and serves as an umbrella for all and everything under him

- RV 10.88.15: This rc (mantra) states a theme stated from time to time in early Vedic scripture. There are two paths that the soul of the worshiper can take upon death: The soul of the worshiper and each person in the universe, in whichever path is taken, meets its karmic result. This has been repeated several times, both in the Veda and in the other scripture. There is the path of the gods, Devayana (RV 1.183.6, 1.184.6, 3.58.5, 6, 4.37.1, 5.43.6, 7.38.5, YV 19.47, SPB 12.8.1.21, NB 12.525, BU 6.2.2), and there is the path of the ancestors, ptryana. (3.12.7, 3.35.6, 7.7.2, 10.14.2, YV 19.47, SPB 12.8.1.21, NB 12.525, BU 6.2.2.) This is a binary system, implicating the Two-Dimensional Universe. In the Two-Dimensional Universe, the world is divided into two halves, with one side on the left side, the other on the right side. There are astronomical and astrological connotations in this binary system, better left to a future installment. It is here that the seeds of the transmigration of souls originated. For the intents of the Veda the path of the gods is to heaven, and the path of the ancestors is the ptryana.

- RV 10.88.16: The two paths, *devayana*, the path of the gods, and the path of the fathers, *ptryana*, are united into one by Agni Vaisvanara. The Northern and Southern Paths play a crucial role in the Vedic path to salvation and liberation. The Northern and Southern Paths are intricately tied to the most important aspects of the worshiper's spiritual journey. In fact, it concerns the greatest of all issues, whether concerning the Vedic astrologer, the worshiper, or any other person's life — the destination of soul after death. There are only two places the soul may travel upon — the Northern Path or the Southern Path. at death the worshiper's soul will encounter a fork in the road in the path towards Vedic salvation. At that juncture, the departing soul of the worshiper will take one of two paths. (SPB 1.9.3.2.) One direction leads to the path of the gods, devayana (RV 1.183.6; 1.184.6; 3.58.5, 6; 4.37.1; 5.43.6; 7.38.5; YV 19.47; SPB 12.8.1.21; NB 12.525), and the other the path of the forefathers, pathi a/nu. (RV 10.88.16; 3.12.7; 3.35.6; 7.7.2; 10.14.2; YV 19.47; SPB 12.8.1.21; NB 12.525.) The Northern Path belongs to the gods and is the path leading to the liberation of the soul. In the worshiper's ultimate spiritual journey, Agni, the Sun, the Fire of Change, aligned with the Sun, the dispenser of the inner secret of yajna and divine response through the asterism of Krittika and the zodiacal houses of Mesa (Aries) and Vrsabha (Taurus), presides over the Path of the gods (*devyama*), Northern Path, with the worshiper's liberation of the Soul.

- RV 10.88.17: The upper (heaven) and lower (earth) powers contribute to the Sacrifice.
- RV 10.88.18: The Rishiis issue the rhetorical questions: How many Agnis are there? How many Suns? How many dawns? How many waters?
- RV 10.88.19: As long as Agni shines the Dawn will appear and there will be a Sacrifice.

Coda

Agni Vaisvanara is a tremendous Vedic force and pervades the Vedic dharma. What can be said about its powers?

- Agni Vaisvanara is the personification of Light.
- Agni Vaisvanara is the inner light of responsible for spark of consciousness in the worshiper and all sentient beings.
- Being in the nature of Light, Agni Vaisvanara scatters and casts away the Darkness.
- In portions, Agni Vaisvanara is an expression of the Sacrificial Fire.

- In portions, an expression of the Fire of Divine Will.
- In portions, Agni Vaisvanara is an expression of the Mystic Fire.
- In other portions, Agni Vaisvanara is an expression of the Fire of Self-Surrender.
- In other portions, Agni Vaisvanara as an expression of the Fire of Creation.
- Agni Vaisvanara is the first principle that created Surya (the Sun).
- The collective Vedic forces created Agni Vaisvanara after initially creating the sacrificial ritualistic chants, then offering Agni Vaisvanara as the sacrifice
- Agni Vaisvanara is the collective Vedic forces themselves.
- Agni Vaisvanara is the unifying agent, the bridge, between Heaven and Earth.
- Agni Vaisvanara is the Creator and Destroyer.
- Agni Vaisvanara creates the world in an instant.
- Agni Vaisvanara is the destroyer of Evil.

In many respects, Agni Vaisvanara is the personification of the many fires of Agni, indeed, with the Vedic dharma.

FIRES OF THE
FIRMAMENT

This part describes the fires of the firmament, the mid-world. Taken literally, these fires connect the worshiper with Heavenly Fires. In the material world they are the atmospheric fires covering the atmospheric the sensible world of perceptions. They are the fires which enlighten the stellar population that appears at night. Thus, in the Upper Heaven, the Upper Ocean, the AtharvaVeda calls these fires the "Starry Heaven." In the Rg Veda it is madhyama. Madhyama in the context of Soma is that feeling of unimaginable Bliss and Joy. That Bliss and Joy is lit with the Fires of the Firmament.

The word "firmament" isn't commonly used much anymore. The word appears many times in Shakespeare's plays, which may give you an idea of the antiquity of the word. Modern Physicists use the word, but only sparingly. Just about the only people who use the word are philosophers, occultists, cosmologists, and commentators of the Vedas. It is, however, a significant word in the Vedic dharma.

The ancients understood they lived on the earth, and that the air they breathed clearly belonged to the sky hovering above the earth. They clearly understood the difference between the profane and the divine and therefore knew that the gods or God could not simply live in the sky. If God lived anywhere, it was somewhere beyond the simple sky they saw every day. Thus was born the firmament.

This was the cosmological layout for many, if not all, cultures in the ancient world. There was a Vedic gloss on this system. We have seen that water or the Waters is a frequent feature in the history of the Vedic force of Agni. There is a reason for this role. In the Vedic dharma, Water is material cause of the universe. Water is the root (i.e., the cause) and the shoot sprouted (the result) therefrom. (AA, 8.1.) Water is the agent for creation and generation. (SPB 3.7.4.4.) Creation is ritualistically represented through sprinkling. The creative powers of water are testified in the various stages of Vedic creation. Water is everywhere, not only as a physical presence but as the subtle basis of matter. The character of the indeterminate, unmanifested mass of neither existence nor non-existence, before the very creation of the Natural Order, *Rta,* the Vedic dharma, was fluid, indeed, it was, water. (RV 10.129.1.) This accounts for the seemingly infinite references, similes, metaphors, renderings, or symbols regarding everything consisting of water: rivers, lakes, oceans, ponds, creeks, you name it. The references to the Waters are reflected in the cosmology:

In the Vedic dharma the sky is the Firmament, otherwise known as Sky or the Mid-Earth. It is the Mid-Earth, because the Firmament is sandwiched between the Waters Above and the Waters below. A more precise definition of these two terms is subject to interpretation. Sri Aurobindo interpreted this cosmology as The Waters Above meaning the Super-Consciousness or Universal Self, the Atman, and the Waters Below as the Unconscious. For our purposes in knowing the Fires of the Vedic dharma, the Waters Above signifies the Celestial Fire. We just finished with that. The Waters Below are the Terrestrial Fire. This will be discussed after the fire we are going to examine now, the Fires of the Firmament.

Saunaka identifies three manifestations, Vedic forces and energies, which are located in and preside over the firmament:

- The Maruts. (BD, 1.103.)
- Agni Jatavedas. (BD, 1.67.)
- Rudra. (BD, 1.103.)

The Fire of the Firmament shines by discharging rain. (BD, 1.93.) This has as much to do with the atmospheric constitution of the firmament as much as it is to the symbolic purchase of rain. The Veda says, "The Fire Enlivens the Heaven." (RV 1.164.51.) The process of enlivening the earth is a reference to the Five Fires doctrine. The Five Fires is the Vedic precursor to the Hindu concept of reincarnation and transmigration of souls. The Five Fires describe the transmigrational journey as the soul travels from one body to another.

Like smoke wafting upwards, when a person departs from this world, the soul travels upwards in the air. (BU 6.2.15.) In his commentary of this stanza of the Upanishad, Sankara states that this destination is the Hiranyagarbha, the cosmic egg or germ.

Whether the concept of reincarnation was recognized in the Vedic world is a topic of scholarly debate. If this mantra does not settle that debate in favor of recognizing reincarnation, it certainly provides its ideological basis. The cycle of fire can be repeated over and over forever. This entire process is characterized by Fire, but not just the physical fire. Fire is the

230

process of the changes from the Heavenly Fire, to the Fire of Prajanya, to the Vegetative Fire, then to Digestive Fire, and finally to the Female Fire. Fire, Agni, is the medium of Change and Transformation from one stage to another. To any stage. This fire becomes the basis for any change and transformation, not simply the recycler of souls. This is the essence of dharma, the natural order *(rta)*.

Some people do not understand this process and do not understand that everything is subject to change and transformation. Heraclitus certainly understood this. So, when a worshiper understands dharma, the natural order *(rta)*, and incorporates that learning into his or her life, the endless cycle of rebirth and transmigration is broken. The worshiper's soul gains immortality and perfection enters the world of the Hiranyagarbha, never to return to the material world again. (BU 6.2.15.)

All manifestations are empowered by the Terrestrial Agni. (BD, 1.103.) Because they are empowered by Agni, they received the spiritual qualities inherent in Agni. One such quality is Bharata. RV 1.64.13 speaks of the Celestial Fire, Bharata, and of the Maruts. The Vedic force and energy of Agni leads the worshiper towards the qualities of Bharata, or spiritual riches, in this case, deep knowledge and understanding. The qualities of Bharata in turn are endowed to the worshiper with the help of the Maruts.

231

THE MARUTS

The Divine Vedic energies of the Maruts originate in Agni. Even though they are known to be closely associated with the divine force and energy of Indra, the Maruts are essentially aligned with and obtain their energy from Vanaspati, the Terrestrial Agni. (BD, 1.103.) The genealogy of the Maruts has something to say about the nature of the Maruts.

- The father of the Maruts is Rudra, another Celestial manifestation of Agni. (RV 1.114.6, 9.)
- The mother of the Maruts is Prsni. (RV 2.34.2; 5.50.5.)

The Veda lists the Maruts' energies. The Maruts are closely aligned to Indra. They are associates of the divine force of Indra. (TB, 1.5.5.6, 8.) The Maruts are divine attributes aligned with the Principle fueling the Vital Dynamics of Knowledge, creating the Speech and Grace (Indra). (BD, 1.127.) The Maruts present a strange presence in the Rg Veda. Seemingly ubiquitous, they appear to be "janitors," called upon whenever special assignments are required. It is tempting to view the Maruts as the Valkyries of the Vedic World. They are described as "fierce" and menacing, they swarm with the Vedic forces and forces as a group, in packs, but their specific qualities belie this threatening facade. They are closely associated with Indra, who summons them frequently in the Vedas. Their qualities are described in Sukta RV 1.19. This Sukta describes the seven qualities of the Maruts. Those qualities are: They are:

- RV 1.19.3:

The Maruts encapsulate the knowledge of how to cause the waters to descend. The descending waters is symbolic speech for the fire of purification. The sprinkling of water is a frequent feature of the Vedic sacrifice. The purification is accomplished through the sprinkling of water. There are numerous references in the Vedas to the purification of the object of sacrifice through the sprinkling of water. (RV 1.34.1, 1.85.1, 2.34.3, 1.114.7, 1.85.2, 2.16.1, 2.21.3, 5.55.3, 9.72.7, YV 1.28, 1.13, 2.5, 2.1, 4.22, 7.11, 8.32, 13.32, 22.19, 25.39.) There are also numerous references of the sprinkling of water in the Brahmanas. (S.P.B. 1.3.3.2, 1.3.3.3, 1.3.10.11, 1.1.3.12, TS 2.6.5.11.) The pouring of water, uksa/nam, also accomplishes the same purifying effect. (RV 1.64.2, 1.135.9, 1.129.10, 1.166.3, 2.2.4, 2.7.5, 2.34.3, 3.7.7, 4.42.4, 4.56.2, 5.27.5, 5.42.14, 5.57.8, 5.59.1, 6.66.4, 7.79.1, 8.55.1, 10.86.13, 10.91.14, 10.92.5, 10.122.4.) Water used in this manner is a feature not only in Vedic sacrifice and ritual, but in religious ceremonies throughout the world.

- RV 1.19.4:
Ferocity (ugra). Ferocity is the most common feature about the Maruts. The Maruts are ferocity incarnate. It is not the garden-variety ferocity, however. The Maruts are fierce and know how to cause the descent of waters (Vigor and purification). Ugra, not only means "ferocity," also connotes heat, passion, intensity, a close relative to *Tapas*, which is intense meditation. Thus, the ferocity addressed in the original Sanskrit is the tremendous heat emanating from the Maruts' intensity, both in mind and in spirit.
- RV 1.19.5: The Maruts are radiant and powerful.
- RV 1.19.6: They live in the heaven above the Sun. Attention should be paid on the precise residence of the Maruts. That they reside in the heaven above the Sun signifies that they are located above the firmament — the Mid-World. That places them squarely in the Seven-Dimension Universe, the most subtle area of the Vedic dharma. There they reside with the other Vedic forces and energies, including that which empowered them — Agni.
- RV 1.19.7: The Maruts moves mountains. In this context, "mountain" should be understood as symbolic of dead, inert

matter. In the Samkhya Karika, when purusha, the universal consciousness, makes contact, "conjoins," with *Prakrti*, primordial, inert, matter, consciousness appears in the world. The moving of mountains, therefore, signifies this conjoining, and, as a consequence, the beginning of Consciousness. Put in the proper symbolic context, this rc (mantra) signifies that the Maruts are responsible in their own way to the establishment of Consciousness in the Vedic dharma.

- RV 1.19.8: The Maruts spread and expand with the rays of an ocean. The "ocean" stated is symbolic speech for a higher consciousness. As their defining characteristic is intensity, the force of their Vedic energy spreads, literally, like rays across the Vedic dharma, spreading the power of their consciousness.
- RV 1.19.9: The Maruts drink Soma.

The Maruts, the Janitors: Helpers of Agni in his Aspect as the Fire of Light

Among the more unrecognized films is Michael Clayton. In this movie George Clooney plays a down and out attorney, once at the top of his game, but now relegated to a "janitor." In the vocabulary of this movie, a "janitor" was a "fixer," someone who was called at specific times to clean up the messes left by other attorneys or from other situations. This job title fits neatly in role the Maruts play in the Vedic dharma, and describe in a very general way what exactly they do. They are the "janitors" of the Vedic dharma, serving primarily the Vedic forces of Agni and Indra.

Earlier it was explained that the Maruts assisted Agni in his aspect as the Fire of Light. Their actions in this regard bear repeating. This capacity is in keeping with the Maruts' essential nature as effulgent, brilliant, adamantine. (RV 1.19.5.) Both reside in Heaven to shine down on the worshiper. (RV 1.19.6.)

- Together the Maruts and Agni in his aspect as the Fire of Light move mountains, cross oceans, and acquire the essence of the Vedic dharma, the Waters. (RV 1.19.7.)

- The Maruts are described as the caretakers of the Fire of Light. (RV 1.19.1.)
- The Maruts work with Agni to sustain his aspect as the Fire of Light. (RV 1.19.2.)
- The Maruts assist Agni in his aspect as the Fire of Light and are the Knowers of the All-Gods, the Visvedevas, the collective forces and energies of the Vedic dharma. (RV 1.19.3.)
- The Maruts and Agni in his aspect as the Fire of Light spread knowledge. (RV 1.19.9.)
- The Maruts and Agni in his aspect as the Fire of Light bathe the worshiper in Light (RV 1.23.23), thereby heaping Increase upon the worshiper. (RV 1.22.10.)

At this point we discuss another manifestation of Agni's powers in Agni Jatadevas.

AGNI JATAVEDAS

Jatavedas means "Knower of All Things." Jatavedas is that manifestation of Change (Agni) presiding the Mid-Earth, the firmament, also known as Agni Vanaspati, "Middle Agni." (BD, 1.67; 1.99.) This manifestation of Agni, Jatavedas, is part of the trinity consisting of three aspects of Agni. Agni Suci presides over the Celestial aspect of Agni, Agni Pavamana presides over the terrestrial sphere (BD, 2.29), and Agni Jatavedas presides over the Firmament. (BD 1.66.) Jatavedas deserves its own separate treatment. Agni, as the Fire of the Mid-World, is Agni Jatavedas. Jatavedas is a prevalent presence in the pervasion of Agni. Jatavedas signifies that manifestation of Agni as the "Knower of all things born." This manifestation of Jatavedas has the following properties:

Jatavedas has these aspects:

- Jatavedas is "The light of consciousness." (RV 3.17.4.)
- Jatavedas also "holds the materials of the sacrifice" together, (TB 1.2.1.22) meaning Jatavedas serves as the guide for the personal changes which are produced by the insights gained through the sacrifice.
- Jatavedas also "controls the hearts of the Maruts," (TB 1.2.1.18) meaning that this manifestation of Agni Vanaspati serves as a conduit to inform and sustain the divine power of Indra.
- Jatavedas is the seed which produces the energy of the world, (TB 1.2.1.40) a major manifestation of the Fire of Change.

- Jatavedas protects the prana, (TB 1.2.1.52) the Vital Principle of Breath.
- Jatavedas is the primary or "First Fire," (TB 1.4.4.10), before all others. The phrase "First Fire" is self-evident. Among the Fires of the Firmament, Jatavedas occupies a special place. Jatavedas represents the most vital functions of the firmament — prana, Vital Breath, the source of energy in the material universe, the very source of power for the Maruts — that its breadth and scope place it first among the other fires in the firmament.
- Jatavedas through its inherent strength is that purifying agent bestowing the expiation of sins of the worshiper. (TB 1.4.8.17.)

"The Light of Consciousness" is a broad statement and by itself can mean anything. Specific characteristics of the Light of Consciousness, how it arose and how it operates, is found in a summary of those characteristics is found in Sukta 29 in the Third Mandala. This Sukta implicates issues of the Light of Consciousness, the role of sacrifice in the creation of that light, and how the Light of Consciousness is created and others. Steeped in meaningful symbolism, it is by far the most concise exposition of this aspect of Change (Agni) found in one place.

RV 3.29.1: The sticks are placed in the fire and create the sacrificial fire. This rc (mantra) refers to the physical aspect of fire. The physical fire is the center of the Fire Sacrifice. At that point the sacrificial fire is Manthama, literally, the agitated, fledgling, flames of fire attempting to grow into a greater flame of light. While the fire is a physical presence, the light emitted therefrom is symbolic. Light is symbolic of the rays of the sun, which represents knowledge. Light represents the brilliant glow of Consciousness. This rc (mantra) subtly juxtaposes two extremes: the physical flame and the effulgence of Consciousness, the physical and the mental, and thereby represents the beginning stages of a deeper, fuller knowledge which is the goal of the sacrifice. Both extremes inhere in the divine force of Agni in its aspect of the Fire of Change. Consciousness will always be associated with brightness, effulgence, brilliance, adamantine and shining like a diamond. Is it no mistake that a smart person is called "bright" and the opposite is called "dull"?

RV 3.39.2: Jatavedas is the two sticks impregnating the embryo. Jatavedas is "all knowing." In this rc (mantra) there are several themes. This rc (mantra) may be viewed as a precursor to the Absolute Self of Vedanta Jatavedas is an epithet of Change (Agni). RV 3.17.4 interprets Jatavedas as "The light of consciousness," but whose name literally means "All Knowing." Change (Agni) has elsewhere been described as the "embryo." (RV 1.70.3, 1.95.4.) The sticks thus act as the penetrating vehicle conveying the seed of Knowledge to the embryonic Change (Agni). This rc (mantra) alludes to the kindling of Change (Agni). Kindling is a concept pregnant with meaning in the Veda. It is symbolic of the digestive fire, the process of creation when purusha makes contact with prakriti, infusing in prakriti the spark of consciousness, the light of consciousness, the conscious energy, the fire by which the divinity of the principles inherent in the gods are conveyed to the individual worshiper, and the ultimate liberation of the soul. More than this, when Agni, via the manifestation in Jatavedas, is "kindled," the qualities and energies from the universe are channeled into the Fire, wherein those qualities are subsumed to be conveyed to the worshiper. All these concepts are all inherent in Change (Agni), and especially in its manifestation as Jatavedas.

RV 3.29.3: Once the embryo is impregnated, the sticks are lowered face up and then turned face downwards, giving birth to Change (Agni). Even the Vedic deities must answer to a higher order. The import of this and the previous rcs (mantras) is that Jatavedas informs the light of Consciousness to Agni, which is thereby communicated to the worshiper via the Fire Sacrifice.

RV 3.29.4: Change (Agni) is Jatavedas and in his manifestation of Jatavedas is placed in the center of the earth as Ila to receive the offerings. Jatavedas is the impregnator responsible for the appearance of Change (Agni). This rc (mantra) states there is a fundamental identity between Change (Agni) and Jatavedas. The paradox inherent in this rc (mantra) is that Change (Agni) is the primary divinity and Jatavedas, while imbued with divine powers, is at best a mere attribute of Change (Agni), and is responsible for its birth. It is also significant that after its birth Change (Agni) is placed in the "center of the earth." Nabhi, is mentioned elsewhere in the Veda, and signifies the subtle, psychic center, and implicates the Eternal Law of Energy and the energy of Change (Agni). In this rc,

Change (Agni) is placed in the subtle, psychic center of the earth, prthvi, which signifies the earth and anything material, be it animal, vegetable or mineral, and especially. Ila is an epithet of Change (Agni) representing the Power of Consciousness to envision the truth. (RV 1.13.9,1.31.11, 1.40.4, 1.149.9, 2.1.11, 2.3.8, 3.4.8, 3.7.5, 4.50.8, 5.5.8, 5.41.8, 7.2.8, 7.16.8, 8.31.4, 10.36.5, 10.110.8.) Change (Agni) thus is at the heart of the material realm. The worshiper is a member of the material realm, and Change (Agni) lies in the subtle, psychic center of the worshiper. The offerings given by the worshiper at the sacrifice resides in the material realm. The worshiper surrenders the material element at the sacrifice to gain the spiritual. The change is mental and spiritual. The change effected in this manifestation of Agni's divine force is in the worshiper through the power of consciousness who finds the truth — even the worshiper's personal truth — steeped in deep concentration at the core of the worshiper's being.

RV 3.29.5: Manthata, those that stir the fire, give birth to Change (Agni) in his manifestation of Jatavedas, which inhere the qualities of undifferentiated, nondual Unity (a/dvayantam), Higher Intelligence, Immortality (amR/taM), and the light of consciousness. This rc (mantra) establishes the second stage of the sacrifice. When the sacrificial fire is stirred, Change (Agni) leaves the material world and is reborn to the realm of undifferentiated, nondual Unity, Higher Intelligence, and Immortality. The rcs (mantras) implies that this region is the light of consciousness. Of course, Change (Agni) works to transform the worshiper through the sacrifice and the sacrificial fire. The fire of Change (Agni) in his manifestation of Jatavedas is initiated when the sticks are rubbed together. (RV 3.29.6.) Once it is born, the fire of Change (Agni) transforms the worshiper to acquire divine qualities. (RV 3.29.7.)

RV 3.29.8: When offerings are given to the sacrificial fire the minds and souls of the worshipers acquire a higher state of consciousness (*bhrad*) found in the region of the svar. This rc (mantra) speaks of the spiritual change in the worshiper. In the spiritual journey of the Fire Sacrifice, the worshiper acquires a higher state of consciousness (*bhrad*) found in the region of the svar.

RV 3.29.9: Smoke (*dhuuma/M*) generates the benefits which is produced at the sacrifice. The "benefits" meant here are the spiritual endowments conferred at the sacrifice. This conveyance of spiritual endowments is a power possessed by all Vedic forces and energies, each in their own way. In the case of Agni, those spiritual endowments are the characteristics possessed by the aspects and manifestations of Agni, as well as those possessed by Agni proper. The significance of this rc (mantra) is that the carrier of those spiritual endowments is conveyed by the smoke produced by the Fire Altar at the sacrifice. One of those spiritual endowments is the gift of consciousness.

RV 3.29.10: There, at the sacrifice, is where Change (Agni) in his manifestation of Jatavedas conveys its benefits and belongs. At the sacrifice the focal point is the worshiper, whose principal concern is to channel those spiritual endowments and incorporate those endowments for use in the spiritual journey. The worshiper becomes consciousness at the sacrifice, or, at least, that is the aspiration.

RV 3.29.11: When Change (Agni) in his manifestation of Jatavedas is its embryotic stage, it is called Tanunapat, and when it is created it is called Narasamsa. When the energy of Change (Agni) in his manifestation of Jatavedas radiates it is called Matarisvan. Tanunapat is called imperishable, Narasamsa is called strong and popular with people, Matarisvan is called a cosmic force. (RV 3.29.11, translation of Swami Satya Prakash Sarawati (2011, Delhi).) These are the principle agents of Change and appear later as aspects of the Terrestrial Agni. The energy of Matarisvan takes many forms. The energy of Matarisvan is the wind, the Vital Air, it is the means of movement of Agni in its manifestation as Jatavedas. This is rather significant. There are literally innumerable references in Vedic and Hindu scripture or writings of the movement of prana or of the Vital Air; prana, apana, vyana, udana, samana. At bottom Agni in its manifestation as Jatavedas is responsible for that movement. More significantly This rc (mantra) sets forth the three components to Consciousness. One, like Tanunapat, Consciousness is imperishable. Two, like Narasamsa, Consciousness displays the strength to which people, and the worshiper, are attracted and seek. Three, like Matarisvan, Consciousness both requires energy, expends energy, and emits energy.

RV 3.29.13: In this manner do immortal beings (*amR/tam*) create divinity in mortal beings (ma/rtyaaso), much like a doctor delivers a newborn. The worshiper's spiritual journey is a personal endeavor, but the general goal is to confer the spiritual endowment of divinity.

"Divinity" should be properly understood. There are many references in Hindu scripture and writings of this practice "conquering death" or that understanding making the worshiper "like gods." This should not be taken in its literal meaning. "Divinity" and "immortality" has more to do with "liberation" or "salvation." In the context contained in this rc, "divinity" means being spiritually reborn. Specifically, "divinity" and "immortality" are terms associated with Consciousness.

RV 3.29.14: The seven priests (*sapta/hotaa*) similarly allow the splendor of Change (Agni) in his manifestation of Jatavedas to shine eternally on the earth. There is a likely astronomical meaning, a veiled reference to the Big Dipper and the seven stars contained therein. The "seven priests" here refer to the Seven-Dimensional Universe, hinting at the transcendent existential level. Perhaps, but not suited for a Fire from the firmament. Still, the import of This rc (mantra) is that the Light of Consciousness is a gift from and shines down from the Seven-Dimensional Universe, the domain of the Vedic forces and energies.

RV 3.29.15: The Kusikas are enlightened to the Universal Self and are the guardians against evil. The Kusikas are enlightened sages. They "possess the energies of the vital principles," comprehending the universe, in the process both igniting and offering homage to the aspect of Agni as the divine fire. (RV 3.39.15, translation of Swami Satya Prakash Sarawati (2011, Delhi). This is another aspect of Change (Agni). In this way, Evil is confronted and as a result of the fire of Change, vanquished.

RV 3.29.16: When Change (Agni) in his manifestation of Jatavedas consumes and is conjoined with Soma, he conveys the offerings to the divine sphere. Remember what we said much earlier about the root derivation of Agni signifying charcoal? Charcoal, once burned (transformed, changed) becomes embers. Those embers signify the Vedic force of Indra. Indra, in all the panoply of his of powers, is commonly associated with the force of Mind and Consciousness.

"The Knower of All Things"

There are other contexts where Agni Jatavedas has been defined in the Vedas. Agni Jatavedas is the "Knower of All Things." This epithet is also used with other aspects of Agni, most notably Agni Vaisvanara, but with

Agni Jatavedas, the "Knower of All Things" is more clearly defined. That definition is made as an accumulation of attributes. These are the most notable:

- In RV 1.77.5: Agni in its manifestation in Jatavedas is called *rtaa/vaa*, the possessor of the inner truth of the Vedic dharma. This title, *rtaa/vaa*, is a coveted and limited to only the most prominent Vedic forces. Agni is the most prominent titleholder. Agni is the presiding Vedic force possessing the inner truth of the Vedic dharma approximately nine Suktas. (RV 1.77.1, 2, 5; 3.13.3; 4.2.1; 5.1.6; 5.25.1; 6.12.1; 7.3.1; 10.7.4.) As the Knower of all Things, Agni in its manifestation in Jatavedas gives strength to the worshiper during the spiritual journey.
- RV 2.4.1: Agni in its manifestation in Jatavedas wipes away the sins of the worshiper. He knows all things born in humanity. As the Knower of all Things Born, Jatavedas is the Godhead, the accumulation of all Vedic forces and energies in One.
- RV 3.1.20: Jatavedas is the "knower of all births," knowing the eternal births of the Vedic force of Agni and knowing the birth of the worshiper who attends the sacrifice. Note that the births of Agni are in the plural. There is only one Vedic force of Agni, but under that umbrella there are many fires, Jatavedas being simply one of them.
- RV 4.1.20: Agni in its manifestation in Jatavedas is aditi, which, in addition to being the lunar mansions, signifies that which is boundless, immense, inexhaustible, abundant, unimpaired, perfect, the essence of the creative power in the universe.
- RV 4.58.8: In incredibly evocative language, the Veda reveals that the streams flow to Agni in its manifestation as Jatavedas. As the Knower of all Things Born, Agni in his manifestation as Jatavedas is constantly in the worshiper's thoughts.
- RV 6.4.2: It is revealed here that the Light of Consciousness emanated by Agni in its manifestation of Agni Jatavedas is "wide." As the Knower of all Things Born, Agni in his manifestation as Jatavedas is the Godhead.

- RV 6.15.13: Agni in its manifestation as Jatavedas is Lord and Master of the house. This has been stated in other rcs (mantras) and has differing levels of meaning. It can be taken to mean literally, the home, residence, the presiding Vedic force of the worshiper's dwelling. House can also be taken to mean the Lunar Mansions, the zoological houses of the zodiac. A reasonable interpretation, given that Jatavedas is the functional equivalent of Aditi. As the Knower of all Things Born, Agni in its manifestation as Jatavedas is strengthened as a result of the Sacrifice for the benefit of the other Vedic forces and energies and the worshiper. Agni in its manifestation as Jatavedas is imbued with *Rta,* the inner essence of the Vedic dharma.
- RV 7.9.4: As the Knower of all Things Born, Agni in its manifestation as Jatavedas has perfect vision. This is not eyesight, but the capacity to reveal the real essence of the Vedic dharma.
- RV 7.12.2: As the Knower of all Things Born, Agni in its manifestation as Jatavedas overcomes all evils.
- RV 10.45.1: Agni in its manifestation as Jatavedas is a Vedic force of many births. The first birth occurred above Heaven. In the second birth Agni in its manifestation as Jatavedas became the Knower of All Things. The third birth occurred in the Waters. The Waters is the fundamental Essence of the Vedic dharma. At that point, Agni in its manifestation as Jatavedas became the Godhead.
- RV 10.61.14: Bharga is synonymous with Rudra-Siva, and it is descriptive of radiance, splendor, effulgence and is seated at the summit of Heaven. Bharga is the alter ego of Agni in its manifestation as Jatavedas.
- RV 10.88.4: Agni in its manifestation as Jatavedas is anointed with Light.

As previously mentioned, as the "Knower of All Things," Agni Vaisvanara, both as an aspect and manifestation of the Vedic force of Agni, serves as the early precursor to Atman, the Absolute Self in Vedanta. It also serves to demonstrate the supreme Omnipresence of the Vedic force of Agni. The width and breadth of Agni indeed is great, as demonstrated in the next manifestation, Rudra.

RUDRA

Rudra is more commonly known today as the harbinger of death, closely aligned with Siva. Indeed, Rudra is more commonly recognized as a pivotal deity in Shaivite traditions or as belonging to its own Tantric cult, not as a Vedic force or energy. There are two manifestations of Rudra in Agni:

- *Rudraya angaye.* (RV 1.127.10.)
- *Tvamagne rudra.* (RV 2.1.6.)

Both essentially imply that this manifestation is the alter ego of the Vedic force of Agni. Dichotomy is the nature of Rudra. On the one hand, it dwells within the sphere of Agni. (BD, 1.67; 7.142); on the other hand, it belongs to the divine sphere controlled by Indra. (BD, 1.122.) On the one hand, Rudra is the Healer and forgives the worshiper's sins; on the other hand, it is a fierce wild animal. This dichotomy would serve as the inspiration to the essential natures of not only to Shiva, but to Kali, Shiva's consort, as well. Yet, Rudra is an integral part of the original Vedic dharma and is more closely associated with the Vedic force of Agni (SSS, 4.29.1) and a manifestation of Agni in the fire of the firmament. (BD, 1.103.)

The Brahmanas explain the origins of Rudra; from these origins it is evident how Rudra became a presiding Vedic force in the firmament. In the beginning, when the Vedic dharma *(rta)* was first established, the Rudras were one of the first classifications of Vedic forces and energies. (SPB, 4.5.7.2.) So when Prajapati created the world he united his mind with Speech *(vak)*. The result of this union was that he became pregnant with and created eight, eleven and twelve drops. The eleven drops were the

Rudras. (SPB, 4.5.7.2; 6.1.2.7, 10.) Prajapati thereupon placed these deities in various sectors of the universe. Rudras were placed in the air and found its place in the firmament. (SPB, 6.1.2.7, 10.)

Rudra is the presiding deity in several Suktas of the Rg Veda. The most revealing Sukta is found in the Second Sukta, 2.33. Far from being the fearful, vengeful, Vedic force in Tantric traditions, Agni in his manifestation as Rudra is seen as an agent for healing and salvation, although shadings of Rudra's ferocity can be seen from the language and imagery used to describe his character:

- RV 2.33.1: Agni, in his manifestation as Rudra, is the father of the Maruts. We have seen the Maruts earlier. The Maruts is another manifestation of the fire of the firmament. While the fire of the Maruts have elements of ferocity, the fire is on whole uplifting and elevating. Agni, in his manifestation as Rudra, is also a source of Bliss, a source of mercy and a source of the "sight of the Sun." This last appellation should be taken metaphorically, of course. On a terrestrial level, the Sun is the source of all life, on a celestial level the Sun is the gateway to the Northern Path, the path leading to the eternal world of liberation and salvation (devayana)(MB 13.1082; Chand.Up., 5.3; SPB 6.6.2.4.)

- RV 2.33.2: Agni, in his manifestation as Rudra, is endowed with the powers of healing and drives away evil for the benefit of the worshiper.

- RV 2.33.3: Here, Agni, in his manifestation as Rudra, is spoken with language usually reserved to the Vedic force of Indra. Agni, in his manifestation as Rudra, is the "Chief of all born," attacks all battles with Evil. Agni, in his manifestation as Rudra also wields Vayra, Indra's weapon used against Vrtra.

- RV 2.33.4: The worshiper however approaches this manifestation of Agni cautiously and with trepidation. With a pleading voice the worshiper here hopes that Rudra is not angered as the worshiper surrenders to this Vedic force.

- RV 2.33.5: Agni, in his manifestation as Rudra, is described as the "Mighty One," he who is the personification of the mortal mind (*maal no*). This is a significant distinction in the allocation of powers of which the Vedic forces are responsible for supporting. For example, the Vedic force of Indra presides over the Buddhi. The Mahat or Buddhi is the first principle of individualization, wherein resides the individual intellect, will, judgment, the faculty which directs awareness out into the objects of the world. In the context of Consciousness, Indra is the active, dynamic Vedic force representing Mahat, Buddhi. That Indra is the Buddhi is indicated by his epithets: Shakra, The Mighty (RV 1.10.6; 5.34.3; 6.47.11; 7.104.20, 8.1.19; 8.32.12; 8.50.1;8.69.14; 8..78.5; 8.93.18; 10.43.6; 10.104.10; 10.167.2; SV 1.1.140) ; Maghavann, the "Victor" (RV 1.23.3; 2.32.13; 11.55.5;1.73.5; 1.77.4; 1.98.3; 1.103.2, 4; 1.136.7; 1.141.13; 1.146.5; 1.157.3; 1.171.3, 5; 1.174.1, 7; 2.6.4; 3.30.3, 22; 3.31.22; 3.32.7; 3.34.11; 3.51.11; 3.36.11; 3.38.10; 3.39.9; 3.43.8; 3.48.5; 3.49.5; 3.50.5; 3.51.1; 3.53.8; 4.16.1; 4.17.8, 9, 11, 13; 4.20.2; 4.22.1; 4.24.2; 4.27.5; 4.31.7; 5.31.1; 5.34.2, 3, 8; 5.42.8; 5.61.11; 5.79.6; 6.24.1; 6.27.8; 6.47.11; 6.58.4; 7.16.7; 7.20.10; 7.21.10; 7.26.1, 2; 7.27.4; 7.28.5; 7.29.5; 7.30.3; 7.31.4; 7.32.12, 20; 7.60.11; 7.29.5; 7.30.3; 7.31.4; 8.1.12; 8.21.10; 8.26.7; 8.33.9; 8, 13; 8.46.13; 8.49.1; 8.52.5; 8.61.1, 18; 8.65.10;8.70.15; 8.95.20; 8.96.20; 8.97.13; 8.103.9; 9.81.3; 9.96.11; 9.97.55; 10.23.2, 3; 10.10.27.4; 10.33.8; 10.42.6, 8; 10.43.1, 3, 5, 6, 8; 10.49.11; 10.74.5; 10.81.6; 10.89.18; 10.104.11; 10.113.2; 10.160.4; 10.162.2); Shatakratu, the Possessor of Many Powers (RV 8.93.16); Satraaji, the Perpetual Lord. (RV 8.3.15; 9.89.4; 9.27.4); Mahan, the Mighty. The ultimate paradox is that while these appellations may be equally applied to Rudra, Indra presides over the Buddhi while Rudra presides over the Manas. This paradox is intensified in the next rcs (mantras) with language reserved only to Indra.

- RV 2.33.6: Rudra, the Bull (*vrsabho*), with the assistance of his helpers, the Maruts, endows the worshiper with Bliss, frees the worshiper of sin, and showers the worshiper with brilliant light. The identification with Indra is inescapable. The Maruts are intimately associated with Indra. Indra — as well as Agni, for that matter — is called "the Bull." Indra, and all Vedic forces and energies as well as the fundamental philosophy of the Vedas, is founded on light, brilliance, effulgence, and Bliss. Mutual interdependence is an essential element of Vedic forces. This interdependency is no better demonstrated than in Agni, in his manifestation as Rudra

- RV 2.33.7: Agni, in his manifestation as Rudra is the Healer, is the expiator of the worshiper's sin.

- RV 2.33.8: Here Agni, in his manifestation as Rudra is again described as the Bull and the "Knower of Mortal Mind." The brilliant light of Agni, in his manifestation as Rudra wipes away all of the worshiper's impurities.

- RV 2.33.9: Agni, in his manifestation as Rudra, is again described as Mighty, again takes an appellation from Indra, here, Shakra. Rudra is described as having a ruddy color in a bright golden form. Red, or Ruddy Brown, in esoteric, alchemical, traditions represents Rebirth. In these same traditions, yellow, Gold, called Xanthosis, represents Immortality. While the fire of immortality and rebirth represent one process of spiritual renewal, this color scheme betrays the dichotomous character of Rudra. By virtue of this fire, Agni, in his manifestation as Rudra is the Supreme Ruler and the Lord of the Vedic dharma.

- RV 2.33.10: The strength of Agni, in his manifestation as Rudra is emphasized. This rc (mantra) describes Agni, in his manifestation as Rudra as the most mightiest force in the Vedic dharma.

- RV 2.33.11: Agni, in his manifestation as Rudra is described as terrible, destructive and fierce. We know that fire has a destructive and beneficial side. On balance — even though Rudra is also described as "sitting in the car seat" and possessing "inspired knowledge" which hopefully is conveyed to the worshiper — Agni, in his manifestation as Rudra represents more the destructive side. Rudra is portrayed as a "dreaded beast of the forest." This caricature will serve in later millennia to supply the basis for the character of Kali, Shiva's consort and the dreaded deity of death:

- RV 2.33.12: Rudra is presented as the Healer. A plea, repeated elsewhere in this rc (mantra), is that the worshiper surrender wholly to Rudra. This is an example of the give-and-take of Vedic sacrifice. In exchange for the complete surrender to Rudra, the worshiper seeks to be healed of all impurities and sins and physical ailments.

- RV 3.33.13: The Maruts, associates of Indra, the offspring of Agni, another manifestation of the fire of the firmament are also seen as Healers. They are also described as providers of Bliss, called the Bull (*vRSaNo*). This fire of Regeneration is the appellation for the Vedic forces of Agni, Indra, and Soma, as well as for Rudra. The Maruts are mentioned in this rc (mantra) in the same breath as Rudra, which is not surprising considering that both are manifestations of Agni as fires in the firmament.

- RV 3.33.14: As soon as the Rishiis reveal the healing, benevolent powers of Rudra, they return to his ferocity. He is described as "terrible," having "great wrath," and destroying enemies. It is perhaps in this context that this fire of the firmament should be understood. He is the Vedic force of Wrath to the worshiper's enemies, the Healer and expiator of sins for the worshiper.

- RV 2.33.15: Rudra, the Bull (*vRSabha*), is the supporter of the worlds. As the Bull, the symbol of Regeneration, it is the fire of Rudra that perpetuates the continued existence of the various existential levels of Agni provides the articulation of forms in the wider Vedic dharma. Rudra borrows this power from Indra, in whom all names are deposited, all smell and odors are deposited, all forms are deposited, all sounds are deposited, all mind and thoughts are deposited. (SA, 5.1.)

Omnipresence is the controlling characteristic of these manifestations of the Vedic force of Agni, Agni Vaisvanara and Rudra. A different aspect of the omnipresence of Agni is indicated in the next manifestation, Saraswati.

SARASWATI

Saraswati is a manifestation of the Middle Agni. (BD, 3.13.) Saraswati is many things in the Vedic world.

- The River Saraswati has been cited as proof of the great antiquity of the Rg Veda. Historically, there once indeed existed the great River Saraswati. The consensus of modern scholarship is that this river completely dried up over four thousand years ago in an early example of climate change, precipitating the end of the great Indus Civilization which relied on its presence. This river is mentioned several times in the Veda. How else could the Rishiis have known of this great and mighty river? All indications are that it is indeed a wide and sweeping river, akin the Mississippi River today. What better simile was available to the Rishiis of the magnitude and strength of Consciousness.

- Saraswati in this rc (mantra) is described as the Power of Consciousness to Hear the Truth (*mahii*). (RV 1.13.9.)

- Saraswati is also a manifestation of *Vrsaa*, the Bull, the active Principle of Regeneration. This attribute is found in the Vedic force of Saraswati. (RV 7.95.2.)

- Saraswati, the mother of the Floods. (RV 7.36.6.) Here is a good example of Vedic imagery. The Saraswati was a river, it is paradoxical that a river which has since completely evaporated would cause floods. The association is to consciousness, and a flood of consciousness is where the mind becomes overwhelmed with the rush of inspiration from the Word, which Saraswati symbolizes.

- Saraswati is also a dynamic Vedic force. As a Vedic force, it primarily represents the Word, Logos.

There is a special relationship between Saraswati and the Fire of Agni. RV 1.164.52 states "The divine bird, the child of the waters, brings satisfaction in the rainy season. I invoke Saraswati again and again." This rc (mantra) demonstrates on a deep level the intimate relationship between Saraswati and the Fire of Agni. "The Divine Bird" refers to the Agnicayana, which purports to form the outline of a Falcon. The Falcon carries special meaning to the Vedic divine forces and principles:

- Indra, the divine Vedic force of Articulation and Divine Speech, represents the Falcon. (RV 3.43.7; 4.26.1; 6.46.13; 8.34.9; 8.84.3; 10.146.4, 5.)
- The falcon brings empowering the divine Vedic force of Soma to Indra. (RV 4.26.6, 7; 5.95.9; 8.89.8; 9.48.3; 9.38.4.)
- Soma Pavamana, the highly distilled product of the Soma sacrifice, is indeed compared to a falcon. (RV 9.38.4; 9.61.21; 9.67.14; 9.48.3; 9.68.6; 9.71.6, 9; 9.72.3; 9.77.2; 9.86.24; 9.87.6; 9.96.6.)
- The Maruts are thought of as the "most supreme" falcon. (RV 4.26.4; 8.20.10; 10.37.5.)
- The Asvins, symbol of the Divine Duality of the universe, are associated with the falcon. (RV 5.74.9; 5.78.4; 8.62.4.)
- Mitra-Varuna, dual Vedic forces, are also associated with the falcon. (RV 7.63.5.)
- That most formidable Vedic forces, Agni, the fire of Change and Flux, is the "Falcon of the Sky," (RV 7.15.4; 10.11.4) and is otherwise compared with the falcon.

That most formidable Vedic forces, Agni, the fire of Change and Flux, is the Falcon of the Sky, (RV 7.15.4; 10.11.4) and is otherwise compared with the falcon. (RV 4.6.10.)

Agni is "the Child of the Waters." At the same time Agni is the Vedic force of Fire. That the personification of fire is associated with the Waters is no simple exercise in Vedic paradox. The Rg Veda explains elsewhere Agni as the fire of Change is kindled (*idhyase*) in the waters. (RV 3.25.5.) This is highly symbolic language running at the heart of the Vedic dharma. In the coded language of the Veda, the essential paradox of the binding of water and fire is major characteristic present in the fire of Change (Agni). This expression is expresses the active principles of Agni: On the one hand as the child, germ, or kinsman, of the waters, the ultimate nature of the Vedic dharma, and on the other hand its progenitor. The juxtaposition of this ambiguity points to the unifying powers of the fire of Change (Agni) in creating the purifying powers of the Vedic dharma —the Waters, the germination powers unleashing the latent potential of the Seed, but also providing the essential purifying properties of fire. This is the reference point of Agni, the Fire of Change. There is then an inextricable connection between The Fire of Change (Agni) and the Waters. This is expressed in many ways:

- A well-known epithet for Agni the Fire of Change is that he is the son of the waters (RV 1.22.6; 1.122.4; 1.143.1; 1.145.1; 1.186.5; 2.31.6; 2.35.1, 2, 3, 7, 9, 13; 3.9.1; 5.41.10; 6.50.12, 13; 7.34.15; 7.47.2; 10.30.3; 10.92.13.)
- Change (Agni) lives in the waters. (RV 1.65.3, 4, 9, 10; 1.67.3, 4, 9, 10; 170.3, 4; 1.95.4, 5, 8; 1.44.2; 1.149.4; 2.4.2; 3.1.3; 3.72.2; 3.55.12.)
- An entire Sukta, RV 2.35, is devoted to the "Son of Waters," which is the Fire of Change (Agni).
- Change (Agni) was born in the waters. (RV 1.95.4, 5, 8; 3.1.4; 3.5.8.)
- Not only is Agni the child of the waters, but he is carried by the celestial waters. (RV 1.59.4; 1.71.2; 2.35.3.1.4; 9, 14; 9.92.4.)
- Change (Agni) is the "grandson" of the Waters. (RV 1.122.4, 6; 1.143.1; 1.186.5; 2.35.3; 3.9.1; 3.29.11; 5.32.4; 5.41.1; 7.34.15.)
- .The active Fire of Change (Agni) has been described as the kinsman of the waters (RV 1.65.7, 8) and the germ of the waters (RV 1.70.3; 1.95.4; 3.5.1), the latter signifying the initial stages of the powers of purification.
- The Fire of Change (Agni) bestows peace through the waters. (AV 2.10.2.)

- The active principles of Change (Agni) produces the waters. (RV 3.4.2.)
- Fire, the essential quality of Change (Agni), protects the water. (AV 11.2.8.)
- .The Fire of Change (Agni) is described as the "Bull (*vRSabha*) of the Standing Waters." (RV 7.5.2; 2.35.13.)
- The Bull is the symbol of Regeneration; the "standing waters" is another expression of the essential nature of the Vedic dharma. The Vedic force of Agni perpetuates the continued existence of the Vedic dharma.

The two principal epithets typifying the evolutionary process of the waters is *apaa garbho*, seed of the waters:

- Agni is described as the child or the germ of the waters, apaa garbha. (RV 1.70.3; 3.5.3.)
- Agni is born of the waters. (RV 2.1.1.)

The waters are the mothers, the creator, of the universe. (RV 1.95.4; 3.92; 6.50.7; 10.35.2.) The waters thus become the material embodiment of the Fire of Change and Transformation (Agni), the subtle vital creator of the world. (RV 3.1.12, 13.) This Vedic energy is the first principle or cause of the material world.

Logos, the Word, is the first principle of the material world. The Word articulates the material world by ascribing names to objects in that world, thus beginning the formation of the material world. The Veda says in this connection that the worshiper "invokes Saraswati." This divine Vedic force is the representation of Vak, Logos, the First Principle, Paratman. (RV 3.5.15, 16; AV 5.10.8; TB 1.6.2.2; TS 2.1.2.6; AB 3.1.2, 3; KS 10.1.) As RV 1.164.45 teaches, there are four elements to Vak, and they correspond to the four, broad, dimensions of the multi-universe. According to that tradition, there are four levels of articulation of the names of forms in creation, each level evolving into the other.

- *Vaikhari* is the gross aspect of articulated speech

- *Madhyama*, which consists of subtle and gross states. The subtle state consists of the seven primary notes. These are the seven notes of the saman chant. Externally these are the notes chanted during the sacrifice; esoterically these notes are the rhythm and vibration of the universe.
- *Pasyanti*, which is the all-perceiving state of Brahman full of energy.
- *Para* is the paratman, Logos, the Word.

While this is nominally concerning the levels of speech, on a deeper level this pertains to the levels of reality, from the gross material level, to the spiritual level of the Atman, and beyond the Atman. The process begins with articulated speech, such as one person to another, and raises to a level of abstraction wherein, depending on that particular school of Hinduism, bindu, parabindu, nada, or AUM — all of which are manifestations of the primal sound emitted at the beginning of creation.

Coda for the Fires of the Firmament

The firmament is nestled between heaven and earth. If anything can be said about the fires of the Firmament, it is that the presiding Vedic forces move ever upwards towards the Heavenly Fire. Rudra is a good example. Rudra is very much a mixed bag; it is atmospheric by nature, consistent with its placement in the firmament, yet has a dark side. It is only appropriate then that the Fires of the Firmament share in qualities which are both profane and qualities which are divine.

There are the Maruts. The Maruts are typically portrayed as a half-celestial, half-terrestrial example of the Fires of the Firmament. The ferocity of the Maruts belie their divine nature, yet they are overwhelmingly divine by nature. The Maruts have these divine characteristics:

- Divine (deva) and know how to cause the waters to descend (purification).
- Fierce (ugra) and know how to cause the descent of waters (Vigor and purification). Ugra, not only meaning "fierce," also connotes heat, passion, intensity, a close relative to Tapas.

- Radiant and powerful (Vigor and Consciousness).
- Live in the heaven above the Sun.
- Moves mountains (purification), where mountains are symbolic of dead inner matter.
- They spread and expand with the rays of an ocean (higher consciousness).
- They drink Soma (purification).

Then there is Agni Jatavedas. With Agni Jatavedas the push proceeds to a Decidedly upward trajectory and approaches the celestial realm closer than any other firmament deity. Agni in its manifestation as Jatavedas can be summarized as having the following characteristics:

- First and foremost, Jatavedas is the "Knower of Things." But what does that really mean? Just as there are many fires of Agni, there are many areas in which the Knower of Things touch. As the Knower of all Things, Agni in its manifestation in Jatavedas gives strength to the worshiper during the spiritual journey; is strengthened itself as a result of the Sacrifice for the benefit of the other Vedic forces and energies and the worshiper; is the Godhead, the accumulation of all Vedic forces and energies in One; knowing the eternal births of the Vedic force of Agni and knowing the birth of the worshiper who attends the sacrifice; is constantly in the worshiper's thoughts; has perfect vision; overcomes all evils; and other powers. Indeed, the "knowing" power of Jatadevas has more to do with providing the subtle essence of the material universe in which the worshiper and we all live. Viewed in this manner, Jatavedas is another precursor the Universal Self, the Atman, that Sri Adi Sankara revealed millennia later.
- Jatavedas is the "Light of Consciousness." Like aditi, that light is boundless, immense, inexhaustible, abundant, unimpaired, perfect — the essence of the creative power in the universe — and like Bharga that light is radiant, splendorous, effulgent and is seated at the summit of Heaven.
- Jatavedas is the kindling, the two sticks impregnating, which gives birth to the Vedic force and energy of Agni.

THE TERRESTRIAL FIRES

The Terrestrial Fires are, as the name connotes, the Fire existing in the bottom rung of the existential ladder — Earth. Saunaka, the Medieval Vedic scholar and author, in his textbook treatise on the Vedic forces and energies, the Brhata Deva, contains an extensive list of the terrestrial fires of Agni. These are manifestations of Agni. As manifestations, these are the different forms of Agni as they appear in the material world. Some are straightforward and uncomplicated. Others have a deeper meaning. These terrestrial fires are manifestations of Agni, this is how Agni appears in the material world. They appear in the material world in their own right and through the various aspects of Agni —the Fire Altar, the Sacrificial Fire, the Fire of Self-Surrender and the other aspects covered in a companion volume. Each represent a small element of Agni's essential nature. They all impact the material world, and they include the following:

AGNAYE

Agnaye is the ultimate paradox. Agnaye is the Fire of Transcendence. Yet, it is a terrestrial fire found in the material world. (BD, 1.112.) Agnaye belongs to and possesses the nature of Agni or Fire. (MB 1.2.538.) Having elements of transcendence, Agnaye represents the subtle basis of the material world. The fire of Agnaye is an agent for the worshiper's Increase. The fire of Agnaye is the necessary impetus to elevate the worshiper's spiritual journey from the Three-Dimensional Universe, the material world, to the subtle basis of the material world, the Five-Dimensional Universe.

APVA

Apva is also a manifestation of the terrestrial Fire of Agni. (BD 1.112.) Meaning "filled," it has the quality of Pervasiveness. (RV 10.103.12.)

ATITHI

Atithi, meaning the "Guest" of human dwellings, a constant presence. (RV 5.1.8, 6.2.7, 7.8.4, 7.9.3.)

While not strictly a terrestrial manifestation of Agni, Atithi is sometimes known as Agni Jatadevas. (RV 1.44.4.) We had just seen earlier that Agni Jatadevas "knows all things born, created, or produced." As the all-seeing guest Agni Jatadevas on the surface appears to be a "Big Brother." In reality Agni Jatadevas, the All-Knowing, provides the subtle under-girth which superimposes the material world for the worshiper's enjoyment and perception. Agni Jatadevas, however, an element of the various aspects of Agni, the subtle essential nature of Agni. Atithi, as the guest, is the physical manifestation of Agni Jatadevas, then becomes the umbrella Vedic energy which engenders the terrestrial fires of Agni.

ARANYANI

Aranyani is also a manifestation of the terrestrial Fire of Agni. (BD, 1.112.) Aranyani is the Vedic Goddess of the Forests and the Animals that dwell within them. (*https://en.wikipedia. org/wiki/Aranyani.*) In her capacity she supplies the raw material, the food, upon which Agni, as the Eater, may consume and purify.

THE ARROW

The Arrow is also a manifestation of Agni. (BD, 1.111.) There are several archery elements named as manifestations of Agni's terrestrial fires. There is the arrow, the quiver, the bowstring, and here, the bow. These metaphors relate to the fire of karma, later discussed millennia later in Vedantic literature and scripture in greater detail. There are three kinds of Karma: Sanchita, this is the vast storehouse of yet unseen, unresolved mental impressions which constitute the sum of one's past karmas – all actions, good and bad, from the worshiper's past lives that follow through to the present incarnation and which create havoc in the worshiper's present life. Kriyamana, those currently in front of us to decide or act on; and Prarabhda, consequences that have already playing themselves out in past lives, literally the "brunt seeds" of past mental impressions. Similarly, there are three kinds of arrows: Quiver: Arrows in the Quiver (Sanchita karma); Hand: Arrows in Hand (Prarabhda karma); Flight: Arrows in Flight (Kriyamana karma). The form of terrestrial fire here, the Arrow, is the Fire of Kriyamana Karma, literally, those actions played out and created in this present life and carried over to later lives.

BARHI

There are numerous references of Barhi grass in the Veda. Representing the inner seat (of grass) wherein the vision of Agni Pavamana is made, Barhi is a manifestation of the terrestrial Fire of Agni. In a sacrificial setting the Barhi is the seat of grass whereupon sits the worshiper, the supplicant, the visiting Vedic forces and energies from which the worshipers and supplicants seek divine inspiration. The terrestrial fire of Barhi is more than simply the grass circling the Sacrificial Fire:

- Barhi is subsumed in Narasamsa, itself a manifestation of the terrestrial Fire of Agni. (BD 1.107.) Nara is the Primeval Man, the Purusa, Manu, Adam in the Abrahamic religions. Nara is also the Universal Spirit pervading the Universe. The terrestrial fire of Narasamsa is the most excellent, most exalted, manifestation of Nara. Given this equivalence, in a very macrocosmic manner, the terrestrial fire of Barhi has cosmic implications. Yet, because it is a terrestrial fire, it also has implications to the material world.
- On a personal level, the terrestrial fire is born from the personal self-surrender of the worshiper. In this regard, the Veda states that the terrestrial fire of Barhi is made from the worshiper's self-surrender. (RV 6.11.5.) On a physical level, the Barhi grass resembles foliage. On a mystic level, when the worshiper surrenders totally to the Sacrificial Fire, the heat merges to be conveyed and communicated to the seat of Barhi grass.

The most prominent of the Vedic invitees is the Vedic force of Agni. Agni arrives in his many capacities:

- The Vedic force of Agni arrives as the Messenger, summoning the other Vedic forces and energies. (RV 1.12.4.)
- As the Messenger, the Vedic force of Agni asks the other Vedic forces and energies to sit on the middle of the Barhi. (RV 3.13.1.)
- At the same token, the gods invite Agni to sit on the Barhi grass. (RV 3.9.9.)
- Most times, the Vedic force of Agni sits on the Barhi simply to complement the presence of the forces of the Vedic dharma. (RV 5.26.5; 7.11.2; 8.44.14.)
- Consistent with his capacity as the summoning Vedic force, the Vedic force of Agni sits on the Barhi as the hotra, the reciter of invocations and litanies. (RV 6.16.10.)
- The Vedic force of Agni occasionally acts as a "middle man" and sits on the Barhi alone, sending oblations, offerings, thoughts, prayers, supplications, to the other Vedic forces and energies. (RV 4.9.1; 8.23.26.)
- Agni in his capacity as the unifier of Heaven and Earth. (RV 1.144.6.)
- When the Vedic force of Agni arrives at the Sacrifice, the worshiper experiences Bliss and contentment. (RV 7.11.2.)

That the Vedic force of Agni is the "messenger of the gods" is somewhat of a misnomer. RV 7.2.3 emphasizes that Agni is the messenger between Heaven and Earth. This would necessarily presuppose that the worshiper and other sentient beings in the material world benefit from this capacity. Primarily, this wisdom indicates that those Vedic forces and energies which are channeled to the worshiper, including to the worshiper, are so conveyed through the offices of Agni. RV 7.2.3 adds that

- Agni speaks to and is the very embodiment of the inner essence of the Vedic dharma.
- The worshiper is to pray to Agni.

- Through the act of prayer or other religious or meditational austerity Agni is kindled.
- Agni itself is Increased through these austerities. In return, the Vedic force of Agni will grant Increase to the worshiper during the spiritual journey.

That place of arrival, whether Agni summons the worshiper, the gods, or both, is the same: The terrestrial fire of the Sacred Grass, Barhi. The terrestrial fire of the Barhi, the sacrificial grass, is an integral part of the Sacrifice. RV 7.43.2 explains:

- When the invitees arrive the Sacrifice moves forward with dispatch.
- The thoughts of the worshiper are enriched by Barhi's terrestrial fire.
- The flames of the terrestrial fire rise high to seek the divine (*devayuu/ny*).
- The worshiper's thoughts are conjoined with and move upwards following the flames in unison and as one.
- The terrestrial fire of Barhi thereby becomes the sacrificial representation of the fullness of the Vedic dharma.

The religious-philosophical foundation of this terrestrial fire are revealed in RV 6.11.5. According to RV 6.11.5, there are four bases to the terrestrial fire of the sacred grass. Those bases are:

- The terrestrial fire of Barhi is grounded from the self-surrender to the Vedic force of Agni. While this may be self-evident, this speaks to a deeper truth. Sitting on a pad of grass is a physical act of resting, but it is also a representative act of total surrender and acceptance of that physical space.
- This basis says that the ladle of purification is set in motion. The terrestrial fire of Barhi, like all forms of fire, is an agent for purification. Once the physical space is taken, once the worshiper accepts that place, the process of purification begins.
- This portion states that the home is established in the "home of earth." This portion of RV 6.11.5 emphasizes that Barhi is a fire

firmly grounded on the material world and operates as a terrestrial fire.

- This portion reveals that the Sacrifice is lodged in the "eye of the Sun." (*suu/rye na/ ca/kSuH*) This portion speaks of a fundamental truth of the nature of Sacrifice. The Sacrifice is focused on the Sun. The Sun is the source of all life and symbolic of illumination, enlightenment, and the source of knowledge. This is a primary purpose of the Sacrifice, that the worshiper gain some insight and awareness.

It is evident from these rcs (mantras) that Barhi is the terrestrial manifestation of a very specific but important facet of the Vedic force of Agni. Barhi is one terrestrial manifestation of the fire of purification. This is due to the general equivalence between two elements —— Fire and Water. Fire and Water originate from the same essential nature and origin. The essential equivalence of fire and water is reflected in the elements found in the sacrifice, the sacrificial grass, fire and water.

- The sacrificial grass is considered to be the cosmic, primeval, Water. (Gonda, *The Ritual Functions and Significance of Grasses in the Religion of the Veda*, (1985), p. 36.)
- Fire (Agne) is produced out of the water from which the grass is represented. (SPB 2.2.3.1; 1.2.3.9; BSS 5.19.8.)
- The sacrificial Agni fires are established in the rainy season.
- This is how the Fire of Agni is kindled (*idhyase*): in the waters. (RV 3.25.5.)

In the symbolic language of the Rg Veda, the sacrificial grass, Barhi, represents the Cosmic waters, and in the case of Barhi, those cosmic waters are expressed in the sacrificial grass. From this sacrificial setting a host of other characteristics are allowed to be presented. This role of the terrestrial fire of Barhi is elaborated further in other rcs:

- When Indra drinks Soma on the Barhi grass the limits of worldly knowledge are broken, allowing the mind to understand and appreciate the world of the Svar, the region of Light. This state of mind is conveyed to the worshiper. (RV 6.23.7.) This is a recurring theme in the Veda, Indra drinking, quaffing, Soma, and this is one of the meanings connected to that theme. There are many levels of meaning that can be taken for the image of Indra consuming Soma. One meaning, the interpretation taken here, is that by consuming Soma Indra becomes representative of the worshiper's mind expanding and transcending the bounds of mortal existence and finding a connection with the realm of the Vedic forces and energies. The Barhi becomes the seat, that place where the moment of awareness occurs, and thus signifies the worshiper's seat, the Body, where the Soma is consumed. When the Soma is consumed, the digestive fire is transformed to the terrestrial fire of Barhi.

- There are many properties to the Soma drink. Not limited to Bliss or divine ecstacy, anyone wanting vigor, strength, divine luminous vision should imbibe. (RV 7.91.4.)
- The terrestrial fire is where the Soma drink is consumed and what confers these properties.

In addition to Agni, his various aspects and manifestations are invited to sit on the Barhi grass.

- The Maruts, a manifestation of Agni's Celestial Fire. (RV 1.85.6;5.46.5.)
- The Waters, a manifestation of Agni's terrestrial fire. (RV 10.30.15.)
- Usasanakta, a manifestation of Agni's terrestrial fire. (RV 1.13.5;7.42.5.)
- Agni together with his incarnation, Indra. (RV 1.108.4.)
- The Three Goddesses, a manifestation of Agni's terrestrial fire. (RV 2.3.8.)
- Rudra, and the children of Bharata, all manifestations of Agni's terrestrial fire. (RV 2.36.2.)

Other Vedic forces and energies sit on the grass surrounding the fire.

- The Ashvins. (RV 1.116.1.)
- Vayu. (RV 1.135.1)

- Indra. (RV 1.142.5; 1.177.4.)
- Visvedevas, the combined Vedic forces. (RV 2.41.13.)

There is obviously more going on with this fire than a simple invocation to sit down for the sacrifice. Much like the Fire Altar, the Barhi is a focal point, a point of concentration and meditation, which plays an integral part of the sacrificial experience. Whereas, however, the Fire Altar is the focal point for the worshiper's mind, the Barhi is the fire which situates the worshiper's body. In this respect, the fire of the Barhi is an appropriate terrestrial fire. Barhi is terrestrial in that much like the material world itself, it is the one element of a two-step process, a duality which is so typical of the material world. Barhi is also properly considered as a Fire. The Barhi grass is fuel and is considered as such in the Vedas. (VS, 2.1; SPN 1.3.3.1 – 3; KS 2.7.9.) As fuel, Barhi is in the nature of fire:

- The priests officiating the sacrifice when igniting the Fire Altar prepares the fuel with the Barhi grass. (MS, 4.1.3.4, 8.)
- The officiating priest ignite the Fire Altar by bringing the kindling with the Barhi grass. (BSS, 10.9.8.13.)
- The priest then sprinkles the fuel with the Barhi grass onto the fire. (KS, 25.5.107.17.)
- As a result of this sacrificial act, the Barhi itself is increased and the fuel is made larger. (KS, 11.4.147.19.)
- As a further consequence the Barhi as fuel is thereby conjoined and unified. (TB 3.2.10.2.)

Thus conjoined, while sitting on the Barhi grass the Vedic forces and energies channel the incendiary power of the Fire Altar. On the Barhi grass the Vedic forces present at the sacrifice resemble birds sitting on a perch. (RV 1.85.7.) This leads to the next manifestation of the terrestrial fire.

THE BIRD

The Bird is a manifestation of the terrestrial Fire of Agni. (BD, 1.109.) In the Asyavamasya Sukta, 1.164.20, the Veda uses symbolic language to say, "There are two birds sitting on a tree. One is eating, and the other one is not eating but merely looks around." Sayana interprets the two birds in this rc (mantra) as the individual soul, the jiva (the bird eating) and the other bird sitting and looking as the Supreme Spirit, the Atman. This is a common, accepted interpretation. The number two is a cardinal number in the Vedic dynamic cosmic order. When the One created the multiplicity of forms, it created the Two-Dimensional Universe. The Two-Dimensional Universe is the material world itself. This universe is premised on opposites. As soon as the One is established its opposite appears. Once it arrives, the opposite moves to return to its counterpart. It is a process that does not have a beginning and goes on forever. This is the terrestrial fire. This microcosm is interpreted as a binary, Two-Dimensional Universe. The Two-Dimensional Universe is the gateway to the material universe. What is seen, heard, felt and experienced is done so through the prism of the Two-Dimensional Universe. It is the substrate of the sensible world as experienced by the worshiper/subject. There is a deeper aspect to duality. According to the Pythagoreans, the binary numbers, one and two, represented the subtle essence of the world. The Monad, the unitary Ekam, and Dyad, the Two-Dimensional Universe, was the essence of Plato's Unwritten Doctrine. This Unwritten Doctrine was not unknown to the Rishiis of the Vedas or other ancient knowledge. The two binary numbers, one and two and their combinations, is the foundation of the mathematical laws that inhabit a priori existence of the material world. These binary numbers and their combinations represent the unassailable spiritual order that is "completely self-contained and leaves no room for anything equivocal or half-way in between." (Richard Wilhelm, Understanding the I Ching, p. 101.) The Monad, the unitary One and the binary Two, would make its appearance thousands of years later in Computer Science. Computer programs, for all the complex tasks it is capable of, is essentially code consisting of Ones and Twos.

As for the terrestrial manifestation of Agni, as with the Pythagoreans, the Vedic dharma is ruled by number. The terrestrial sphere especially so, because this level is ruled by the back-and-forth of binary dyads. The duality of the motions back and forth is reflected in the fire which is produced. The duality of this fire necessarily gives rise to the existence of Opposition, the sometimes-maddening adversity and conflict which infects the material world. Other fires on the terrestrial realm resolve this conflict, unify the polar opposites, and are found in Usasanakta and other terrestrial fires of Agni.

THE BOW

The bow is a manifestation of the terrestrial Fire of Agni. (BD, 1.111.) This is an element of the fire of karma. Prarabhda karma are those actions undertaken in this present life in creating new karmic impressions and consequences which must be resolved in a new incarnation. The Bow and the next manifestation of the terrestrial Fire of Agni, the Bowstring, are those actors which create these new impressions and consequences. The Bow and the Bowstring are the fires of Prarabhda Karma. The Bow is appropriate as a terrestrial fire; the unresolved issues in the transmigrational journeys of the worshipers' lives are resolved on this earth, at this moment. It is through this fire that those issues are burnt.

THE BOWSTRING

The Bowstring is a manifestation of the terrestrial Fire of Agni. (BD, 1.111.) This terrestrial fire should be considered with that fire from which it follows, the Bow.

The Bowstring was one of several products made from the hide of cattle. (Srinivasan, *Concept of Cow in the Rig Veda* (2017), p. 14.) Srinivasan identifies instances in the Veda in which a bowstring was defined as being a leather strap wrapped around the point of the arrow, securing the point "to the shaft. (RV 6.75.11.) Srinivasan hypothesizes that perhaps vajra itself, Indra's sword which felled Vrtra, was made from cow leather. (Id.) The Cows, not surprisingly, represent various items made out of leather. While there is a pedestrian meaning to this aspect of Cows, they all refer to items like the leather straps and joists used in chariots in the chariot simile used in the Katha Upanishad. (RV 6.47.11.) The Cows also refer to the leather used for the leather string for the bow. (RV 8.20.8.)

If correct, Srinivasan raises many interesting possibilities with the terrestrial manifestation of Agni. The symbol of the Cow means many things in the Vedic dharma. It also represents the potentiality of many ruling concepts in the Vedic dharma:

- Cows represent the inner illumination of the rays of knowledge. (RV 2.24.6; 4.1.16 (glory of the cow of light discovered after meditation of the supreme name of the milch cow.)
- Cows also represent consciousness as knowledge. (RV 3.30.20; 3.39.6 (Indra finding meath (empirical knowledge) in the cows); 10.92.10 (inspired knowledge); 3.31.10; 3.31.11.)

- According to Sri Aurobindo, cows represent the power of consciousness, discrimination, and discernment. (See also, RV 2.11.2; 2.15.10; 2.16.9; 2.34.15 (right-thinking); 3.31.11; 10.92.10.) In recognition of this meaning, some English translations render gobhir, as "Ray-Cows," signifying the rays of knowledge. (RV 1.7.3; 1.16.9; 1.23.15; 1.53.4; 1.62.5; 1.95.8; 1.151.8; 2.15.4; 2.30.7, 20; 2.35.8; 3.1.12; 3.50.3; 3.3.3, 4; 8.7; 2.24.6; 2.20.5; 6.19.12; 6.45.20, 24. 6.66.8; 6.64.3 (red rays); 10.92.10; 4.5.5; 4.17.11; 4.23.10; 4.27.5; 4.30.22 (Indra, lord of the ray-cows); 4.31.14; 4.32.6, 7, 18, 22; 4.40.5; 4.42.5; 4.57.1; 5.1.3; 5.2.5;5.3.2; 5.45.8; 5.80.3; 6.44.12; 6.47.27; 6.53.10; 3.55.8; 3.30.10, 21; 2.55.8; 3.35.8; 1.36.8; 9.31.5; 6.1.12 (herds of light); 6.17.2; 6.17.6; 6.43.3 (ray-cows within the rock); 6.28.1 (ray-cows bringing bliss); 6.28.3; 9.31.5 (ray cows yielding light and the milk of knowledge); 7.18.2; 7.41.3; 7.54.2; 7.90.2; 8.2.6; 8.20.8; 8.24.6; 9.62.12 (Soma pours the ray-cows and life-energies upon us); 9.67.6; 10.7.2; 10.16.7; 10.31.4; 10.68.2; 10.108.7; 10.111.2.)
- *Gobhir,* the ray-cows, figured prominently in the Ninth Mandala, is the presiding divinity of Soma Pavamana. (RV 9.2.4; 9.6.6; 9.8.5; 9.10.3; 9.14.3; 9.32.3; 9.43.1; 9.50.5; 9.61.13; 9.66.13; 9.68.9; 9.74.8; 9.85.4; 9.85.5; 9.86.27; 9.91.2; 9.97.15; 9.103.1; 9.107.2, 2, 9, 18, 22.)
- The milking cow, kine, is the source of truth, essence, and knowledge.
- Kine are also representative of the union of heaven and earth.
- Kine are finally representative of the Waters, the essence of the Vedic dharma. (RV 1.32.2; 1.130.5; 3.33.1; 5.53.7; 10.5.4.)

This terrestrial manifestation of Agni thus becomes a by-product of all these qualities. The terrestrial surface of this world upon which we all and the worshiper tread contains elements of these qualities. The Bowstring thereby affirms the spiritual and subtle basis of the world, even though it originates from that most terrestrial of animals.

THE BULL

The Bull is a manifestation of the terrestrial Fire of Agni. (BD, 1.111.) The Bull is a wide, broad, concept, and is able to signify many interpretations, one concept feeding to the other: the Bull represents the Male Principle.

- The Bull is *Vrsti*, signifying Rain. The Bull is *Vrsan(aa)*, signifying the Showerer, the Bestower of Benefits.
- The Bull is *Vrsabha*, signifying the Bull, as related to *Purusa*. For its many regenerative properties the Fire of Change in Agni is described as the "Bull (*vRSabha*) of the Standing Waters." (RV 7.5.2; 2.35.13.)
- The Bull is finally *Vrsaa*, signifying the Bull, as the Principle of Regeneration.

These different manifestations of the Bull lead to paradoxical results. Consider vRSabha, the Bull of Purusa.

- For its many regenerative properties the Fire of Change in Agni is described as the "Bull (*vRSabha*) of the Standing Waters." (RV 7.5.2; 2.35.13.)
- Indra is also *vRSabha*, the Bull of the Standing Waters. (RV 6.44.21.)

This is not so much contradictory, but a matter of shared responsibility. The Bull is associated with several Vedic forces and energies. The Bull is *vrsanaa*, the "Showerer of benefits." These benefits, as has been mentioned in this book, are not material, but spiritual endowments bestowed on the worshiper during the Sacrifice. Not only Agni, but nearly all of the principal Vedic forces distribute these benefits as the Bull:

- Indra. (RV 1.7.6,7; 1.52.23; 1.108.3, 7, 8, 9, 11, 12; 2.17.8; 4.50.10; 5.33.2; 6.22.8; 6.33.1; 6.44.20; 7.31.4; 8.85.7; 10.153..2.)
- Agni. (RV 1.112.8; 3.27.25; 6.1.1; 8.73.10; 10.191.1.)
- Agni-Soma. (RV 1.93.6.)
- Indragni. (RV 1.108.3, 7, 8, 9, 11, 12.)
- Indra-Soma. (RV 7.104.1.)
- Indra-Varuna. (RV 6.68.11; 7.60.9; 7.82.2; 7.83.9.)
- The Asvins. (RV 1.112.8; 1.116.22; 1.117.3, 4, 8, 12, 15, 18, 19, 25; 1.118.1, 6; 1.119.4; 1.157.5;1.158.1; 1.180.7; 1.181.8; 1.183.1; 1.184.2; 2.41.8; 5.74.1; 5.75.4, 9; 6.62.7; 7.70.7; 7.71.6; 7.73.3; 7.74.3; 8.5.24, 27, 36; 8.22.8, 9, 12, 16; 8.26.1, 2, 5, 12, 15; 8.35.15; 10.39.9.)
- Mitra-Varuna. (RV 1.151.2, 3; 1.151.2; 7.60.9, 10; 7.61.5.)
- Maruts. (RV 2.33.13; 7.56.18, 20; 7.58.6; 8.20.16; 10.93.5.)
- Soma. (RV 2.40.3; 8.93.19; 9.5.6; 9.19.5; 9.64.2.)

All of these aspects place the Bull firmly as a fire on the terrestrial level. There are other significations which jettison the Bull outside the terrestrial sphere.

- The zodiacal houses of Mesa (Aries) and Vrshaba (Taurus) rule over the Nakshastras of Krittikas, Rohini, and Mrgishira. (TB 3.1.1.1.) This is a most auspicious role in the Vedic astrological dharma. Krittikas is when the Vernal Equinox, begins, and when the Divine Doors begin to open. Rohini signals the commencement of the Sacrificial year when the rituals begin. Mrgishira is where Orion is situated in the evening sky, a constellation of great significance.
- There are five Bulls in heaven, referring most likely to the constellation Taurus. (RV 1.105.10.)

The worshiper will not encounter a more formidable terrestrial fire as the Bull.

THE CAR

The Car is a manifestation of the terrestrial Fire of Agni. (BD, 1.111.) This fire consists with many components to chariots — the car, the reins, the handrail, and the whip. According to the Vedic Astrologer, the "Car" is symbolic for "planet." In the Bhagavad Gita the car, the chariot, was representative of the worshiper's body and soul. In the Upanishads it is an allusion to the metaphor made in the Katha Upanishad which compared the Self with the worshiper's mind in an extended comparison between the charioteer and the horse to the mind and the sense perceptions. In that famous passage (Kath. U., 3.3 – 10), the Katha Upanishad states:

> Know the Self to be sitting in the chariot, the body to be
> the chariot,
> the intellect [i.e., Buddhi] the charioteer,
> and the mind the reins.

> The senses they call the horses,
> the objects of the senses their roads.

> When he [i.e., the Highest Self] is in union with the body,
> the senses, and the mind,
> then wise people call him the Enjoyer.

> He who has no understanding and whose mind [i.e., the
> reins] is never firmly held,
> his senses [i.e., horses] are unmanageable,

like vicious horses of a charioteer.

But he who has understanding and whose mind is always firmly held,
his senses are under control, like good horses of a charioteer.

He who has no understanding, who is unmindful and always impure,
never reaches that place but enters into the round of births.

But he who has understanding, who is mindful and always pure,
reaches indeed that place, from whence he is not born again.

But he who has understanding for his charioteer,
and who holds the reins of the mind, he reaches the end of his journey,
and that is the highest place of Vishnu.

Beyond the senses there are the objects, beyond the objects there is the mind,
beyond the mind there is the intellect, the Great Self is beyond the intellect.

This highly influential passage accomplishes much to the esoteric understanding of the symbol of the horse and its place in its cosmological structure. It delineates the various elements within which the consciousness resides:

The Self, the subject, sits with the charioteer.

The Chariot is the body

The intellect (Buddhi) is the charioteer.

The mind, Manas, is the reins.

The senses, the indriam, are the horses.

The object of the senses is the road.

So is the image of the horse in the Veda.

This passage defines the esoteric meaning of horses in the Veda. Horses in the Veda has the metaphorical meaning of the "senses," sight, touch, hear, smell, and feel. Horses represent the senses, the mind's perception of the senses, in all their unbridled glory. Unyoked, the Horses represent the Monkey Mind, distracted, unfocused, confused, going from one thought to another.

The fact that the chariot metaphor is analyzed to mean the various components of the chariot demonstrates that the fires exercise their powers in separate areas. The metaphor used here, the car, is the chariot itself, which, in the Katha Upanishad metaphor, stands for the Body, guided by the Self. This fire is aspect of the terrestrial fire is the fire of the Body. It is a testament of the possibilities of the human condition.

DHUMAKETU

Dhumaketu is an aspect of consciousness. Dhumaketu, "Special Vibratory" (*dhuma*) + "knowledge" (*ketu*), the vibration of Knowledge envisaging Agni Pavamana as the "smoke bearer." (RV 1.27.11, 10.4.5, 10.12.2.) Just as where there is smoke, there is fire, Smoke indicates the presence of consciousness Dhumaketu is an epithet for Agni (MB 1.8174) and an epithet for Agni's brother, Surya (MB 3.155.). The Light of Consciousness is personified in Agni Vaisvanara. The Light of Consciousness (Agni Vaisvanara) is channeled to the worshiper on the worshiper's death. On death, the worshiper's body is torn from its mortal coil into three parts; one part going to the Seasons, one pat to the air, and the third part to the terrestrial world. (JB 1.46.) The Jaiminiya Brahmana (JB 1.46, 49) sets out how the worshiper returns to the terrestrial world as Light. First there is the Fire of Agni:

- When Agni Vaisvanara burns the corpse the smoke shakes off his body.
- From the smoke the worshiper goes into the night.
- From the night the worshiper goes to the day.
- From the day the worshiper goes to the half-month of the waning moon.
- From the half-month of the waning moon the worshiper goes to the half-month the waxing moon.
- From the half-month of the waxing moon the worshiper goes to the month.
- From the month the body and life-force of the worshiper unite.

- When the body and life-force of the worshiper unite, the worshiper shines upon the World as Light. The worshiper returns to this world.

This manifestation of Agni accomplishes several things. Not only does it account for the progression of the soul after death, but it also gives an early account for the transmigration of souls. It begins the doctrine espoused later in the Upanishads regarding the Five Fires of the Vedas. In so doing, it further supports a bedrock belief in the immortality of the Soul and of the terrestrial, material world.

THE DICE

One of the most amazing Suktas in the Rg Veda is that which is called, "The Gambler's Remorse," RV 10.34. The "Presiding Deity" in this Sukta is The Dice. The dice is a manifestation of the terrestrial Fire of Agni. (BD, 1.110.) Given the mundane topic, there is a connection with the Vedic force of Agni. The refrain in every stanza is that the worshiper "puts his welfare" in the hands of Agni. The eminent Vedic scholar R.L. Kashyap notes there are two interpretations to this Sukta. One, that the Sukta indeed is about the misery of a gambler. Two, it is about a worshiper who desires a more austere life and wants to play with the mala beads rather than tossing the dice. There is, of course, a third interpretation. Dice is gambling, a game of chance. When the gambler throws the dice on the ground, instead of placing his trust to faith, he, as the refrain goes, places the trust in Agni.

Given the symbolic nature of the Vedas the Dice are the symbol of the fortuitous nature of life in the Vedic dharma.

THE DRAUGHT

The Draught is a manifestation of the terrestrial Fire of Agni. (BD, 1.111.) A draught (draft) can either be a current of air or the act or instance of drinking.

DRAVINODAS

Dravinodas is a manifestation of the terrestrial Fire of Agni. (BD, 1.106.) Dravinodas is the "Giver of Strength." In the Vedic dharma, Agni in his manifestation as Dravinodas is known as the Giver of Treasures." (RV 1.96.1 – 9.) The treasures given are not material; they are spiritual endowments of which Strength is one.

THE DRUM

The drum is a manifestation of the terrestrial Fire of Agni. (BD, 1.111.)

THE FROGS

The Frogs are a manifestation of the terrestrial Fire of Agni. (BD, 1.109.) The Frogs are the Presiding Deities in 7.103, with Parjanya, a deity associated with the Rains. Parjanya made its appearance in RV 1.164.51, and earlier in the introduction of this book. In the Vedic dharma Parjanya is a deity associated with the rains. It was in this context that RV 1.164.51 described, paradoxically, as the replenishment of the earth though the Five Fires. The Five Fires have been mentioned a few times in this book. It is an important part of the Vedic dharma and bears repeating. As has been reiterated several times in this treatment, those five fires are:

- The Heavenly Fire. Humans are sacrificed at death by cremation, becoming food for the divine Vedic energies and principles and transformed by the heavenly fire into Soma, the purified mind. This fire transforms the human body at death and upon the funeral pyre. The smoke, ciders, and ashes carrying the soul upwards to the heaven.
- The Fire of Parjanya. This fire transforms Soma and the souls in its command into rain. Parjanya is the Vedic divine force for rain. The soul carried upwards to the heavens to be met by Parjanya.
- The Vegetative Fire. Soma, the divine food, releases the rain, its essence, to earth, where it is transformed into vegetation. Rain is the essence of Soma (Purification), as divine food, falls to the earth with the souls in transmigration.
- The Digestive Fire. When these food plants containing the human should are eaten, they are transformed into seamen by the

man-fire, the digestive fire. The rain containing the seeds of the souls in transmigration are transformed to semen and are absorbed by the plant life and fauna and eaten by man or animal.

- The Female Fire. The semen is transformed into a Purusa, a person, by the woman-fire. The semen is transformed into a Purusa.

The frogs are associated with Parjanya no doubt based on the perceived appearance of frogs following the rains. Regular like clockwork, they appear, assuring the Vedics at the time that there is a continuity of life. The frogs thereby became representative of the perpetuity of life; later, in the Upanishads Parjanya became the simile of the reincarnation and transmigration of the worshipers' lives. The frogs are made a manifestation of the terrestrial fire because it is on the terrestrial level where all this transformation takes place.

THE HANDGUARD

The Handguard is a manifestation of the terrestrial Fire of Agni. (BD, 1.111.) This is symbolic language of the another part of the chariot/Self metaphor.

IDHMA

Idhma, the manifestation of Agni Pavamana representing the sacrificial fuel for fire. Idhma is a manifestation of the terrestrial Fire of Agni. (BD, 1.106.) Idhma is that aspect of the terrestrial fire bringing Increase. (BD, 3.4.) It is an important part of the terrestrial fire. The terrestrial manifestation of Idhma is one of the basic elements of the Vedic dharma. When the Purusa was created and created the seasons, the fuel of fire consisted of the Summer. (RV 10.09.6.) Agni is the guiding force for the power of Increase.

- The heat from the Fire of Agni that provides the fuel of the worshiper's increase. (RV 4.2.6.)
- There is a symbiotic relationship with regard to the increase the worshiper receives from Agni's Vedic force. The worshiper brings the fuel to kindle the Fire of Agni, which provides the worshiper the energy to proceed in the spiritual journey. (4.12.2.)

There can be no development, spiritual or otherwise, without Increase. Increase is the practical means by which the worshiper gains the spiritual endowments provided in the Vedas, but more generally the only means by which the fire of Change and Transformation may occur.

The fire of Idhma provides the very basis for Change and Transformation. In eons past, in the beginning of creation, when the Sacrifice was first created, Purusa was put forward as an offering. The Vedic forces performed their sacrifice and from the sacrifice of Purusa the seasons were created. Spring became *aiya*, Summer became the fire of Idhma, and autumn became the Offering. (RV 10.90.6.) This passage implicates several aspects of this terrestrial fire and beyond. It implicates Idhma, placing this terrestrial fire as one of the most ancient. It also demonstrates an important characteristic of the Sacrifice.

ILA

Ila is a manifestation of the terrestrial fire and is subsumed in Narasamsa, itself a manifestation of the terrestrial Fire of Agni. (BD 1.107.) Even without the subsumption with Narasamsa, Ila follows the terrestrial Agni. (BD, 3.13.) Ila is an epithet of Agni Pavamana representing the Power of Consciousness to envision the truth. (RV 1.13.9.) Ila is an important manifestation of the terrestrial Fire of Agni:

- When the Vedic force of Agni was first born, he was transformed into the personification of the Divine Vision, Ila, that the mysteries of the Vedas and other mysteries of the Vedic dharma may be conveyed to the Rishiis. (RV 1.31.11.)
- The Rishiis are not the only beneficiaries to the divine vision of Agni. Agni is transformed to Ila, so that the worshiper may invoke these powers for the spiritual journey. (RV 1.40.4.)
- Ila is the fire that collects the mighty powers of the Vedic dharma, such as its vastness and plentitude and luminosity, and translate these forces into common speech. (RV 3.7.5.)
- In this capacity Ila is the fire which speaks the truth. (RV 7.16.8.)

KAVI

Kavi, another name for the power of revelation possessed by the Rishiis. Kavi and the other Rishiis Bhrgu and the Angiras, sprang from the coals of the Sacrificial Fire. (MB 13.85.4142.)

THE LITTER AND
THE DIVINE DOORS

The litter and the Divine Doors. The litter and the Divine Doors are subsumed in Narasamsa, itself a manifestation of the terrestrial Fire of Agni. (BD 1.107.) The litter can refer to one of three things.

- One, it can refer to the implements and remnants from the Sacrifice. It includes items such as Soma stalks left over from the distillation of pavamana, charcoal and other embers from the Sacrificial Fire, or animal parts discarded from the Horse Sacrifice. As all things Vedic, there is an esoteric meaning to the litter. Charcoal provides the clearest example. Charcoal are the remnants from the Fire Altar. The spark ignites wood; the wood smolders and is fanned into flame, fire; the wood is transformed into energy; wood becomes friction, light, heat, hot coals, embers, and ash. Just as when fire consumes wood, leaving its essential elements in the form of charcoal and ash, that same fire is in operation in the sacrificial ritual and reduces the form and substance of the universe to its most essential elements. As the Fire Altar represents the focal point of the worshiper's concentration, the charcoal represents the most basic elements of the worshiper's mental concentration. The charcoal becomes the terrestrial symbol of pure thought and the purified mind.
- Two, it can refer Barhis, itself a terrestrial manifestation of Agni's fire, denoting the litter of grass strewn on the sacrificial ground on which the gods are summoned to seat themselves. Since it is the

Vedic forces summoned, the area is considered something more than simple seating arrangements. It is holy, sacred ground, and that is how it is defined in one rc, where it is called the altar of strewn grass, barhi/r u tistiraaNaa/. (RV 1.108, 4.)

- Three, on a somewhat more graphic mode, the litter is grass called Eleusine indica. It is mentioned in the Atharvaveda (AV 14.2.22, 23) and is said in the Yajurveda Saṃhita (TS 2.2.8.2) and elsewhere (MS 2.2.5) to be produced from the excrements of cattle. In the Kathaka Saṃhita (KS 10.10) it is stated to be used for the sacrificial litter (Barhis) and for fuel. Baskets or other products made from this grass are referred to in a Danastuti ('Praise of Gifts') in the Rigveda. (RV 8.55.3.) While all these uses no doubt had their real-life correlates, there is also an esoteric meaning to all this. We had just seen in the first meaning that charcoal represents the remnants of the Fire Altar, namely pure thought and the purified mind. The litter in this sense represents the remnants of the food from cows. The cows represent knowledge and Speech. The litter in this sense represents pure knowledge or knowledge freed of those elements which had burdened that knowledge previously.

The meat of this terrestrial manifestation are the Divine Doors. The Veda reveals its secrets through riddles, paradoxes, and code words. One code word is the simple "door" or dvar. Bal Gangadhar Tilak states this word signifies the Equinox. Tilak's thesis (Tilak Orion, or the Antiquity of the Vedas, pp. 107-108) is that the Vernal Equinox resided in the asterism of Mrgishira, the principal star of which is Orion. This stellar location marked the beginning of the Devayana, the Path of the Gods, and the termination point of the Piriyana, the Path of the Fathers. The Vernal Equinox is otherwise alluded in the Rg Veda as the "Gates of Heaven." The Equinox — Vernal or Autumnal, but especially Vernal — is the portal to the devayana, the Path of the gods, which is the preferred destination of the soul after the death of the physical body. (Tilak, Orion, p. 165.) This is the higher purpose on which the concentration of the worshiper should be fixed; it is there that which the worshiper should keep its "eyes on the prize." The imagery of the doors is perfect. The Equinox represents the portal wherein from whence the worshiper arrived; it is the door from where the soul appeared on earth; and it is the gateway where the soul will one day return.

The asterism of Krttikas, located in the same cluster of asterisms with the Vernal Equinox, is located at the mouth of the Nakshatras. (T.B. 1.1.2.1.) Krittikas is the asterism of Agni, the Fire of Change. (SPB 2.1.2.1.) Krittikas, the "Divine Doors," is the very embodiment of the transcendent world of the Seven-Dimensional Universe. (RV 1.72.8.) The devayana, the Path of the Gods, begins with the Krttikas and ends with Vaisakhi, and the ptryana, the Path of the Fathers, begin with Anuradha and end with the Apabharanis. (TB 1.5.2.7.) The Divine Doors of Krittikas provide the guidepost to where the Vedic astrologer seeks to reach the spiritual journey — the devayana, the Path of the Gods.

In the Veda there are four themes where the "Divine Doors" are concerned.

- The first theme is where a "door" signifies a physical barrier that keeps the cows or cattle at bay. (RV 1.51.3; 5.45.1; 6.17.6; 6.62.11; 10.120.8; 10.139.6.) In Vedic imagery the "cows" or "cattle" are representative for knowledge or the articulation in speech. When the doors are opened, the fruits of knowledge blossom. The Equinox, especially the Vernal Equinox occurring at Spring, is the cosmic analogue of the renewal of life.

- The second theme is when a Vedic force or principle "opens a door" and "finds food." (RV 1.130.3; 2.2.7; 7.9.2; 8.39.6.) "Food" here is any source which provides support, nourishment, or sustenance.

- Third is where the a "door" is any means or method to assist in the sacrificial rite or worship. (RV 1.13.6; 1.128.6; 5.5.5; 8.39.6.) This is an important meaning. The Vernal Equinox is located at the constellation of Krittikas, Orion. It is an important, perhaps most important, commencement date for sacrificial rituals.

- Four, the Divine Doors carry astrological significance. RV 4.18.9, 8.6.7, 5.34.2, and 8.93.14, Indra cutting off Vrtra's head is symbolic of the cutting off of the head of Prajapati, the symbol reflected in this Nakshatra, Mrgishira, the closing phase of the Vernal Equinox, the "Antelope's Head", the English correlate of the constellation Orion. (SPB 2.1.2.8.) Further, the slaying of

Vrtra opens the gates of heaven to allow the soul to enter devayana, the gates of heaven, articulated symbolically by the association with the Nakshastra Mrgishira (Orion). (RV 10.73.7.)

A significant equivalence is created. The Divine Doors equate to the Vernal Equinox, which is equated with the devayana, the path of the gods, which leads to the worshiper's liberation and salvation. These themes are reflected in many passages in the Veda:

- The Vernal Equinox (the "Divine Doors") signals the beginning of the sacrifice and enhances its performance. (RV 1.13.6.)
- The Vernal Equinox (the "Divine Doors") is the astrological correlate of the spiritual awareness that bestows benefit. (RV 1.48.15.)
- The Fire of Change (Agni) confers blessings on the worshiper which emanate from the powers of the Vernal Equinox (the "Divine Doors"). (RV 1.128.6.)
- Bala (Indra) releases the energies of the Vernal Equinox (the "Divine Doors") that lay concealed by the clouds. (RV 1.130.3.)
- The Vernal Equinox (the "Divine Doors") is the portal through the room from where the world of divinity is found. (RV 1.142.6.)
- Spiritual benefits are obtained when the powers of the Vernal Equinox (the "Divine Doors") are released. (RV 2.3.5.)
- The powers of the Vernal Equinox (the "Divine Doors") are kindled when the Fire of Change (Agni) is conjoined with Awareness (Usas). (RV 3.5.1.)

Awareness (Usas) furnishes the luminosity of the Vernal Equinox (the "Divine Doors.")(RV 4.51.2.)

- When kindled by the luminosity of Awareness (Usas), the Vernal Equinox (the "Divine Doors") releases the waters. (RV 8.5.1.) In this context, "releasing the waters" means releasing the powers of religious ecstacy. (Soma.)
- The Vernal Equinox (the "Divine Doors") heralds the arrival of the gods. (RV 7.17.2.) In this regard, the "arrival of the gods" is

an obscure reference to the beginning of the sacrifice and the sacrificial rituals.

"Vernal Equinox" is Veda-Speak for "day." The Vedic Rishis were very cognizant that the Day should refer to the equinox at that period during the year when the Sun shines for the longest duration of time. Just as the Dawn signals the beginning of a new day, the longest period of daylight indicates the true beginning of a new year. "Day" (RV 1.54.3; 1.71.5; 1.129.3; 1.136.6;1.185.10; 2.13.5; 2.24.14; 3.54.3; 3.54.5; 4.3.5; 5.47.7; 5.59.1; 6.18.14; 8.70.2; 9.109.5) therefore becomes the code word for the "Vernal Equinox." This is consistent with the interpretation put forward by Plato in the Timaeus — which Plato himself stated was a repository of mysteries originating from "the East" rather than his own personal philosophy. The purpose of the Equinoxes are to delineate the progression of the days and nights. (Weil, Imitations of Christianity, p. 94.) The Vernal Equinox has great spiritual power to transform the worshiper and is formidable implement in the worshiper's path to salvation. This has as much to do with the intense meditative practice described in another terrestrial fire, Usasanakta. According to that practice, the worshiper meditates on the constant regularity of the passage of days, nights, weeks, etc., and as a result of this intense meditation concludes there is no difference between the future and the past. In arriving at this conclusion the worshiper pierces through time to eternity and dwells in the eternal present. The Vernal Equinox (the "Divine Doors") has great spiritual power according to the specific injunctions in the Veda:

- The worshiper is transformed spiritually when the worshiper's being and essence is given up to that place in the celestial sphere where the Vernal Equinox (the "Divine Doors") is located. (RV 1.71.5.)
- The worshiper praises the Vedic force and energy of Indra when meditating on the Vernal Equinox (the "Divine Doors"). (RV 1.129.3.)
- The worshiper proclaims veneration and spiritual faith to the Sun, Vernal Equinox (the "Divine Doors") and to the earth. (RV 1.136.6.)

- Understanding its place in the universe, the worshiper surrenders its soul and being to the Vernal Equinox (the "Divine Doors") to receive its protection. (RV 1.185.10.)

- The Fire of Change (Agni) establishes the connection between the celestial sphere (earth) and the Vernal Equinox (heaven). (RV 2.13.5.) This rc (mantra) reveals another dimension in the relationship of heaven and earth. Heaven and earth could mean the planetary earth and stellar atmosphere. Other meanings could be father/mother, masculine principle/feminine principle, or as here, the celestial sphere/ Vernal Equinox. Whatever juxtaposition is used, the Vernal Equinox, the Divine Doors, is an agent for the unification of opposites.

- The conjoining of the celestial sphere (earth) and the Vernal Equinox (heaven) is the repository and declaration of the inner essence of the Vedic dharma, *Rta*. (RV 3.54.2, 3.) Just as friction occurs whenever two sticks are rubbed together, and the same type of friction occurs whenever the two existential planes of Heaven and Earth come into contact. The friction produces heat. From the heat the Vedic dharma, in all its splendor, is emitted.

- The worshipers glorify the Maruts and praise the shining Vernal Equinox (the "Divine Doors"). (RV 5.59.7.)

- The Vedic force of religious ecstacy, Soma, spreads joy and divine ecstasy to the celestial sphere and Vernal Equinox (the "Divine Doors"). (RV 9.109.

THE MALLET

The Mallet is a manifestation of the terrestrial Fire of Agni. (BD, 1.111.)

THE MORTAR

The Mortar is a manifestation of the terrestrial Fire of Agni. (BD, 1.111.) The Mortar is defined as a cup-shaped receptacle made of hard material, in which ingredients are crushed or ground, used especially in cooking or pharmacy, anciently used in Alchemy, and more anciently during the time of the Vedas to pulverize and distill Soma juice.

The noted Vedic scholar, R.L. Kashyap, interprets The Mortar to symbolize "the Body." (Kashyap, *The Secrets of The Rig Veda*, (2003), p. 205.) On a certain level it certainly does represent the body of the worshiper. As a manifestation of the terrestrial Fire of Agni The Mortar represents something else. To understand this aspect of The Mortar it is helpful to recall the mechanics of the distillation of Soma juice during the Soma Sacrifice. The original Sanskrit for the Mortar is *ulukhala*. Ulukhala is properly defined as the receptacle in which Soma stalk is ground and the juice extracted. The Mortar thus becomes the vessel in which the terrestrial fire burns. The Mortar thus can mean the body, or it can mean the Fire Altar, or it can be interpreted in a very general sense to mean any vessel wherein the terrestrial fire is located. The Mortar is paired with the Pestle, and the Pestle is another manifestation of the terrestrial fire of Agni. In that discussion there will be more about this terrestrial fire.

Truth be told, aside from its purely ritualistic interpretation and use, the Mortar can be interpreted in any of a number of ways. If Soma Pavamana is the undiluted, purified Soma juice which induces the feeling of religious ecstacy, the Mortar can be interpreted as the receptacle storing that feeling of religious release. Whether that receptacle is the worshiper's body, mind, or spirit is academic and subject to reasonable disagreement. That it is a receptacle of this feeling is the important concept to hold.

NARASAMSA

There are many sides to Narasamsa. Nara is the Primeval Man, the Purusa, Manu, Adam in the Abrahamic religions. Nara is also the Universal Spirit pervading the Universe and is associated with the Supreme Vedic force from whom the Vedic dharma was born. (MB 1.1.72.).

Narasamsa is the terrestrial (B.D., 1.107, 1.110) manifestation of Agni. Narasamsa subsumes several other manifestations of the terrestrial fire: Barhi, Ila, and the Litter and the Divine Doors. That these implements of the sacrifice should be subsumed in Narasamsa is fitting. Narasamsa is the terrestrial fire of the Sacrifice. (B.D., 3.2.) As the terrestrial fire kindling the sacrifice, Narasamsa is the driving force of the give-and-take process which pervades the sacrifice. This is due as much from the inherent nature of Narasamsa as to the nature of Narasamsa as the Purusa.

- Narasamsa is the efficient cause of the Sacrifice. (RV 5.5.2.) As the efficient cause, Narasamsa is the guiding light and rationale behind the sacrificial rituals.
- Agni in his terrestrial manifestation of Narasamsa creates the offerings which are presented at the sacrifice. (RV 1.13.3.) In the same way, Purusa, through his own self-sacrifice, created the seasons (RV 10.90.6), knowledge and the life-force of the Vedic dharma (RV 10.90.8), and the rcs and samans (mantras) of the Vedas. All these emanate from the terrestrial Fire of Agni in his manifestation of Narasamsa.
- Narasamsa provides the subtle basis for the sacrifice. Agni in his terrestrial manifestation of Narasamsa officiates the sacrifice in

300

his priestly capacity from Heaven. (RV 1.18.9.) In the same way, Purusa is the incarnation of the Sacrifice. (RV 10.90.7.)

- The sins of the worshiper are expiated through the terrestrial fire of Narasamsa. (RV 1.106.4.)

The terrestrial fire of Narasamsa is the most excellent, most exalted, manifestation of Nara. Indeed, the most exalted status of Agni in his manifestation as the terrestrial fire of Narasamsa is indicated by the vast array of Vedic forces and energies which spring from its "pregnant seed" (RV 10.92.11):

- The four Agnis.
- Yama.
- Aditi.
- Tvastr, a manifestation of Agni as a terrestrial fire.
- Dravinoda, another manifestation of Agni as a terrestrial fire.
- Rbhukshana.
- Rodasi, a manifestation of Heave.
- Vishnu.
- The Maruts, a manifestation of Agni as a fire from the Md-World.

While the fire is terrestrial, Narasamsa is divine in nature

- Narasamsa is perfect in form and firmly established in its thought. (RV 7.2.2.)
- Narasamsa is the godhead, the spokesman for the Vedic forces and energies. (RV 5.5.2.)
- Narasamsa is perfect in his knowledge. (RV 2.3.2.)
- Narasamsa is the most perfect articulation of the godhead. (RV 10.70.2.)

The fire of Narasamsa is also the Universal Spirit pervading the Universe.

- The vast Vedic dharma is kindled, energized, through the terrestrial fire of Narasamsa. (RV 1.106.4.) "Kindled" here should be given the meaning attributed to the Mystic Fire of Agni. It is more than a simple igniting; when Agni is kindled or, as here, when Narasamsa is kindled, the mystic powers are triggered, energizing the subtle powers of the Fire.

- When Narasamsa shines down on the world, the terrestrial fire reveals the seven existential planes of existence (Sat, chit, ananda, svar, dyu, Antariksha, bhuvah, and bhumi) and the three levels of heaven (uttama(m) or uttame, madhyama or madhyame, and avama.)

The qualities of Narasamsa is summarized in RV 3.29.11:

- Narasamsa is the child in the womb. The "womb" is the Vedic dharma itself.
- Narasamsa is the son of the body.
- Narasamsa is the logos, the articulation, of the godhead.
- Narasamsa grows in the mid-word.

It can thus be said that Narasamsa is the terrestrial representative of the Celestial fires on earth. But it is basically a terrestrial fire. It provides both for the worshiper.

PESTLE AND MORTAR

The Pestle and Mortar are manifestations of the terrestrial Fire of Agni. (BD, 1.113. If the Mortar is the vessel of the terrestrial fire, the Pestle is instrument engaging the point of contact generating the terrestrial fire. Monier Williams provides an alternative definition of "Pestle" with "Vanaspati," which is itself a terrestrial manifestation of the Fire of Agni. Vanaspati is one word for Pestle because in the practice of the Soma Sacrifice both the Mortar and the Pestle were made out of wood. (Kashyap, *The Secrets of The Rig Veda*, (2003), p. 205.) Indeed, Kashyap appears to interpret the Pestle as the sword of Indra. What are we to make of all this? The situation is not improved any, because the only portions of the Rg Veda which reveals anything substantial about the Pestle and Mortar is in RV 1.28.1 – 6.

Remember the Five Fires doctrine described in the beginning? Two of those fires were the following:

- The Digestive Fire.

   When these food plants containing the human should are eaten, they are transformed into seamen by the man-fire, the digestive fire. The rain containing the seeds of the souls in transmigration are transformed to semen and are absorbed by the plant life and fauna and eaten by man or animal. (BU, 6.2.12.,)

- The Female Fire.

> This semen is transformed into a Purusha, a person, by the woman-fire. The semen is transformed into a Purusha. (BU, 6.6.2.13.)

These fires may have more application other than explaining reincarnation. Hanns-Peter Schmidt, in Ŗgveda 1.28 and the Alleged Domestic Soma-Pressing, Electronic Journal of Vedic Studies (2009, Vol. 16:1), cites the work of other previous scholars, in theorizing that the Soma Sacrifice, at least the portion which pertains to the grinding of the Soma plant with the Pestle and Mortar and Pressing Stones, are all imagery grounded in sexual innuendo. In other words, the Pestle becomes the penis; the Soma juice becomes the semen; the Mortar becomes the uterus; the Pressing Stones become the testicles; and the planks which crush the Soma stalks the thighs.

Interesting hypothesis, but this also misses the point. If one really tried, one could find phallic symbols anywhere. There is fire in sexual passion, that is undeniable; that is the whole point of what a terrestrial fires of Agni should be concerned. Collectively, the Pestle and Mortar represent the phallus and uterus and the sexual fire.

THE PLANT

The plant is a manifestation of the terrestrial Fire of Agni. (BD, 1.111.)

Plato compared mortal humans to a plant, whose roots reached to Heaven. The Plant was sprinkled with celestial waters, "a divine semen, which enters the head." Water, with fire, is symbolic of the process of purification, and just as water is sprinkled to purify the subject, so must a fire take place to clear the dry, dead brush, and rejuvenate the forest and allow the forest to grow taller, stronger and in a more healthy manner.

PRTHVI (EARTH)

Earth, Prthvi, is an element in the Vedic dharma. Prthvi is also a manifestation of the terrestrial Fire of Agni. (BD, 1.111.) Prthvi is the Earth, the flip side of Heaven. Fire is a terrestrial agent, and the Jaiminiya Upanishad Brahmana gives the best summation of the subtle influence of the Fire of Change (Agni) to the Earth. The Fire of Change is speech and speech is the earth and the Fire of Change and the other emanations of the Three-Dimensional Universe are reposed in OM. (JUB 1.2.1-8.) The Fire of Change, Agni, pervades the sensible universe, the *vyahrti*. The fire of The Principle of Change (Agni), or pervasion of consciousness, is expressed in triplets and reaches to the three levels of the sensible universe:

- The sensible universe, vyahrti, consisting of bhuh, the lower world;
- Antarikstra, the mid-world, sometimes called bhuvah, the upper world; and
- Svar, the sun-world, bindu, is the hub, the gateway, the vortex which inverts and turns the sensible world on its head into tridhaatu, or mahii, the upper three levels of the world beyond the manifest universe.

The Three-Dimensional Universe holds special significance to the Principle of Change (Agni):

- The Fire of Change (Agni) has a three-fold nature. (RV 1.95.3; 4.1.7.)

306

- This three-fold nature has sometimes been referred to as the "three brothers, (RV 1.164.1; 10.51.6), a representation of the three altars
- The divine fashioned the Fire of Change (Agni) to have this three-fold nature. (RV 10.88.10.)
- The Fire of Change (Agni) has three heads (RV 1.146.1), residing in three stations, tongue or bodies. (RV 3.20.2.)
- The Fire of Change (Agni) resides in three abodes (RV 8.39.8), meaning heaven, earth and water. (RV 8.44.16; 10.2.7; 4.6.9.)
- The Fire of Change (Agni) is lit with three kindlings. (RV 3.2.9; 3.26.7.)
- The Fire of Change (Agni) has three births (RV 1.95.3; 4.1.7), the first from heaven, the second from men, and the third from the waters. (RV 10.45.1.)

The element of Prthvi, Earth, is foundational. In the Sabalopanishad, 2.4, it is the starting point for the evolution of the rest of the elements:

- Earth dissolves in water.
- Water dissolves in fire.
- Fire dissolves in air.

Mithuna (Gemini) is the zodiacal house belonging to Agni and is the source of the unifying powers of the Vedic force of Agni.

- Agni, Fire, represents the Masculine Energy; Prthvi, Earth, represents the Feminine Energy. Through the pairing and mating (*mithuna*) of Agnim (Fire) with Prthvi (Earth), the two elements are melded together, interchangeably, to provide the Regenerative Principle.

Thus does this terrestrial manifestation of fire accounts for the heat of this material world, assist in its creation, and allows it to subsist and continue.

THE PRESSING STONES

The Pressing Stones are manifestations of the terrestrial Fire of Agni. (BD, 1.110.) The Pressing Stones hold great significance to Soma. It is through the pounding of the pressing stones on the stalks of the Soma plant — whatever that plant actually was — that the purified Soma juice is produced. The purified Soma juice is an entheogenic drink which induces a powerful religious experience of the mystical union with the divine. The nearest contemporary vegetation today is peyote, which is consumed and used for similar purposes.

As a terrestrial manifestation of Agni, the Pressing Stones is the fire which transforms the ordinary crushed juice obtained from the Soma plant into the exhilarating drink that it is today known. The terrestrial fire is premised on the impact of the stones. On impact, the clashing stones create their own heat (*Tapas*) and the heat therefrom produce the sparks which ignite the physical fires and kindle the mystic fires. The terrestrial fire is also premised on the nature of the divine experience itself. To experience the divine is an intense, transformative event, nothing like the mundane day-to-day of life in the material world. Mystics have commonly likened the divine as fire. It is incendiary, destroying the previous way of thinking into a new way of living. This is why that moment of insight, spiritual renewal, or enlightenment is frequently described as being "born again."

The pressing stones provide the raw material for the spiritual endowments and entitlements provided to the worshiper. Soma juice is pressed out by the press stones. The Pressing Stones could be left at that, simply a ritualistic stage of the Soma Sacrifice. Instead, as in all things in the Vedic dharma, even every-day phenomena possess several layers of meaning. So it is for the Pressing Stones. On a sacrificial level,

- Soma is pressed out by the stones.
- Soma is purified by those who pass the plant through the press.
- Soma is pressed out by the stones.
- Purified Soma is pressed out of the purifier.
- Soma needs to be purified because the initial purchase of the soma plant is a crime. This is a curious epithet. The Soma plant must be obtained in some manner in order for the preparation of the Soma juice. It is beyond the scope of this treatment to give a step-by-step process of obtaining the Soma plant Suffice it to say there have been other references of the "crime" of purchasing Soma. For example, Soma had to be purchased from the Panis, the merchant class identified with Evil incarnate. (RV 6.51.4; 6.44.22; 8.75.7; See, generally SPB, 3.2.4.1-7.) Be that as it may, this served another reason why Soma was required to be purified, to cure the defilement caused by its purchase from the Panis.

The press stones are premised on the fuel which rule the Vedic dharma. This a return of the give-and-take present in the sacrificial rite. This is illustrated by the following rcs (mantras).

- "Soma is Pressed Out by *Tapas*." (RV 9.113.2) *Tapas* is intensity of many forms, here, interpreted as the intense rays emitted by the Sun.
- Once pressed out, Soma thereupon is offered back for the rays of Surya, the Vedic divine force of the Sun. (RV 9.61.9.)
- From there, the pressed-out Soma supports the world. (RV 9.63.6.)

The Pressing Stones are instrumental in this give-and-take. Soma is pressed out by Vayu, the Vedic force which breathes in the midworld. In a marvelous "he who breathes." From this ritualistic interpretation, these epithets speak of the psychological state induced as a result of the Pressing. Soma is Milked to Produce the Intense Essence. From there, the rcs (mantras) further explain:

- Upon being pressed, Soma make people glorious.
- When pressed Soma supports the gods' blissful state. While the rc (manta) speaks of the gods, this thought applies equally to mere mortals.

There is a purely sacred meaning to the Pressing. Here,

- The out-pressed Soma is divine.
- Soma is pressed by the divine Vedic powers.
- Upon being pressed, Soma destroys all enemies. Here, "enemies" in the black-and-white world of the Rg Veda is taken to mean "Evil-doers."
- The pressed-out Soma is luminous.

Finally, the pressing stones are associated with Soma: "The thrice-seven cows (*tri/r asmai sapta/ dhena/vo*) milk (*duduhre*) Soma with infusions of Truth." (RV 9.70.1.) Mystically shrouded in symbolic language, this epithet touches to the heart of the Soma's place in the Vedic dharma.

The culmination of these epithets and descriptors is that the pressing stones represent Soma Pavamana, Soma in its purified and pristine form, and all the meanings contained therein. The pressing stones thus symbolize both the spiritual journey and provide the means to undertake that journey. (RV 10.92.15.)

"Thrice Seven" is a phrase which makes recurring appearances in the Vedas. "Thrice Seven" combines the essential qualities of the cardinal numbers three and seven. The Three-Dimensional universe is the subtle aspect of the material world. The Seven-Dimensional Universe is the transcendent universe. "Thrice seven" is the metaphorical leap from the subtle aspect of the material world to the transcendent.

In this respect "Thrice Seven" implicates the collective microcosm and macrocosm. The concept of the "Thrice Seven," trih sapta, recurs throughout the Vedas, in the Rg Veda in several rcs (mantras) (RV 1.72.6; 1.191.12, 14; 4.1.16; 7.87.4; 8.46.26; 8.96.2; 9.86.21; 10.64.8; 10.90.15) and in the Brahmanas. Its meaning is tantalizingly obscure and varied. The Brahmanas unanimously indicate that "Thrice Seven" refers to:

- 12 months;
- 5 seasons;
- 3 worlds;
- One Sun,

and further state that the Sun is the world. (TS 7.3.10; 5.4.12; AB 30.4; TB 3.8.10; KB 11.6; PB 6.2.2;SPB 1.3.5.11.) This interpretation from the Brahmanas implicates the macrocosm, the Vedic dharma. It encompasses both a division of time and its assignment to the physical worlds. The occult meaning of "Thrice Seven" according to these passages could be said to include both the "spatial and temporal expanse of the physical universe" and that area beyond the spatial and temporal boundaries of the material world.

"Thrice Seven" is an extension of the "Rule of Three" referenced in the Lagadha Vedango Jyotisa. (RVJ, 24; YVJ, 42.) This "Rule of Three" must be viewed against the many references in the Veda of the number seven which were listed above. References of this number have been widely interpreted as representative of the seven levels of existence, both the macrocosm and microcosm, the Seven-Dimensional Universe.

There are seven levels to the macrocosm and microcosm, and three different fuels impelling each level. (AV 19.6.15.) "Thrice Seven" communicates a deeper aspect of the macrocosm and microcosm. On one level it provides a cosmological framework for the transcendent Seven-Dimensional Universe where each level contains three different subdivisions. On another level it provides a mechanism whereby the worshiper can jump start from the material world to the transcendent world. This process is symbolized in the construction of the Fire Altar. The Fire Altar represents the whole world and the bricks the regions (SPB 7.3.1.13) and the vedi sacrificial altar, the entire sacrificial enclosure, represents the earth. (SPB 7.3.1.15.)

Specifically, when constructing the fifth layer of the Fire Altar with Stamobhaga bricks, twenty-one bricks are used to symbolize the three worlds and the regions. (SPB 8.5.3.5, 6.) Each level of the fifth layer contains three layers and represents a different, progressively elevated, layer of the cosmic order:

- The first three layers, one through three, is symbolic of the world;
- The second three layers, four through six, is symbolic of the mid-earth;
- The third three layers, seven through nine, is symbolic of the heavens.
- The fourth three layers, ten through twelve, is symbolic of the eastern quarter;
- The fifth three layers, thirteen through fifteen, is symbolic of the southern quarter;
- The sixth three layers, sixteen through eighteen, is symbolic of the western quarter; and
- The seventh three layers, nineteen through twenty-one, is symbolic of the northern quarter

You have probably noticed there are seven layers to the Fire Altar. Those seven layers are representations of the Seven-Dimension Universe. There is, in addition to all that, an intricate give-and-take going on. The Vedic sacrifice ritual is intended to demonstrate a fundamental truth of the universe: that there is a give-and-take between the Microcosm (humankind) and the Macrocosm (the universe), of every object therein, encompassing the process from creation to dissolution. (Sannyasi Gyanshruti, Sunnyasi Srividyananda, *Yajna, A Comprehensive Survey* (2006), pp. 84 – 85.) This give-and-take process is the essence of how the natural order (*rta*) operates. Here, Soma bounces back and forth between these different levels of existence, from the macrocosm to the microcosm, all through the context of the Sacrifice, through its different constituent parts. The altar, the sacrificial bricks, all represent these worlds. "Thrice Seven," does not simply indicate the Seven-Dimensional Universe but reveals different aspects of this Seven-Dimensional Universe after taking into consideration its triplicate nature with respect to an aspect in some level in the divine, dynamic cosmic order *(rta)*, in conjunction with the Three-Dimensional Universe of this material world. Soma, the product of the Pressing Stones, infuses these worlds with Truth, *Satyam*, in this cosmic give-and-take.

THE QUIVER

A quiver is a container for holding arrows, bolts, or darts. It can be carried on an archer's body, the bow, or the ground, depending on the type of shooting and the archer's personal preference. The quiver is also a manifestation of the terrestrial Fire of Agni. (BD, 1.111.) The Quiver is the fire of Kriyamana karma. The quiver is a part of the fire of karma. As the quiver is, of course, the container which contains the arrows for the archer, Sanchita, is this vast storehouse of yet unseen impressions and is the sum of one's past karmas – all actions, good and bad, from the worshiper's past lives that follow through to the present incarnation. Just as in the new incarnation of the worshiper a vast amount of past mental impressions (vasanas) are deposited, those mental impressions become the arrows in the archer's quiver. The quiver is a terrestrial fire because the arrows taken from the quiver take place on this earth.

RATRI

Ratri is a manifestation of the terrestrial Fire of Agni. (BD, 1.111.) Ratri is the Vedic force representing the Night and is the sister of Usas, the Vedic goddess of Dawn.

THE REINS

The reins are the manifestations of the terrestrial Fire of Agni. (BD, 1.111.) A named element to the chariot/Self metaphor of the Katha Upanishad, the reins stands for the mind, Manas. In the Vedic dharma the reins signify the terrestrial fire of Manas, the mind.

THE RIVERS

The Rivers are the manifestations of the terrestrial Fire of Agni. (BD, 1.112.) It is easy to see how the Rivers are a terrestrial manifestation of Agni. When the Vedic dharma is thought of as a living organism, it is easy to believe that the Rivers represent the vessels of the Vital Life Force, Prana, circulating the entire system like blood veins. In addition it is easy to imagine the system of rivers representing the synapses of the mind sparking and igniting the expanse of the brain. This is exactly how the Rivers are represented in the Rg Veda.

This attribute in the Vedic dharma is mentioned many times in the Rg Veda with the simile of a river flowing. The eb and flow of rivers and waters symbolize the flow of Consciousness. This manifestation of Agni addresses one of the primary paradoxes posed in the Vedas — how can two diametrically opposed elements like fire and water be so inextricably linked together? Indra figures prominently in this manifestation of Agni's terrestrial fire. It was mentioned earlier that in his struggles with Vrtra Indra acts as an incarnation of Agni. (Mikhailov, (2001) *RgVedic Studies*, p. 14.) Both Indra and Agni dwell in the midst of struggles. (RV 8.40.3.) This includes every aspect of that struggle, including the struggle itself as well as the results. Agni, indeed, is the alter ego for Indra:

- Agni assumes the title so often attached to Indra, maghavan, the Mighty Showerer of Spiritual Endowments. (RV 1.73.5.)
- Indra and Agni are called the "White Gods" because they descend from the heaven bathed in lights. (RV 8.40.8.)

- Both Indra and Agni cause the Rivers (Consciousness) to flow from all quarters of the Vedic dharma. (RV 8.40.8.) In symbolic language this means the Vedic forces of Agni and Indra are responsible for the proliferation of Consciousness throughout the Vedic dharma, but primarily Agni since Indra acts in this capacity as Agni's incarnation.
- Indra and Agni cause the Rivers (Consciousness) to flow in accordance with their subtle practices and laws (vrata). (RV 8.40.8.)

The Rivers, as a terrestrial fire, are especially the result of the subtle processes generated from Agni and Indra.

- Indra increases the flow of the Rivers flowing to the ocean. (RV 8.6.35.) In symbolic language, this is the increase of the level of consciousness in the worshiper towards Self-Realization.
- Through the subtle processes and laws (vrata) of Agni, the words of the worshiper move like cows and like rivers flowing to the ocean. (RV 8.44.25.) Symbolically, the Vedic force of Agni bestows knowledge (cows) and enhanced levels of consciousness (Rivers to the ocean).

Whenever two Vedic forces or energies come into contact, tension, friction and heat result. Fire is a necessary result of this interaction. This terrestrial fire operates in its own version of the creation of the Vedic dharma, patterned seemingly from other more well-known narratives. The following rcs (mantras) present a lineal progression from the very beginnings of the Vedic dharma to the present. While subtle, the Rivers provide the fire to fuel this progression. This is because the subtle basis of The Rivers consists of Water, the very essence of the Vedic dharma.

- In the beginning darkness enveloped the flowing rivers. Indra, Agni's incarnation, eventually caused the wave of consciousness to spread in every existential level or world. (RV 1.52.10.) The resemblance to the creation narrative found in RV 10.129 is inescapable. The meaning is mutually consistent both with Vrtra's nature, RV 10.129, and this rc. Etymologically, Vrtra means "the enveloper." This is what he does, he conceals the waters (read, "the inner essence of the Vedic dharma"), in a word, conceals the better natures of humankind. Vrtra is an etymological derivative of *Rta*, the cosmic order. "Vrtra" is derived from the composite of three parts: *vi* + *Rta* + *ra*. "Vi" is a Sanskrit prefix meaning "not" or "negation of" or "away from;" *Rta* means "to place in motion;" "ra" means "to give or grant." It can be concluded from this that Vrtra represents *Prakrti* in a state of rest, inert matter, devoid of any change of place in motion. *Rta* is, of course, also the inner essence of the Vedic dharma. Vrtra, then, obscures the inner secret of the Vedic dharma. However you look at him, Vrtra can be viewed as a fallen angel of sorts. Indra, however, Agni's incarnation, recovers the inner essence of the Vedic dharma for every existential level or world for the worshiper and all sentient beings and objects found therein.

- Savitr is the child of the waters. (RV 1.22.6.) Symbolically speaking, this is the way the Vedas articulate how the creation of the Vedic dharma began as a product of Consciousness. This rc (mantra) features the Vedic version of creation according to the Samkhya dharana. According to Samkhya, the world evolved when Purusa made contact with *Prakrti*.

- The waters rolled off Vrtra when he was killed by Indra. This rc (mantra) presents the flip side to the previous narrative at RV 1.22.6. Whereas pursuant to RV 1.22.6 the Vedic dharma commenced when Consciousness (Purusa) made contract with the inert matter of the Vedic dharma (*Prakrti*), immediately thereafter according to RV 1.32.10 the waters (consciousness) "rolled off." This rc (mantra) is the Vedic version of the evolution of Consciousness according to Samkhya. According to the Samkhya philosophy, after Purusa and *Prakrti* made contact, Consciousness appeared, first with the development of Mahat or Buddhi (intellect, discernment), then with Ahamkara (ego), and finally with Manas (Mind). In the symbolic language of the Veda, Consciousness spilled out of Vrtra was slain by Indra.

- RV 1.33.11 expresses an essential truth about Consciousness. This rc (mantra) says that the rivers (Consciousness) flow on their own accord, based on their own essential, inherent nature. That "own essential, inherent nature" is svadha, another terrestrial manifestation of Agni's fire. This terrestrial fire has a personal dimension. The worshiper, having his or her own essential, inherent nature, begins the spiritual journey according to the several, different paths to liberation and salvation. The worshiper also begins this spiritual journey according to the mental place that is occupied at that time. The spiritual journey may commence when the worshiper is already half-way there; the spiritual starting place may be at a different place when the worshiper is not so spiritually developed. All stages are governed according to the terrestrial fire of Svadha.

- The Vedic energy of Indra forces the flow of the waters (Consciousness). (RV 1.52.4.) This is a primary function of Indra's force and energy. This is metaphorical of Indra's function of stimulating the impulsion of Consciousness. Indra not only provides the initial spark of Consciousness. That spark is also the impetus which allows the mental activity to flow.

- Continuing from the previous selection, the energy of Agni's incarnation, Indra, "desires the course" of the rivers in slaying Vrtra. (RV 1.52.8.) This is metaphorical not only to underscore his function in stimulating the flow of consciousness but to guide and provide direction to that flow. Specifically, Indra, Agni's incarnation, guides the course of the worshiper's spiritual journey.

- Once they begin, the Rivers proceed swiftly, spread unceasingly, they never stop, and pervade everywhere within the Vedic dharma. (RV 2.28.4.) This brings us to another metaphor which frequently appears in the Vedas — the Floods. Conceptionally, they are a variety of River, a River of course incredibly swift and engorged with many Waters. Symbolically, the Floods represent the first heady experience of realization and awareness, metaphorically equivalent to a wild fire.

- When they are released, the Rivers desire, like a mosquito to a light bulb, to flow into the Ocean. (RV 3.36.7.) The accepted consensus is that the "Ocean" is symbolic of the Higher Self, Ekam, the transcendental level of consciousness.

- When freed by Indra, the incarnation of Agni, and like salmon instinctively from the moment of their birth wanting to return to those same waters, The Rivers desire to return to the Ocean, that place from where they were born, not matter what the personal cost. (RV 3.36.6.)
- This is because The Rivers urge the inner truth and essence of the Vedic dharma *(rta)* on the worshiper and to the material world. (RV 1.105.12.)

The stream of consciousness paradoxically flows in both directions.

- The flow of consciousness (rivers) moves down to Indra from below the sky. (RV 1.54.7.)
- The Rivers flow from the higher regions to the worshiper. (RV 5.51.7.)
- The glory of Indra, Agni's incarnation, is so great the rivers flowing upward do not reach him. (RV 1.52.14.) This rc (mantra) is not simply counter-intuitive. The meaning is similar to the meaning of an early song from the English rock group, The Who, "I Can't Reach You." In this song, Pete Townshend plaintively sings the title of the song in the refrain over and over. The lyrics are ambiguous enough that one can interpret the song's meaning to be addressed to his love interest, a sophisticated pop song. The "You" can just as easily be addressed to God. He tries and tries, but cannot reach God, the divine, the unreachable. So is it here. The flow of the rivers is the worshiper's awareness, and while they reach upwards the flow cannot reach the divine. This rc (mantra) informs that Indra, the incarnation of Agni, is unknowable.
- An enhanced level of Consciousness is bestowed to the worshiper who practices with earnest austerity or who will so worship. (RV 1.125.4.) This is one of the many "treasures" or "riches" mentioned in the Veda, the spiritual endowments.
- The flow of Consciousness is one of the many spiritual gifts bestowed by Indra, in his incarnation as Agni. (RV 2.11.1.

One may wonder what relation The Rivers, the waters, may possess to be Agni's terrestrial manifestation of fire. These rcs (mantras) give us a look

- The blazing flames of Agni are compared with the flow of rivers. (RV 1.143.3.) Those flames have the active force of Light. Those flames are ageless, eternal. They brighten the night.
- Agni releases The Rivers from heaven, not an ordinary level of consciousness but that consciousness beyond (paravatah) the material world. (RV 1.75.6.)
- The Maruts, a manifestation of the Mid-World Fire of Agni, play their own role. As their chariot, interpreted as their subtle bodies, move across the cosmos, waves of consciousness scatter and spread and pervade. (RV 1.168.8.)
- The Maruts cause the Rivers to run in all directions. (RV 5.35.7.)

Metaphors and similes abound in the Veda concerning The Rivers. As a river which ebbs and flows along its course (RV 1.32.12 (the seven rivers); 1.52.7 (rivulets); 1.72.8 (seven rivers flowing from heaven); 1.73.6; 1.83.1; 2.11.1; 2.38.2; 2.28.4; 3.46.4; 4.22.6, 7 (Indra setting the rivers to flow freely); 4.22.6, 7 (same); 5.49.4; 5.62.4; 5.83.8; 6.19.5; 6.20.12; 9.31.3), this simile depicts the thoughts flowing one after another in the conscious mind much like water flowing through a waterway. This is the flow of individual mental consciousness. The thoughts and sensations flow one after the other, seemingly and hopefully to and with a specific goal. The transformative nature of Consciousness then is its malleability, its constantly changing nature. This quality of transformation is captured in sindhavah, the symbol of the flow of the rivers, Sindhava, representative of Consciousness. The fire of Change (Agni) also causes the river torrents to flow, meaning, of course, that this is the power source behind mental activity. (RV 1.95.10.)

SRAUDDHA

Srauddha, faith, is a manifestation of the terrestrial Fire of Agni. (BD, 1.111.) Srauddha literally means anything or any act that is performed with all sincerity and faith, or "Srauddha." In the Vedic dharma, it is the ritual that one performs to pay homage to forefathers, the ptrs, especially to one's dead parents. "Conceptually, it is a way for people to express heartfelt gratitude and thanks towards their parents and ancestors, for having helped them to be what they are and praying for their peace. It can be considered a 'day of remembrance'." (*https:// en. wikipedia. org/ wiki/ Śrāddha.*)

Saunaka, the Medieval Vedic scholar and author, understood Srauddha to be a terrestrial manifestation of the Fire of Agni. An entire Sukta is devoted to this terrestrial fire, RV 10.151. The dynamics of the sacrifice support Saunaka's conclusion that Saunaka is a terrestrial fire. The Sacrificial Fire burns and sends its smoke — another terrestrial fire, Dhumaketu is an aspect of consciousness expressed as a vibration of Knowledge envisaging Agni Pavamana as the "smoke bearer." As the smoke with its smoke, ciders, and ashes wafts up the atmosphere, in conjunction with the Heavenly Fire, Srauddha carries the soul of the worshiper upwards to the heaven. Binding this process is the subtle concept of Kindling. Physical fire is "ignited," but the aspect of Agni in the Sacrificial Fire is "kindled." Kindling imparts all those qualities and energies from the universe and channeled those qualities and energies into the Fire. The Sacrificial Fire plays a central role in the Sacrificial ritual, it is the center of attraction. Once kindled it is beheld by the worshiper, or, as in the Soma Sacrifice, the principal means of producing the Soma juice to be consumed by the worshiper. In all sacrificial settings, the central fire is the means by which the worshiper is transformed spiritually. With the terrestrial fire of Srauddha, the physical body of the worshiper is thereafter transformed from its mortal coil to ashes. The few rcs (mantras) demonstrate this process in some detail:

- The Mystic Fire of Agni is kindled by the terrestrial fire of Srauddha. (RV 1.151.1.)
- After being kindled, the Mystic Fire conveys that great fire of faith to the worshiper. (RV 1.151.3.)
- The collective Vedic forces and energies worship this terrestrial fire, which is protected by the wind (Vayu). (RV 1.151.4.) This statement is, of course, consistent with simple physical laws of nature. Without air the terrestrial fire, indeed all fire, would extinguish and die.

The Fire of Sraddha (Faith) carries its own energy. On a personal level, writes Deepti Dutta, in the Yoga Sutras Patanjali refers to reverential faith as "generating in the seeker an unusual energy (virya)" and as a "yearning to realize the truths in the life" which creates a "sustained effort." "This energy and diligence is again and again described as the primary requisite for spiritual fruition." (Dutta, *Samkhya, A Prologue to Yoga* (2018), pp. 51 – 53.)

On a grand macrocosmic level in the Vedic dharma, Srauddha encompasses the regeneration of souls. This entire process of regeneration is accomplished through fire. The most prevalent simile for regeneration is rain. The Vedic god Prajanya recycles the worshiper's soul as well as and in the manner of rain. This process is described in the Five Fires of the Vedas. According to the Upanishads there are five fires:

- The Heavenly Fire.

  Humans are sacrificed at death by cremation, becoming food for the divine Vedic energies and principles and transformed by the heavenly fire into Soma, the purified mind. This fire transforms the human body at death and upon the funeral pyre. The smoke, ciders, and ashes carrying the soul upwards to the heaven. (BU, 6.2.14, Ch.Up., 5.4.1.)

- The Fire of Parjanya.

This fire transforms Soma and the souls in its command into rain. Parjanya is the Vedic divine force for rain. The soul carried upwards to the heavens to be met by Parjanya. (BU, 6.2.10, Ch.Up., 5.5.1, 5.6.1.)

- The Vegetative Fire.

Soma, the divine food, releases the rain, its essence, to earth, where it is transformed into vegetation. Rain is the essence of Soma (Purification), and as divine food, falls to the earth with the souls in transmigration. (BU, 6.2.11, Ch.Up., 5.4.2.

- The Digestive Fire:

When these food plants containing the human should are eaten, they are transformed into seamen by the man-fire, the digestive fire. The rain containing the seeds of the souls in transmigration are transformed to semen and are absorbed by the plant life and fauna and eaten by man or animal. (BU, 6.2.12.)

- The Female Fire.

This semen is transformed into a Purusha, a person, by the woman-fire. The semen is transformed into a Purusha. (BU, 6.6.2.13.)

Faith moves mountains, goes the popular expression. Those mountains are moved from the personal energy generated by the fire of faith.

THE STEED, THE HORSES

As you should realize by now, the rcs (mantras) of the Rg Veda speak in symbols. The Steed is a manifestation of the terrestrial Fire of Agni. (BD, 1.109), and is a good example of the incredibly rich meaning of the symbolic vocabulary of the Veda. There are no shortage of interpretations as to what the "Steed" or "Horses" signify.

R.L Kashyap has interpreted the "Horse" to mean "energies." Through linguistic and textual analysis of the Sanskrit word for Horse which links it to the Ashvins, Yogi Baba Prem interprets as signifying prana, karma and Speech. (*http://vedicpath.com/Articles/ Ashvamed-ha.html.*)

Subhash Kak, in his book, *The Asvamedha, the Rite and its Logic*, offers a few other interpretations. According to Kak, the Horse and the Horse Sacrifice represent

- Prana, the Sun, and time.
- The Universe. The Horse has thirty-four ribs, and according to RV 1.162.18, thirty-four represents the twenty-seven Nakshastras, the five planets, the Sun and the Moon.
- The process by which Time progresses and transcends all else.

The worshiper recognizes these as valid interpretations of Horse. The symbol of the Horse is vast and encompasses many subjects and themes in the Vedic dharma. The worshiper also knows that the Horses represent the fire of sense perceptions, the mind's perception of the senses, in all their unbridled glory. The senses, like all other bodily and mental functions, must be fueled by a fire of energy. Unyoked, this fire represents the Monkey

Mind, distracted, unfocused, confused, going from one thought to another. Trained, this fire is penetrating and focused, whereupon the worshiper mounts the Horses to traverse higher and higher levels of existence with an enlightened mind.

These interpretations, while having merit, miss an important point. There are horses and there are horses yoked. This is primarily the meaning used in this text. There are other interpretations of the meaning which bear mentioning: It is not so important that which is yoked, or restrained, but the act of restraint itself. Thus, Horses may be interpreted as energies, thought progressions, Time, prana, or the universe. Yoked Horses are another matter. The important common feature, restraint, is the goal of the Vedas, and the yoking (restraint) of the worshiper's energy, prana flow, consciousness, is the useful tool the worshiper seeks to learn in the spiritual journey.

SVADHA

Svadha is mentioned in several rcs (mantras) in the Veda. Svadha is defined as an inherent power which upholds its nature, following its own law or nature. Svadha also refers to the essential nature of the fire informing Change (Agni) and the other dynamic forces in the Vedic pantheon. For example

- The fire of the Maruts realize their own nature by supporting the sacrifice. (RV 1.6.4.)
- Once Vrtra was slain, the Waters started flowing due to the svadha (self-nature) of Indra. (RV 1.33.11.)

The Fire of Agni commands special attention. RV 2.35.7 gives a full description of the inherent self-nature of Agni in his manifestation as the Son of Waters:

- In the lunar house of Agni a cow is giving milk. This imagery refers to Kine. An old-English word, not generally used today, but in the Vedas means the milking cow, the source of truth, essence, and knowledge. The imagery is inescapable. Just as just as there is the milk of knowledge, so is the Kine, the milking cow, its symbol.
- With this milk of Knowledge the Vedic force of Agni recycles his svadha, his inherent self-nature. With this milk of knowledge Agni is the Eater of Food. "Eater of Food" is another symbol, representative of the fire of dissolution in the universe. The "Eater" can mean anything from the dissolving entity of the Vedic dharma,

to the Vedic force which superimposes the material universe, to obtaining knowledge, enlightenment, or consciousness. As the Eater, Agni produces food again and again. In the fire of producing food again and again, the entire natural order is created, recycled and re-created. Being the "Eater of Food" is coded language for saying that Agni is the Subject, the Absolute Self. The "Eater" is part of the essential nature of Agni.

- The Vedic force of Agni gathers supports in the Waters. "The Waters" is symbolic. The Waters represents of the essential nature of the Vedic dharma. It is from this essential nature of the Vedic dharma that Agni derives his strength.
- Indra has an infinity and indestructible essential nature (svadha) to support the Word. (RV 5.34.1.)

It is clear from these excerpts that Svadha is something more than simply the inherent nature of the Vedic forces and energies. It is the internal fire of each respective Vedic force or energy which powers that force and energy — its internal combustion if you will. It is the essential characteristic of any given Vedic force. It is, for example, the essential nature and characteristics of Agni which make Agni. On a personal level, svadha is a further conversion of that internal fire. Svadha is at its essence the combustion of the heat generated from the internal fire of the Vedic forces and energies. By virtue of this internal heat it is communicated to the worshiper; having received the endowment of this internal heat, the worshiper makes use of that internal heat through the means by which those qualities are present in the Vedic divine forces, thereby implementing those qualities into the life of the worshiper. In the Veda the references of the svadha, or essential nature, of Agni are many, but one of the most concise statements of Agni's svadha is found in RV 1.70.4. According to this rc (manta) there are characteristically three elements to the svadha of Agni:

- The Vedic force of Agni increases in the night that assume various forms. This element of Agni's svadha is a reference to another terrestrial manifestation of Agni in Usasanakta, which is discussed in a few pages. In Usasanakta, while on the surface having a binary structure, Usasanakta is a manifestation of both the unitary nature of Agni and the capacity of Agni to unite polar opposites. The terrestrial fire of Agni confirms the powers of unification of Agni and emphasizes that these unifying powers are a source of Agni's capacity to Increase.

- Agni is the soul of moving and non-moving things. In the symbolic language of the Veda, this element of Agni's svadha signifies that Agni provides the spark of vital life to all objects, to sentient and non-sentient beings and things.
- Agni is born of truth (amr/tah.) In this context, amrta refers to the word most frequently translated or rendered —eternity. However, understood on a deeper level, amrta derives from its root, Rta, meaning the Universal Order or the Vedic dharma. The underlying essence of the Vedic dharma is water. Amrta is the Cosmic Waters, the essence of the essence of the Vedic dharma, if you will.

These are the qualities the worshiper desires to incorporate. It is through the self-nature of the Vedic forces and energies that their self-nature is communicated to the worshiper.

- Through the intrinsic nature (svadha) of Agni, the worshiper receives spiritual endowments. (RV 3.35.7.)The strength of the self-nature (svadha) of the fire of Ila channels the mantra to the worshiper. (RV 1.88.6.)Through the essential nature (svadha) of Usas, awareness is channeled to the worshiper. (RV 4.52.6.)
- The essential nature of Agni illumines and purifies the worshiper. (RV 8.8.3.)
- Through the essential nature of Indra, with the quaffing of Soma, both spiritual endowments are conveyed to the worshiper. (RV 8.32.6, 19.

The essential natures of the Vedic forces and energies do not simply benefit the worshiper.

- The entire material world is supported by the essential nature (svadha) of Indra. (RV 8.88.5.)
- In the initial stages of creation eons ago after the universe was divided between that which was above (macrocosm) and that which was below (microcosm). (RV 10.129.4.) The undifferentiated mass thereupon coalesced through the actions of kama (desire), and afterwards from the essential nature (svadha) of the lower world. (RV 10.129.5.)
- Later, when all the energies and forces of the Collective Gods were brought together, the impulsions of their essential natures (*svadha*) began. (RV 10.157.5.)

The fire of Svadha implicates these issues and touches on the depths of the Vedic dharma. From these depths, the essence and internal, inherent nature of the Vedic dharma is communicated to the material, terrestrial world through Svadha.

SVAHAKRITIS

Svahakritis is a manifestation of the terrestrial Fire of Agni. (BD, 1.109.)
Svahakritis is "the maker of offerings." It is derived from "Offering" (*svaha*)
+ "maker" (*kriti*). (RV 1.188.11.)

TANUNAPI

Tanunapi is a manifestation of the terrestrial Fire of Agni. (BD, 1.106.), Tanunapi is that manifestation of Agni Pavamana meaning "The summer sun" or "Son of the Body of the worshiper." (RV 1.13.2.) This manifestation is a link between the terrestrial and celestial fires. When this manifestation first appeared, Tanunapi was presented to Matarisvan. (RV 1.142.2.) Tanunapi was thereupon brought to the terrestrial sphere by Matarisvan. (RV 1.60.1.) Matarisvan is called the Vedic Prometheus, because the Vedic force and energy of the terrestrial fire was brought to the world by Matarisvan. Matarisvan bears the meaning of "Pervasion." (RV 1.71.4.)

This is how the Vedic force of the terrestrial fire covers the material world. This pervasion is not limited to the link between the celestial and terrestrial worlds. Matarisvan is instrumental in bringing the Agni's fire of the firmament to the Svar, the World of Light found in the upper world. (RV 1.96.4.) The dynamics is therefore intricate: Tanunapi is presented to Matarisvan in the upper world, Matarisvan presents Tanunapi from the mid to the upper world, and then brings Tanunapi to the material worlds. The pervasion of Matarisvan and Tanunapi thus pervades, in one form or another, every aspect of the material world. This is also, indeed, how Tanunapi obtained its name.

The fire of the celestial Agni extends, pervades to the body (tanu) of the worshiper. (BD, 2.26; 3.1.) The dynamics between the terrestrial and celestial fires provides the subtle foundation of the Vedic dharma. This manifestation of Agni, Tanunapi, protects all the processes, forces and energies, in every level or region, of the laws running the Vedic dharma. (RV 10.92.2.)

THE THREE GODDESSES

The Three Goddesses is a manifestation of the terrestrial Fire of Agni. (BD, 1.108.) The Vedas identify the Three Goddesses in RV 1.13.9:

- Ila (another manifestation of the terrestrial fire), symbolizing the fire of divine vision.
- Saraswati (a manifestation of the fire of the firmament), symbolizing divine articulation.
- Mahi, the symbol of the vast power of the Vedic dharma. Mahi is another name for Bharati, a manifestation of the Celestial Fire of Agni. (RV 2.3.8.)

These Three Goddesses create the Bliss created at the Sacrifice that may be invoked and enjoyed by the worshiper. (RV 5.5.8.) Bharati, with her muses; Ila, with gods and men; and Agni with Saraswati to provide inspiration. In creating this Bliss the Three Goddesses act in unison. (RV 7.2.8.)

Since they are terrestrial fires — fires found in the material world — the Three Goddesses represent the three levels of the Lower Ocean. As their identification indicates, the Three Goddesses a paradigm for the three existential levels of Earth, Mid-World and Heaven. The Three Goddesses cover these existential levels with Vision, Articulation, and Power. Without Speech no form could exist. (SB, 2.5.) Without Vision, there is no speech. Without speech, any form could not be known and the worshiper would be bereft of intelligence (SA, 5.7.) Having obtained information from the sensory organs, the worshiper obtains information to be used in the spiritual journey to liberation and salvation. (SA, 5.3; 5.6.) This is not limited to ordinary speech. Without the Word, how can the wisdom of the Vedas be communicated to the worshiper? The intelligence the worshiper gains in this process empowers the worshiper in the spiritual journey to discover the vastness of the Vedic dharma. The Three Goddesses are the source of Vision, Speech, and the vastness of the Vedic dharma from which the three levels of existence may be given form and substance and accordingly represent the three-fold nature of Speech, Vac. (BD, 3.12.) The Three Goddesses provide form to the three levels of existence and yet are empowered by the corresponding levels of Agni. Each level is governed by its own fire. Ila, another manifestation of terrestrial Agni, presides over the terrestrial Agni; Saraswati, a manifestation of Agni of the firmament, presides over the middle Agni; and Bharati presides over the celestial Agni. (BD, 3.13.) The Three Goddesses represent an important fire for the terrestrial realm, because without the articulation of places, objects, and things the material world would be unintelligible. Together, they sit, are present, at the sacrifice, where the worshiper invokes their powers. (RV 3.4.8.)

TVASTR

Tvastr is the Architect, "Fashioner of Forms," (BD 1.84) of the Universe. Tvastr is a manifestation of the terrestrial Fire of Agni. (BD, 1.108.) Tvastr is the fire which gives shape to the manifold appearance of Creation. From a material standpoint Tvastr supplies the fire of the material world. Tvastr is also known as Tvasta. (RV 3.4.9, 5.5.9, 7.2.9, 10.70.9.) Tvastr makes many appearances in the Veda.

- Tvstr is the author of all forms. (RV 1.13.10.)
- Tvastr is the maker of forms and all types of beings in the universe. (RV 3.55.19.)
- Tvastr makes the vessel which is housed the human body; Rbhus transforms this body into four parts. (RV 1.20.6.) The general consensus, among them Adi Sri Sankara, is that the "four parts" refer to the kosas other than the physical body, the vessel in the rc, the Annamaya, Pranamaya, Manomaya, and Vujnanamaya kosas.
- Tvastr is the great victor over the enemies of the world and is terrestrial fires power the internal subtle bodies of the Vedic forces and energies. (RV 2.31.4.)
- Tvastr is the possessor of light and the possessor of the essence of the Vedic dharma *(rta)* and establishes in the worshiper all that is needed for spiritual increase and protection. (RV 3.54.12.)
- Tvastr, the Master Architect, gives shape to all living forms and is Savitr, the Creator. (RV 10. 10.5.)
- Tvastr, the Master Architect, bestows long life to the worshiper. (RV 10.18.6.)

- Tvastr is one in the many Vedic forces and energies which support the essence of the Vedic dharma, *Rta*. (RV 2.23.17.)
- The season Tvastr is associated is the Vedic season of Sukra (RV 2.36.3.)
- Tvastr is the husband of Heaven, his wife. (RV 10.64.10.)

Tvastr renders services to Indra, primarily in fashioning Indra's weapon, Vajra. As Indra is considered an incarnation of Agni in terms with the former's struggles with Vrtra, these references would still implicate the terrestrial manifestations of Agni:

- From the material obtained from Heaven, the terrestrial fire of Tvastr forges the weapon wielded by Indra, Vajra, which is used to kill Vrtra, the serpent which covers and obscures the essential truth of the Vedic dharma. (RV 1.32.2; 1.62.6.)
- Not only did Tvastr produce Vajra, but he also sharpens it for Indra, increasing Indra's strength. (RV 1.52.7.)
- The subtle basis of Tvastr, its secret name, is found in the home of Soma. (RV 1.84.15.) This is probably the key to understanding the essential nature of Tvastr. Soma is the personification of divine ecstacy and is the fuel that fires the feeling of religiosity. If Soma is the secret name of Tvastr, this Vedic force imbues the physical forms found in the material world with an undeniable spiritual element. Many words have repeated this same thought; this rc (mantra) confirms it.

Nonetheless, Tvastr is a terrestrial fire firmly implanted within the purview of Agni. Being a terrestrial fire distinguishes Tvastr from the Purusa. Purusa created the subtle basis of the material world and the forms of all things living in it; Tvastr is the creator of the physical world.

- The Ten Powers begat the Vedic force of Agni with Tvastr. (RV 1.85.9.)
- Tvastr is the father of Indra (RV 1.22.9), which is an incarnation of Agni.

- Agni is identified with Tvastr, who fashioned Agni's Vedic energies for the worshiper to channel, along with the other spiritual endowments that Agni may bestow, for use in the spiritual journey. (RV 2.1.5.) Indeed, the identification is so strong that at one point it was revealed that the Vedic force of Agni came into being through the combined efforts of the Waters ("Son of the Waters"), the energy radiating from the unification of Heaven and Earth, and Tvastr. (RV 10.2.7.)
- The terrestrial fire of Tvastr is golden red in color. While the fire of Tvastr aspires to raise as a Celestial Fire, it is the cause of Increase for the worshiper, and the worshiper benefits from the spiritual endowments brought by Tvastr. (RV 2.3.9.)

Tvastr has the distinction of being the only mortal human to become a Vedic force and energy, much like Hercules in Greek mythology. While Tvastr can certainly be likened to Hercules, he has more in common with the Demiurge found in Plato's Timaeus, the entity creating the World Soul of the Vedic dharma. Tvastr is simply the most manifest expression of the Fire of Change which is personified in Agni.

THE TWO WORLDS

The Two Worlds are manifestations of the terrestrial Fire of Agni. (BD, 1.113.) One world is fire of the terrestrial world which is led by the worshiper, and the other world is fire of the celestial world where Agni leads the world away from this world. (BD, 1.91.) This portion from the Brhata Devata captures the two sides of the Two Worlds. On the one side the Two Worlds are firmly terrestrial fires and identified with the Earth. (BD, 1.83.) On the other, they are identified with Rodasi (BD, 4.6; 17.126; 0.94; McDonnell translation.) Rodasi is the first manifestation of heaven and earth conjoined. (RV 1.52.10; 1.105.1-18; 1.167.4 5; 1.185.3; 3.26.9; 3.54.3, 4, 10; 4.55.6; 4.56.4, 8; 6.50.5; 6.62.8; 6.66.6; 6.70.2, 3; 9.7.9; 9.98.9; 10.12.4; 10.67.11; 10.79.4; 10.88.5, 10; 10.92.11.) *Rodasi*, that element of the Vedic dharma (*rta*) where the Svar is located at is that point where they are conjoined. (RV 1.22.13.). Svar, interpreted in many translations as the Sun-World, or the World of Light, binds the higher and lower worlds and acts as the focal point gaining entry to the one from the other. *Rta* "rises" or "moves upwards" above these three worlds, consists of the Empyrean, and at the same time provides the foundation for all that exists below. The Svar, the sun-world, is bindu, the hub, the gateway, the vortex which inverts and turns the sensible world on its head into tridhaatu, or mahii, the upper three levels of the world beyond the manifest universe.

In the larger Vedic dharma, the Two Worlds represent the Two-Dimensional Universe. The material world is reflected in the Two-Dimensional Universe. The Two-Dimensional Universe is based on polar opposites. The fire of the Two Worlds upholds this Two-Dimensional

Universe, as well as the other dimensions of the Vedic dharma, where opposites abound:

- Big, Small / Little
- Cheap, Expensive
- Clean, Dirty
- Deep, Shallow
- Down, Up
- Early, Late
- Easy, Difficult / Hard
- Far, Near / Close
- High, Low
- Hot, Cold
- Left, Right

The list is endless; the Two-Dimensional World literally exists for opposition. The Two Worlds is the terrestrial fire which empowers the worshiper who engages in the spiritual journey in the material world to enter the transcendent world of liberation and salvation. The fire of the Two Worlds unifies these raging opposites. The manner in which these opposites are unified are explained in greater detail in the next terrestrial fire, Usasanakta.

USASANAKTA

Usasanakta, "Dawn and Night." Night and Day are manifestations of the terrestrial fire of Agni. (BD, 1.108.) Usasanakta, Day and Night (RV 2.3.6; 6.9.1-3), is binary system. As a type of fire, Usasanakta rightly is a terrestrial manifestation of Agni's fire. As a binary system, it is grounded in the Two-Dimensional Universe. Usasanakta however is not a simple fire. On one level this phrase is simply what it literally means, day to night, the progression of day to night. The Rishis equated the shining asterism of Orion with the Vernal Equinox, and the Vernal Equinox exists in juxtaposition to the Autumnal Equinox. On a deeper level, then, "Day and Night" signifies the fire urging from the progression between the two equinoctial asterisms, the Vernal to the Autumnal Equinox.

Any doubt as to the meaning of "Day and Night" is resolved by comparing it with its flip-side moniker, "Night and Day," *na/ktoSaa/saa*. If "Day and Night" is the fire which urges the progression of the Vernal Equinox to the Autumnal Equinox, "Night and Day," *na/ktoSaa/saa*, the fires of the Autumnal to the Vernal Equinox. Armed with this knowledge about the nature of "Day and Night" and "Night and Day," new life is breathed into two groups from the First Mandala:

- RV 1.13.3:
  Here, Narasamsa, itself a manifestation of Agni of the terrestrial fire, arrives to the Sacrifice with "honeyed speech." The "honeyed speech" is divine speech. The fire of Narasamsa subsumes several other manifestations of the terrestrial fire: the fires of Barhi, Ila,

and the Litter and the Divine Doors. The "honeyed speech" is subsumed in these other manifestations of the terrestrial fire.

- RV 1.13.4:
The Vedic force of Agni establishes the mantra. Mantra is a higher expression of Speech.

- RV 1.13.5:
The Barhi, itself also a terrestrial manifestation of Agni's fire, has a shiny surface. The Vedic force of Agni is possessed of divine vision.

- RV 1.13.6:
The collective Vedic forces and energies increase the inner truth of the Vedic dharma, *Rta*. The fire of the divine doors — Vernal and Autumnal Equinoxes — teach the worshiper of the inner workings of the Sacrifice. The inner workings of the Sacrifice is the give-and-take process of the yajna, described earlier in this book. On a personal level it is the communication between the Vedic force of Agni and the worshiper. On a grand cosmic level, this give-and-take gave rise to the Purusa Sukta in the Tenth Mandala.

- RV 1.13.7:
The powers of Night and Day, *na/ktoSaa/saa*, the fires of the Autumnal to the Vernal Equinox, are called to the Sacrifice.

- RV 1.13.8:
These two powers, the fires of the Autumnal to the Vernal Equinox, conduct the Sacrifice. This is more true than you think. Astronomical calculations and the comings and goings of the seasons and the equinoxes were closely followed in order to know when Sacrifices were to commence. "The equinoxes are the only times when the solar terminator (the 'edge' between night and day) is perpendicular to the equator. As a result, the northern and southern hemispheres are equally illuminated." (*https://en.wikipedia.org/wiki/Equinox*.) Days and nights therefore play a part in the travel of the soul to another binary system, the Northern Path (*devayana*) and Southern Paths (*ptryana*). (B.U.,

6.2.16; C.U., 10.5.3.) The two binary systems work together towards the salvation and liberation of the worshiper:

- RV 1.96.3:
  Preliminarily, Agni is the perpetual giver (*srprdanum*). This is one element of the give-and-take process of Sacrifice.

- RV 1.96.4:
  The Vedic force of Agni constructs the path to the Svar, the *devayana*

- RV 1.96.5:
  Night and Day, *na/ktoSaa/saa* —Vernal and Autumnal Equinoxes —nourish the Vedic force of Agni, who becomes radiant, shines, and unites Heaven and Earth.

- RV 1.96.6:
  The Vedic force of Agni bestows understanding of Sacrifice and the give-and-take process of the sacrifice and guides the worshiper during the journey along the Path of the Gods (*devayana*).

The gods are etymologically connected to and associated with "day," as they arrive at their deified status as a result of the eight-day rite, (PVB 22.11.1) or the fifteen-day rite, (PVB 23.6.2) and they became gods in the first place by entering heaven, div. (SPB 11.1.6.8; TB 2.3.8.2.) The word for demon, asura, the antithesis of divinity, is derived from *a* + *surya*, or "not light." (SPB 13.4.3.11 (the King of the demons is *Asita* ("Black")); 11.1.6.8 (after the creation of the demons there was only darkness).) Day thus becomes the Northern Path and night becomes the Southern Path. The soul reaches liberation and release when it travels northward in the path of the gods where there is light (TS 1.1.7) and is condemned to be reborn again and again when it traverses the paths of the forefathers. Thus, Yama, Death, is admonished to go on the path other than the path of the gods so that the worshiper may travel there unmolested. (RV 10.18.1.) This doctrine was later repeated in the Upanishads.

The divine dynamic forces responsible for providing the northern path of the gods is another example of the interchangeable roles between the divine dynamic Vedic forces. Assigning separate responsibilities to separate divine dynamic Vedic forces is ultimately irrelevant because these dynamic forces collectively forge the paths a worshiper may take. (RV 7.38.5; 7.7.2; SPB 2.9.2.28; 4.4.4.13.) The Fire of Change (Agni), Bala (Indra), the Asvins, and Usas all have a role to play in making the path of the gods available to the worshiper. The Fire of Change (Agni) figures prominently in paving the path of the gods available to the worshiper:

- The Fire of Change (Agni) knows the Path of the Gods and where it traverses. (RV 1.72.7.)
- The Fire of Change (Agni) not only knows the Path of the Gods and where it traverses but understands how that path crosses the seasons of the year and the equinoxes of the hemispheres. (RV 10.98.11.)
- The Fire of Change (Agni) leads the worshiper along the path of the gods. (SPB 1.9.2.3; 8.6.3.22.)
- The Fire of Change (Agni) brings the other Vedic energies and by extension the worshiper along the Path of the Gods when after the worshiper offers his or her being through Self-Surrender. (RV 5.43.6.)
- The Fire of Change (Agni) moves the worshiper along the Path of the Gods through his guidance. (RV 10.51.5.)

If you arrive at the impression that Agni operates as a unifier of opposing forces, you are correct. This is another aspect of the power of unification forged by his fire. In Usasanakta is also one fire in two: Usha's name is derived from "Ushi," also meaning "night," (Mikhailov, *Rgvedic Studies* (2001), p. 9.) Thus this fire is called Usasanakta. One may say that Usasanakta's importance arises in the day sacrifices, and that observation holds true. More significantly, Usasanakta provides the fire which assures the orderly progression of creation. But what is the fundamental nature of creation? We know now that the essence of the Vedic dharma is Water. Just as the waves of water in the ocean have its own in-and-out movement, so does the fabric of the Vedic dharma contract and expand with its own cadence. It was on this basis that Sri Abinavagupta concluded in the Tantraloka that there was a synergy between Time, Prana, and the process of breath which is the vibration of the Force dwelling within the Universal Being, the Atman, or God. (T.L., 6.129.)

It is here that Usasanakta has its greatest significance. Night follows day in the fire that provides for regular breath of the universe. Usasanakta is therefore representative of the Two-Dimensional Universe in the terrestrial aspect of Agni. The fire of Usasanakta also does much to regulate the operation of Time in that Two-Dimensional Universe. That regulation is not a simple perpetuation of the running of time, although that regularity of Time places a part. The Pythagoreans believed that in the meditation of the constant regularity of the passage of days, nights, weeks, etc., forced the worshiper to conclude there is no difference between the future and the past. In arriving at this conclusion the worshiper pierces through time to eternity and dwells in the eternal present. (Weil, *Imitations of Christianity*, p. 96.) This is an approach which conjoins and liberates the worshiper from the host of other dichotomies which bedevil the worshiper's mind and impede the spiritual journey, piercing through the conflict of opposition and unifying polar opposites.

Usasanakta employed an unwritten approach that can be taken for any repetition or correspondence found in the Vedas, Brahmanas or Upanishads. It is the meditative practice which elevates the worshiper to higher existential levels, principally, from the Two-Dimensional to the Three-Dimensional Universe. It is an approach which was perfected millennia later in the Yoga Sutras of Patanjali. There was employed a practice which provides, among other things, several ways to disengage from the workings of the material world, and, deep in meditation, move towards samadhi, the ultimate unification with the Absolute Self. One such practice is samyama, the combined exercise of dharana, concentration, Dhyana, meditation, and samadhi. While Usasanakta does not give us the detail found in the Yoga Sutras, the general application is the same: to apply severe meditation to pierce beyond the confines of the material world, whether those confines are, as here, the temporal progression of day and night, or, as in Patanjali, the elements, or any other feature of the material world in which we live. As for this particular fire, Day and Night plays a significant role for the Vedic astrologer who strives to undertake that spiritual journey through the understanding and contemplation of the stellar population. As for the Vedic force and energy of Agni, the fire of Usasanakta is thus the regulator of and liberator from the strictures of Time.

VANASPATI

Vanaspati, defined as the "Lord of Beauty" or "Lord of the Plants." Vanaspati is a manifestation of the terrestrial Fire of Agni. (BD, 1.109.) Vanaspati is a link between the Vedic forces of Agni and Soma, the Vedic force of religious fervor and ecstasy. The Vedic scholar Kashyap notes that "vana" means both "plant" and "delight." He notes that "vana" connotes "delight" in the Upanishads. The double meaning is an appropriate use of wordplay which is so often found in the Veda. This terrestrial fire emphasizes how Soma is spoken of a deity and of the plant from which the juice is extracted. (RV 10.172.1.)

Vegetation is a complex, intricate fire, which cuts through the very heart of an important aspect of the Vedic dharma. Here is where matters really become esoteric, and it is not just about plants. On the surface, this category is straightforward. Soma is Vanaspati. Commentators, among them Kashyap and others, have noted that "vana" means both "plant" and "delight." They note that "vana" connotes "delight" in the Upanishads. The double meaning is an appropriate use of wordplay which is so often found in the Veda. This particular epithet emphasizes how Soma is spoken of a deity and of the plant from which the juice is extracted at the sacrifice. On the surface, then, this category speaks on a simple sacrificial level to represent the plant from which the Soma juice is extracted and to say that the Soma juice is lord of them all.

Here is where matters get esoteric.

"Vegetation" was a concept used by that greatest modern alchemist, Sir Isaac Newton, in his alchemical writings. Yes, the same Isaac Newton. The same Newton who uncovered the physical laws of optics, motion and gravity, was a notorious alchemist. In fact, he was more preoccupied with discovering the link between the physical and subtle worlds through alchemy (than he was with mechanical physics. Newton's discovery the mechanical laws of nature was only half of his endeavors. His work sought to discover those physical laws as complements of God's influence. It was through the alchemical arts that he thought the link between the physical and subtle existed. His alchemical writings, in fact, far outnumber his scientific dissertations, and their page count number literally in the hundreds of thousands. It was through his writings that he developed Vegetation. It is a broad concept, extensively employed, and he sometimes changed the parameters of this idea. But in Newton's alchemical writings, it was a major concept and preoccupation. According to Newton, there were three kingdoms of nature — animal, mineral, and vegetable. These kingdoms operated under two sets of laws: The physical, mechanical laws of nature, and the "Chemical Laws" of God. It was Newton's job to find the link between these two worlds. Newton found this link in the Vegetative Principle, which had these characteristics:

- The vegetable spirit is identified with Light and Illumination, representing the power of God.
- The congealed aether that pervades everything, "interwoven with the grosser texture of sensible matter."
- The "subtle spirit," or "nature's universal agent, her secret fire" or "material soul of all matter." According to Newton the Earth and all matter was a breathing, living organism, "draw[ing] in aethereal breadth for its daily refreshment and transpires again with gross exhalations."
- The Vegetative spirit was the agent which activated inert, dead, matter into living, breathing material.

If all this sounds very familiar, you are right. This all sounds very close to the psychic, subtle powers of Vayu, the Vedic divine force of Prana, the Life-Force and the radiance and effulgence of Soma. Where at one point in his book about Newton and alchemy, *The Janus Faces of Genius*, B.J.T. Dobbs wondered where Newton's ideas about Vegetation originated, it is very tempting to believe that the inspiration came from Soma. While

346

tempting, it is hardly likely. The first English translation of the Vedas did not occur until one hundred years after Newton engaged in his alchemical ruminations. Further, what Newton was attempting to achieve was very different than a spiritual journey of a worshiper to liberation and salvation. Newton tried to integrate alchemy and the mechanical philosophy with his concept of Vegetation, which operates under the premise that metals "vegetate" — that is, grow — in the earth, being changed over time from one substance into another.

Still, with Vegetation both Newton and the Vedas tap into a very basic truth. Both tap into the very essence of the material world and its link with the divine, psychic, and subtle. Both affirm that there is a link and essential sameness between these two worlds.

The story becomes even more esoteric.

Two epithets refer to the color of Vanaspati, Soma, the Lord of Plants. Vanaspati is golden; flaming, conceivably, flaming red; and resplendent, again, likely golden-colored. What do these epithets possibly mean? Was the Soma plant gold in color or flaming red?

Classical alchemical was concerned about color. Joseph Needlham, the noted scholar of Chinese science, writes that the entire purpose of traditional alchemy was to loosen the bonds of temporal existence to achieve perfection. In terms of metals, that meant turning base matter into gold, which, as we have seen here, represents liberation and salvation, but in the area in which Needham studied and wrote, represented longevity, Immortality, and finally grace and redemption. While alchemists attempted to transmute base metals into gold, in their upward journey, the base metals traversed through the color chart. Each color represented a different stage of development, the final color was gold, into which indeed the base metal had been transmuted.

The different schools of Classical Alchemy differed widely. There was general agreement on the change in color base metals underwent in the transmutation process. The base metals began the journey upwards on the color chart, beginning with the color

- Black, called Melansis or Nigreda, representing Death. A case can be made that this was the vast, indiscriminate, undefined mass of matter described in RV 10.129, wherein began the process of evolution of the Vedic dharma.

- White, called Leukosis or Albedo, representing Resurrection.
- Yellow, Gold, called Xanthosis, representing Immortality.
- Red, or Ruddy Brown, called Iosis, representing Rebirth. Other traditions include a further step. The color in this additional step is Green, or Green-tinted, called Verditas.

After these progressions the alchemist is supposed to reach the Philosopher's Stone, the irreducible essence of physical matter, carrying within it life-giving properties, including, but not limited to, Immortality.

The properties of Vanaspati are positively full of color:

- Vanaspati, Soma, is golden.
- Vanaspati, Soma, is resplendent.
- Soma is Green-tinted.

All these colors are high in the color chart. Thus, they are high on the existential level. Vegetation is highly symbolic speech for and a useful tool to achieve the liberation and salvation of the worshiper.

- Soma's glories (*dhamani*) are in the plants or herbs (*o/SadhiiSv*). (RV 1.91.4.)
- Soma is the Axe in the Woods. (RV 9.95.3.)
- Vanaspati, Soma, is flaming (*bhraaljamaanaM*). (RV 9.5.10.)
- Soma is Vanaspati. (RV 9.5.10.)
- Vanaspati, Soma, is golden (*hiraNyalyam*). (RV 9.5.10.)
- Vanaspati, Soma, is resplendent (*halritam*). (RV 9.5.10.)
- Soma manifests (*ajanayas*) all the herbs (*o/SadhiiH*). (RV 1.91.22.)
- Vanaspati, Soma, has a thousand branches (*sahalsravalshaM*). (RV 9.5.10.)
- Soma Is Adept in Herbal Knowledge.(YV 4.37.)
- Soma is Green-tinted. (RV 10.116.3.)
- Soma is Soft (*rdu-udana*) in the Inside. (RV 8.4.8.10.)

In a larger sense, Vanaspati represents yet a deeper meaning. In the Timaeus, Plato the image of the mortal humans were compared to a plant (Weil, *Imitations of Christianity*, pp. 98 – 99), whose roots reached to Heaven. The Plant, another manifestation of Agni's terrestrial fire, as sprinkled with celestial waters, "a divine semen, which enters the head." In a Vedic context, the Bull is the principle which impregnates mortal humans with the divine seed. Plato had always maintained that his teachings were not his own but that he had transmitted doctrines existing in "the East." It is tempting to believe that this terrestrial fire served as the inspiration of this portion of the Timaeus.

THE WATERS

Water is the great Vedic field pervading the stellar population in the cosmos. The Waters is ratna, the essence of the Vedic dharma. (RV 3.21.11.) The Waters is also a manifestation of the terrestrial Fire of Agni. (BD, 1.112.) At first blush it might seem that the inclusion of the Waters as a terrestrial fire is oxymoronic. After considering the essential natures of the Waters and fire, it is clear this is not the case. Both the Waters and fire are purifying agents. More importantly, both the Waters and fire share elements of fluidity that account for the constant change and transformation of the material world. Water possesses the characteristics in forming the basis of the Vedic dharma and consists of the fundamental basis of essential functions found in the Vedic dharma. Water is the Agent for Creation or Generation. Water is material cause of the universe. Water is the root (i.e., the cause) and the shoot sprouted (the result) therefrom. (AA, 8.1.) Water is the agent for creation and generation. (SPB 3.7.4.4.) Water Symbolic of the Process of Evolution and Dissolution. Water is symbolic of the process of evolution. Water is the source of all created beings. (GB, 1.29.) The waters represent the beginning of the world. (RV 2.1.1; 2.20.7; 2.30.) The waters are symbolic to the process of dissolution. (RV 1.143.3; 1.164.42; 1.168.2; 2.1.1; 2.38.2; 3.1.5; 3.5.3, 8; 3.9.1, 2; 10.121.7.) Water Representative of the First Cause of the Universe. These issues — the eternity of the world, the process of dissolution and evolution of the universe, the very recurrence of many universes in this process, plus, the need to designate a first cause or eternal law — are ingrained in Vedic belief. (YV 3.5 (first cause or eternal law); 4.3 (eternity of the world); 4.47 (recurrence of numerous worlds).) The solution is that symbol of the first case or principle of the universe, that foundation of everything. The first principle of the Vedic dharma is water. (SPB 6.7.1.17; 11.1.6.16; 1.1.1.4;11.1.2.3; TS 5.1.3.1; AA, 8.1.8.1.) These bedrock principles are symbolized in the creation of the sacred fire. Starting from the fire of another terrestrial aspect of Agni, Grhapati, where Water represents the Female principle and Fire represents the Male principle, the Adhvaryu priest sprinkles water (Female) on the fireplace and fire implements (Male) of the altar. (SPB, 2.1.13.) The reason this is done is because the Vedic dharma is pervaded by water (Female), and by sprinkling water on the fire altar (Male) the Adhvaryu mates Female and Male, who copulate and further pervade the Vedic dharma. (SPB 2.1.1.4.) This is the eternal dance of the Vedic dharma, as constant as the waves that lap on the shore.

THE WHIP

No, this is not an implement of unconventional sexual practices. The Whip is a manifestation of the terrestrial Fire of Agni. (BD, 1.111.) Not mentioned in the chariot/Self metaphor found in the Katha Upanishad, the Whip is the functional equivalent of another metaphor used in that Upanishad — the charioteer — with an important distinction. The whip serves the same purpose of the charioteer, which is to guide and motivate the movement of the horses. More importantly, the whip is the means of that guidance and motivation; so while the charioteer controls the horses, it also controls the use of the whip. The whip, therefore, has a more specialized meaning. Mind, thoughts, are all forms of mental activity. According to the Vedas, the subtle energies which kick-start the living force of the worshiper is called, isas, usually rendered as "impulse" or "impulsion." Impulsion supplies the very impetus for consciousness, the impulse provides those energies required to run the many other physiological functions of the worshiper. Thought and thinking may be viewed as electrical impulses traveling through the synapses in the brain. The Whip, therefore, becomes the terrestrial fire of impulsion which is integral to function of consciousness.

ABBREVIATIONS

AA	Aitatreya Aranyaka
AV	Atharva Veda
BD	Brhata Deva
BG	Bhavagad Gita
BSS	Baudhayana Srauta Sutras
BU	Brhad Aranyaka Upanishad
GB	Gopatha Brahmana
CU	Chandogya Upanishad
JB	Jaiminiya Brahmana
JUB	Jaiminiya Upanishad Brahmana
KS	Kathaka Samhita
MAU	Mandukya Upanishad
MB	Mahabharata
MUU	Mundaka Upanishad
Nir.	Nirukta
RV	Rg Veda
SA	Sakhaya Aranyaka

SPB	Satapatha Brahmana
SSS	Sakhayana Srauta Sutra
TB	Tattiriya Brahmana
TS	Tattiriya Samhita
VS	Vaisesika Sutras
YTU	Yoga Tattva Upanishad
YS	Yoga Sutras (Patanjali)
YV	Yajur Veda

Printed in the United States
By Bookmasters